Voice over IP Security

Patrick Park

Cisco Press

Cisco Press
800 East 96th Street
Indianapolis, Indiana 46240 USA

Voice over IP Security

Patrick Park

Copyright © 2009 Cisco Systems, Inc.

Published by:
Cisco Press
800 East 96th Street
Indianapolis, IN 46240 USA

Printed in the United States of America

First Printing September 2008

Library of Congress Cataloging-in-Publication data

Park, Patrick, 1971-

  Voice over IP security / Patrick Park.

     p. cm.

  ISBN 978-1-58705-469-3 (pbk.)

  1. Internet telephony--Security measures. I. Title. II. Title: VoIP security.

TK5105.8865.P37 2008

004.69'5--dc22

2008036070

ISBN-13: 978-1-58705-469-3

ISBN-10: 1-58705-469-8

Warning and Disclaimer

This book is designed to provide information about Voice over IP security. Every effort has been made to make this book as complete and as accurate as possible, but no warranty or fitness is implied.

The information is provided on an "as is" basis. The authors, Cisco Press, and Cisco Systems, Inc. shall have neither liability nor responsibility to any person or entity with respect to any loss or damages arising from the information contained in this book or from the use of the discs or programs that may accompany it.

The opinions expressed in this book belong to the author and are not necessarily those of Cisco Systems, Inc.

Trademark Acknowledgments

All terms mentioned in this book that are known to be trademarks or service marks have been appropriately capitalized. Cisco Press or Cisco Systems, Inc., cannot attest to the accuracy of this information. Use of a term in this book should not be regarded as affecting the validity of any trademark or service mark.

Corporate and Government Sales

The publisher offers excellent discounts on this book when ordered in quantity for bulk purchases or special sales, which may include electronic versions and/or custom covers and content particular to your business, training goals, marketing focus, and branding interests. For more information, please contact: **U.S. Corporate and Government Sales**   1-800-382-3419   corpsales@pearsontechgroup.com

For sales outside the United States please contact: **International Sales**   international@pearsoned.com

Feedback Information

At Cisco Press, our goal is to create in-depth technical books of the highest quality and value. Each book is crafted with care and precision, undergoing rigorous development that involves the unique expertise of members from the professional technical community.

Readers' feedback is a natural continuation of this process. If you have any comments regarding how we could improve the quality of this book, or otherwise alter it to better suit your needs, you can contact us through email at feedback@ciscopress.com. Please make sure to include the book title and ISBN in your message.

We greatly appreciate your assistance.

Publisher	Paul Boger
Associate Publisher	Dave Dusthimer
Cisco Press Program Manager	Jeff Brady
Executive Editor	Brett Bartow
Managing Editor	Patrick Kanouse
Development Editor	Dan Young
Project Editor	Seth Kerney
Copy Editor	Margaret Berson
Technical Editors	Bob Bell
	Dan Wing
Editorial Assistant	Vanessa Evans
Designer	Louisa Adair
Composition	Octal Publishing, Inc.
Indexer	WordWise Publishing Services LLC
Proofreader	Water Crest Publishing, Inc.

Americas Headquarters
Cisco Systems, Inc.
170 West Tasman Drive
San Jose, CA 95134-1706
USA
www.cisco.com
Tel: 408 526-4000
800 553-NETS (6387)
Fax: 408 527-0883

Asia Pacific Headquarters
Cisco Systems, Inc.
168 Robinson Road
#28-01 Capital Tower
Singapore 068912
www.cisco.com
Tel: +65 6317 7777
Fax: +65 6317 7799

Europe Headquarters
Cisco Systems International BV
Haarlerbergpark
Haarlerbergweg 13-19
1101 CH Amsterdam
The Netherlands
www-europe.cisco.com
Tel: +31 0 800 020 0791
Fax: +31 0 20 357 1100

Cisco has more than 200 offices worldwide. Addresses, phone numbers, and fax numbers are listed on the Cisco Website at **www.cisco.com/go/offices.**

About the Author

Patrick Park has been working on product design, network architecture design, testing, and consulting for more than 10 years. Currently, Patrick works for Cisco as a VoIP test engineer focusing on the security and interoperability testing of rich media collaboration gateways. Before Patrick joined Cisco, he worked for Covad Communications (a VoIP service provider) as a VoIP security engineer focusing on the design and deployment of secure network architecture and lawful interception (under the Communications Assistance for Law Enforcement Act [CALEA]) with various tools and solutions. Patrick graduated from Pusan National University in South Korea, where he majored in computer engineering. While attending graduate school, he wrote the book *Web Server Programming with PHP*. Patrick lives with his wife and children in Los Gatos, California.

Dedication

This book is dedicated to our God who lifted me up for this opportunity, my wonderful wife, Sun, and my children, Janice and Jayden. Thank you all for making me complete.

Acknowledgments

I'd like to give special recognition to Dan Young and Andrew Cupp for providing their expert technical knowledge in editing the book and working hard to keep the book on time.

A big "thank you" goes out to Dan Wing and Bob Bell for giving great comments during the review process and helping me complete this book.

Thanks to Allan Konar, Yoon Son, and Mo Kang for contributing their technical expertise, which helped me find the right direction in the initial writing of this book.

Last but not least, I'd like to thank my current manager, Shamim Pirzada, who mentors me and encourages me to spend extra time for personal development. Also, thanks to my colleagues, the Photon team, who gave great inspiration and technical information.

Contents at a Glance

Contents

Icons Used in This Book

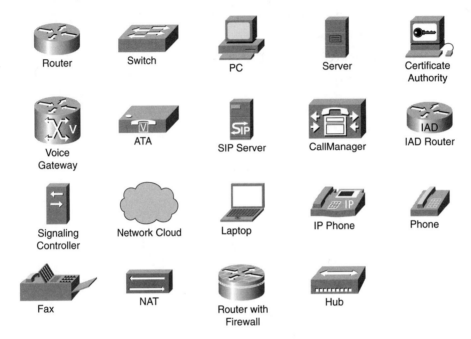

Command Syntax Conventions

The conventions used to present command syntax in this book are the same conventions used in the IOS Command Reference. The Command Reference describes these conventions as follows:

- **Boldface** indicates commands and keywords that are entered literally as shown. In actual configuration examples and output (not general command syntax), boldface indicates commands that are manually input by the user (such as a **show** command).

- *Italic* indicates arguments for which you supply actual values.

- Vertical bars (|) separate alternative, mutually exclusive elements.

- Square brackets ([ ]) indicate an optional element.

- Braces ({ }) indicate a required choice.

- Braces within brackets ([{ }]) indicate a required choice within an optional element.

Introduction

Voice over Internet Protocol (VoIP) has been popular in the telecommunications world since its emergence in the late 90s, as a new technology transporting multimedia over the IP network. In this book, the multimedia (or rich media) includes not only voice, but also video, instant message, presence data, and fax data over the IP network.

Today people commonly make phone calls with IP phones or client software (such as Skype or iChat) on their computer, or send instant messages to their friends. This gives them convenience and cost savings. Many telecommunications companies and other organizations have been switching their legacy phone infrastructure to a VoIP network, which reduces costs for lines, equipment, manpower, and maintenance.

However, the benefits of VoIP are not free. There are disadvantages to using VoIP. The integrated rich media makes it difficult to design the network architecture. Multiple VoIP protocols and different methods of implementation create serious interoperability issues. Integration with existing data networks creates quality of service issues. The fact that so many network elements are involved through open (or public) networks creates serious security issues, because each element and network has vulnerable factors.

The security issues especially are becoming more serious because traditional security devices (such as firewalls) and protocols (such as encryption) cannot protect VoIP services or networks from recent intelligent threats.

This book focuses on the important topic of VoIP security by analyzing current and potential threats to demonstrating the methods of prevention.

Goals and Methods

The most important goal of this book is to give you correct and practical answers for the following questions:

- What are the current and potential threats?
- What are the impacts of those threats?
- Why are current data security devices not able to protect against recent intelligent threats?
- How can you protect VoIP services and networks from those threats?
- What is lawful interception and how do you implement it?

One key methodology used in this book is to give you hands-on experience of current well-known threats by simulating them with publicly available tools. Through the simulation, you can realize the characteristics and impacts of those threats and have a better understanding of mitigation.

Another key methodology is to give you detailed examples of protection methods with protocols, products, and architecture so that you may apply them to real VoIP service environments.

This book also gives you clarification of VoIP security concepts, definitions, standards, requirements, limitations, and related terms.

Who Should Read This Book

This book is NOT designed to give you information about VoIP in general which is available almost everywhere. Instead, this book focuses on VoIP security and gives practical information to people like those in the following list:

- Managers or engineers who are planning to employ VoIP systems in their organizations
- System engineers or architects who design and implement VoIP networks
- Network administrators who administer, upgrade, or secure networks that include VoIP elements
- Security consultants who perform security assessments for VoIP environments
- Developers who implement VoIP products or solutions
- Researchers and analysts who are interested in VoIP security

This book assumes that the readers have some minimal knowledge of networking (such as TCP/IP), operating systems, and VoIP in general (such as IP phones).

How This Book Is Organized

Although this book could be read cover to cover, it is designed to be flexible and allow you to easily move between chapters and sections of chapters to cover just the material that you need more work with.

This book consists of three parts. Part I, "VoIP Security Fundamentals," contains Chapters 1 through 5 and covers VoIP security fundamentals that are essential to understand current threats and security practices. Part II, "VoIP Security Best Practices," contains Chapters 6 through 9 and demonstrates VoIP security best practices with the detailed analysis and simulation of current threats. Part III, "Lawful Interception (CALEA)," contains Chapters 10 through 11 and covers another aspect of VoIP security, Lawful Interception, from basic concept to real implementation.

Chapter 1, "Working with VoIP," provides an overview of VoIP and its vulnerability in general. Chapters 2 through 11 are the core chapters and can be read in any order. If you do intend to read them all, the order in the book is an excellent sequence to use.

The core chapters, Chapters 2 through 11, cover the following topics:

- **Chapter 2, "VoIP Threat Taxonomy"**—This chapter defines VoIP threat taxonomy, based on four different categories: threats against availability, confidentiality, integrity, and social context. This chapter is not intended to provide exhaustive lists of current and potential threats, but to define the taxonomy for identifying the threat in the first place, measuring the current and potential impact, and helping implementers to develop protection methods and secure service architecture. Twenty-two typical threats are introduced with examples and features.

- **Chapter 3, "Security Profiles in VoIP Protocols"**—This chapter introduces the security profiles of VoIP protocols: SIP, H.323, and MGCP. The content shows how each protocol defines specific security mechanisms and recommends combined solution with other security protocols, such as IPSec, TLS, and SRTP.

- **Chapter 4, "Cryptography"**—This chapter provides a high-level understanding of crypto-graphic algorithms with comprehensible figures, avoiding mathematical details. Well-known cryptographic algorithms are introduced, such as DES, 3DES, AES, RAS, DSA, and hash func-tions (MD5, SHA, and HMAC). This chapter also covers the mechanism of key management, focusing on key distribution.

- **Chapter 5, "VoIP Network Elements"**—This chapter covers what devices are involved in the VoIP network architecture, and how they work for secure services. Session Border Controller, VoIP-aware firewalls, NAT servers, lawful interception servers, customer premise equipment, call processing servers, and media gateways are introduced.

- **Chapter 6, "Analysis and Simulation of Current Threats"**—This chapter covers two main topics: detailed analysis and hands-on simulation of most common threats, and the guidelines for mitigation. For the analysis, it examines the detailed patterns, usage examples, and impacts of the threats. For the simulation, it introduces negative testing tools that are available on the Internet so that you can have hands-on experience. The threats that this chapter covers are DoS, malformed messages, sniffing (eavesdropping), spoofing (identity theft), and VoIP spam (voice, instant message, and presence spam).

- **Chapter 7, "Protection with VoIP Protocol"**—This chapter demonstrates the details of how to make VoIP service secure with SIP and other supplementary protocols. It focuses on the methodology of protection in these five categories: authentication, encryption, transport and network layer security, threat model and prevention, and limitations.

- **Chapter 8, "Protection with Session Border Controller"**—This chapter examines security issues on the VoIP network borders, and provides the methodology of preventing the issues with an SBC. This chapter includes the details of SBC functionality (such as network topology hiding, DoS protection, overload prevention, NAT traversal, and lawful interception), as well as the method of designing service architecture with an SBC in terms of high availability, secure network connectivity, virtualization, and optimization of traffic flow.

- **Chapter 9, "Protection with Enterprise Network Devices"**—This chapter demonstrates how to protect the enterprise VoIP network with Cisco devices for practical information. Cisco firewalls, Unified Communications Manager, Unified Communications Manager Express, IP phone, and multilayer switches are used. This chapter includes security features, usage exam-ples, and configuration guidelines for those devices.

- **Chapter 10, "Lawful Interception Fundamentals"**—This chapter covers the fundamentals of lawful interception. The topics are definition, background information, requirements from law enforcement agents, the reference model from an architectural perspective, functional specifications, request/response interface, and operational considerations.

- **Chapter 11, "Lawful Interception Implementation"**—This chapter demonstrates how to implement lawful interception into the VoIP service environment. It focuses on how the intercep-tion request and response work between functional modules, based on industry specifications.

VoIP Security Fundamentals

This chapter covers VoIP strengths and vulnerabilities with the following topics:

- VoIP advantages
- VoIP disadvantages
- Sources of vulnerability
- Vulnerable components
- Myths versus reality

CHAPTER 1

Working with VoIP

Voice over Internet Protocol (VoIP) has been prevailing in the telecommunication world since its emergence in the late 90s as a new technology transporting multimedia over the IP network. It is very common today for people to make phone calls with IP phones or client software (for example, Skype, iChat, and Google Talk) on their computer. Many telecommunications companies and other organizations have been moving their telephony infrastructure to their data networks, because it provides a cheaper and clearer alternative to traditional public service telephone network (PSTN) phone lines.

Even though the VoIP service is getting popular, its technology is still developing. It is growing rapidly throughout North America and Europe, but it is sometimes awkwardly implemented on most legacy networks, and often lacks compatibility and continuity with existing systems. Nevertheless, VoIP will capture a significant portion of the telephony market, given the fiscal savings and flexibility that it can provide.

The context of VoIP service in this book includes not only voice, but also video, Instant Messaging (IM), presence data, and fax data over the IP network. Figure 1-1 shows VoIP service architecture with many different types of services.

In this chapter, you learn about the benefits and disadvantages of using VoIP, its vulnerabilities and components, and this chapter also dispels some myths. The content in this chapter refers to recommendations from the National Institute of Standards and Technology (NIST).[1]

NOTE   This chapter approaches the topics at a high level. The technical details are described in Part II, "VoIP Security Best Practices."

Like every technology, VoIP has many benefits and disadvantages. The following section describes the benefits of VoIP.

Figure 1-1 *VoIP Service Architecture*

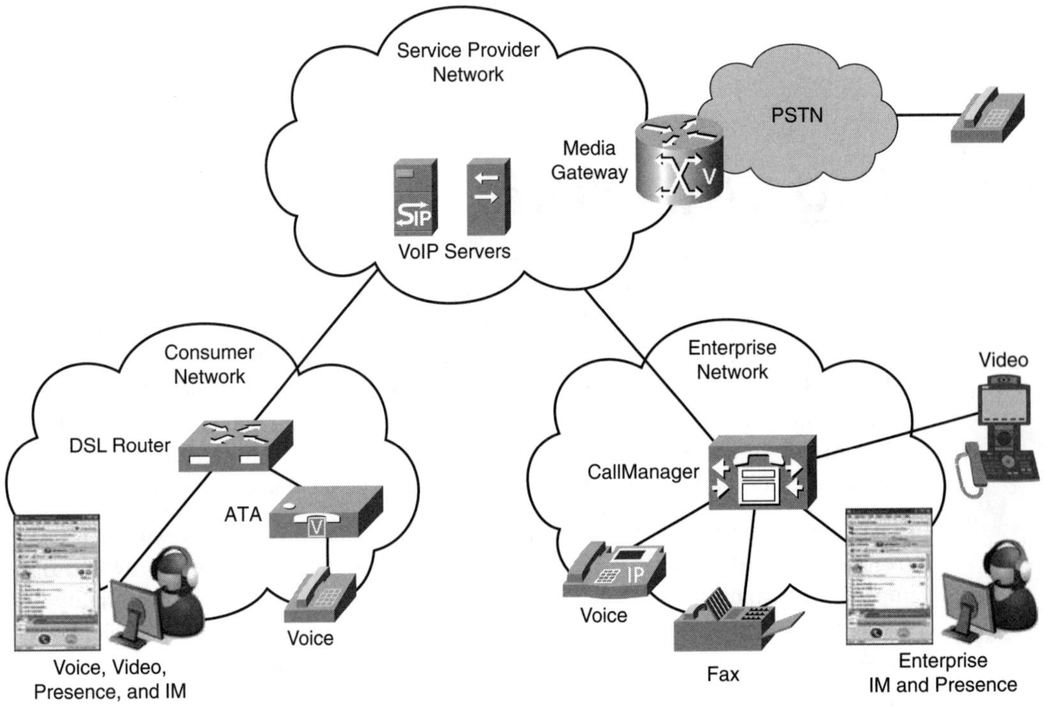

VoIP Benefits

The reason for the prevalence of VOIP is that it gives significant benefits compared to legacy phone systems. The key benefits are as follows:

- **Cost savings**—The most attractive feature of VoIP is its cost-saving potential. When we move away from public switched telephone networks, long-distance phone calls become inexpensive. Instead of being processed across conventional commercial telecommunications line configurations, voice traffic travels on the Internet or over private data network lines.

  For the enterprise, VoIP reduces cost for equipment, lines, manpower, and maintenance. All of an organization's voice and data traffic is integrated into one physical network, bypassing the need for separate PBX tie lines. Although there is a significant initial setup cost, significant net savings can result from managing only one network and not needing to sustain a legacy telephony system in an increasingly digital and data-centered world. Also, the network administrator's burden may be lessened as they can now focus on a single network. There is no longer a need for several teams to manage a data network and another to manage a voice network.

For consumers, VoIP reduces the charge of subscription or usage, especially for long distance and international calls.

- **Rich media service**—The legacy phone system mainly provides voice and fax service even though limited video service is possible. However, the demand of users is much higher than that, as shown in today's rich media communications through the Internet. People check out friends' presence (such as online, offline, busy), send instant messages, make voice or video calls, transfer images, and so on. VoIP technology makes rich media service possible, integrating with other protocols and applications.

  Rich media service not only provides multiple options of media to users, but also creates new markets in the communications industry, such as VoIP service in mobile phones.

- **Phone portability**—The legacy phone system assigns a phone number with a dedicated line, so you generally cannot move your home phone to another place if you want to use the same phone number. It is a common hassle to call the phone company and ask for a phone number update when moving to a new house. However, VoIP provides number mobility: The phone device can use the same number virtually everywhere as long as it has proper IP connectivity. Many businesspeople today bring their IP phones or softphones when traveling, and use the same numbers everywhere.

- **Service mobility**—The context of mobility here includes service mobility as well. Wherever the phone goes, the same services could be available, such as call features, voicemail access, call logs, security features, service policy, and so on.

- **Integration and collaboration with other applications**—VoIP protocols (such as Session Initiation Protocol [SIP], H.323) run on the application layer and are able to integrate or collaborate with other applications such as email, web browser, instant messenger, social-networking applications, and so on. The integration and collaboration create synergy and provide valuable services to the users. Typical examples are voicemail delivery via email, click-to-call service on a website, voice call button on an email, presence information on a contact list, and so on.

- **User control interface**—Most VoIP service providers provide a user control interface, typically a web GUI, to their customers so that they can change features, options, and services dynamically. For example, the users log in to the web GUI and change call forwarding number, speed dial, presence information (online, offline), black/white list, music-on-hold option, anonymous call block, and so on.

- **No geographical boundary**—The VoIP service area becomes virtualized without geographical limit. That is, the area code or country code is no longer bound to a specific location. For example, you could live in South Korea but subscribe to a U.S. phone number, which makes it possible that all calls to the U.S. become domestic calls (cheaper) even though you live in South Korea.

- **Rich features**—VoIP provides rich features like click-to-call on a web page, Find-Me-Follow-Me (FMFM), selective call forwarding, personalized ring tones (or ringback tone), simultaneous rings on multiple phones, selective area or country code, and so on.

Now that you are aware of many of the benefits, the next section takes a look at several disadvantages.

VoIP Disadvantages

The benefits of VoIP do not come free of charge. There are significant disadvantages for using VoIP, as follows:

- **Complicated service and network architecture**—Integrated rich media services (such as voice, video, IM, presence, and fax) make it difficult to design the service and network architecture because many different types of devices for each service are involved, as well as different protocols and characteristics of each media. Rich features (such as click-to-call and FMFM) also make the architecture more complicated because many different applications (such as web and email) and platforms are involved. This complication requires extra time and resources when designing, testing, and deploying. It also causes various errors and makes it harder to troubleshoot and isolate them.

- **Interoperability issues between different protocols, applications, or products**—There are multiple VoIP protocols (such as SIP, H.323, Media Gateway Control Protocol [MGCP], and Skinny), and product companies who choose whatever they like when developing products, which means there are always interoperability issues between the products that use different protocols. Even between the products using the same protocol, interoperability issues still come up because of different ways of implementation, different versions (extensions), or different feature sets. Therefore, it is common for VoIP service providers to spend a significant amount of time and resources for testing interoperability and resolving the issues.

- **Quality of service (QoS) issues**—Voice and video streams flow over an IP network as real-time packets, passing through multiple networks and devices (such as switches, routers, firewalls, and media gateways). Therefore, ensuring QoS is very difficult and costs lots of time and resources to meet the user's expectations. The main factors in QoS are packet loss, delay (latency), and jitter (packet delay variation).

In a comparison of VoIP QoS versus traditional circuit switched networks, Sinden[2] reported data from a Telecommunications Industry Association (TIA) study that showed even a fairly small percentage of lost packets could push VoIP network QoS below the level users have come to expect on their traditional phone lines. Each coder-decoder (codec) the TIA studied experienced a steep downturn in user satisfaction when latency crossed the 150-ms point. However, even with less than 150 ms of latency, a packet loss of 5 percent caused VoIP traffic encoded with G.711 (an international standard for encoding telephone audio on a 64-kbps stream) to drop below the QoS levels of the PSTN, even with a packet loss concealment scheme. Similarly, losses of 1 and 2 percent, respectively, were enough to place quality in VoIP networks encoded with G.723.1 (for very low bit-rate speech compression) and G.729A (for voice compression on an 8kbps stream) below this threshold. At losses of 3 and 4 percent, respectively, the performance of these networks resulted in a majority of dissatisfied users.

- **Power outages**—Legacy home phones continue to work even during a power outage because the phone line supplies 48 volts constantly. However, VoIP phones use regular data network lines that do not provider power in most cases, which means you cannot use VoIP phones during power outages. Of course, there are inline power solutions (such as Power over Ethernet), but these are mainly for enterprise environments.

- **Emergency calls**—Unlike legacy phone connections, which are tied to a physical location, VoIP allows phone portability as described in the previous section, which is convenient for users. However, the flexibility complicates the provision of emergency services like an E-911 call, which provides the caller's location to the 911 dispatch office based on the caller ID (phone number). Especially for users using softphones on their mobile computers, E-911 service is almost impossible unless the users notify the service provider of their physical location every time they move. Although most VoIP vendors have workable solutions for E-911 service, government regulators and vendors are still working out standards and procedures for 911 services in VoIP environment.

- **Security issues**—In a legacy phone system, the security issue is mainly intercepting conversations that require physical access to phone lines or compromise of the office PBX. In VoIP, based on open or public networks, security issues are much more than that. Between a caller and callee, many elements (such as IP phones, access devices, media gateways, proxy servers, and protocols) are involved in setting up the call and transferring the media. Each element has vulnerable factors that are targets for attackers. The next few sections provide examples.

- **Legal issues (lawful interception)**—Legal wiretapping in VoIP, also called lawful interception (LI), is much more complicated than that in legacy phone systems, because of the complexity of VoIP service architecture. For the details, refer to Chapter 10, "Lawful Interception Fundamentals."

Among these disadvantages, the security issues are becoming more serious because traditional security devices (such as firewalls and Intrusion-Detection Systems) and protocols (such as encryption) cannot protect VoIP services or networks from recent intelligent threats.

The following sections look into the vulnerability from the following aspects:

- What are the sources of vulnerability?
- What are the vulnerable components?
- What do people misunderstand about the vulnerability?

Sources of Vulnerability

VoIP has two types of vulnerability. One is the inherited vulnerability coming from an existing infrastructure such as the network, operating system, or web server that VoIP applications are running on. The other is its own vulnerability coming from VoIP protocols and devices, such as IP phone, voice gateway, media server, signaling controller, and so on.

Basically, these vulnerabilities are derived from the characteristics of VoIP that are shown in Figure 1-2.

Figure 1-2   *Sources of Vulnerability*

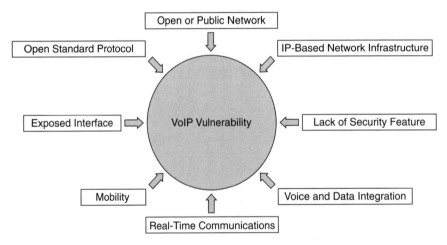

Each source of vulnerability is explained in the following sections.

IP-Based Network Infrastructure

As the name VoIP implies, all traffic flows over IP networks and inherits the vulnerability of IP networks, such as Transmission Control Protocol Synchronization (TCP SYN) attacks, exhaustive floods, malicious IP fragmentation, network viruses, or worms.

Open or Public Networks

In most cases, VoIP traffic flows through open or public networks like the Internet where anonymous people including attackers may send and receive signals or media.

Open VoIP Protocol

Most VoIP protocols, such as SIP or H.323, are standardized and open to the public. Anyone can create client or server programs based on the protocol specification even for malicious purposes. Attackers can utilize the malicious program to communicate with target servers or clients before compromising them. Additionally, the open protocol may expose security weaknesses of the specification, which attackers could take advantage of.

Exposed Interface

A client/server model is the basic architecture of VoIP service. Generally, servers are located in a protected network (the enterprise's or the service provider's), but the interfaces receiving call requests are open to clients that are located in an open or public network. It is possible for attackers to scan random IPs/ports and find the exposed interfaces for sending malicious traffic, such as Denial of Service (DoS), toll fraud, and so on.

Real-Time Communications

Unlike regular data service like email, VoIP services work with real-time media traffic that is very sensitive about packet delay, loss, and jitter (packet delay variation). Even minor packet delay or jitter could be recognized by users and impact the overall QoS. Packet loss also can impact the QoS because VoIP uses User Datagram Protocol (UDP) packets in most cases, and there is no retransmission mechanism.

Mobility

A legacy phone system assigns a dedicated line to a certain phone number and does not provide the users with mobility, It typically requires physical access for an attacker to spoof the identity (the telephone number or line). However, generally, VoIP allows endpoints to be virtually everywhere as long as they have proper IP connectivity, which complicates protection against identity spoofing.

Lack of Security Features and Devices

Although many data security devices like firewalls are adding features for VoIP, it is still not enough to protect VoIP service or network from today's sophisticated threats, compared to regular data security realm.

Voice and Data Integration

Voice (or video) is real-time data in VoIP. The integration of voice and data in the same network gives significant benefits, but it causes new issues; for example, integrating voice and data into a single device (such as a PC) makes it difficult for the network to use network separation (for example, VLANs) to identify "data" traffic and "voice" traffic. VLAN separation is the standard operating procedure for many hard IP phones, but of course does not work well at all when voice and data are integrated.

There are always more sources of vulnerability depending on service types or integrated solutions; however, these are the main sources.

The next section describes the vulnerable components in VoIP service.

Vulnerable Components

All components involved in VoIP service have vulnerable elements that are affected directly or indirectly. The following are VoIP's main components and their vulnerability.

- **Operating system of the VoIP application**—VoIP applications run on many different types of operating systems such as Linux/Unix, Microsoft Windows, or real-time operating system (RTOS), and are affected by the vulnerabilities inherent in those operating systems and network code implementations (for example, IP and TCP). The frequent security patches for the operating systems prove that they always have security issues.

- **VoIP application**—There are many different types of VoIP applications; for example, softphones (Skype, Google Talk), instant messengers (AOL AIM and MSN Messenger), call managers, softswitches, and so on. The application itself may have security issues because of bugs or errors, which could make VoIP service insecure.

- **Management interface**—For management purposes, most VoIP devices have service interfaces such as Simple Network Management Protocol (SNMP), Secure Shell (SSH), Telnet, and HTTP. The interfaces could be the source of vulnerability, especially when being configured carelessly. For example, if a VoIP device uses a "public" community name in SNMP, an attacker can get valuable information (for example, configuration) by using SNMP queries. If a VoIP device uses the default ID/password for its management interface, it is easy for an attacker to break in.

- **TFTP Server**—Many VoIP devices, especially customer premise equipment (CPE), download their configurations from a TFTP server. An attacker could sniff the packets and gather the server information. Or, an attacker could impersonate a TFTP server by spoofing the connection, and then distribute a malicious configuration to the CPE.

- **Web client/server**—Many VoIP applications are embedded into a web client (that is, a browser) to provide web services (for example, click-to-dial service, corporate directory lookup, and timecard services). These services inherit the vulnerability of web client/servers, such as malicious code or worms.

- **Access device (switch, router)**—All VoIP traffic flows through access devices (Layer 2 and 3 switch or router) that are in charge of switching or routing. Compromised access devices could create serious security issues because they have full control of packets. Even minor wrong configuration could be a potential security hole. For example, an attacker compromises a Layer 2 switch and sets up a monitoring port for a particular voice VLAN. The attacker can capture all VoIP signals and media through the monitoring port without any impact on end users. Another example is that wrong configuration on a Layer 3 router could make an unnecessary broadcasting domain where a potential attacker could sniff broadcasted messages that are used for further attacks.

- **Network**—The network itself can be the vulnerable component because of uncontrolled traffic, regardless of malicious or not. For example, the flooded traffic from certain endpoints not only threatens the target server, but also exhausts network bandwidth so that other legitimate traffic cannot go through. The flooded traffic could come from either malicious sources as a part of Denial-of-Service (DoS), or legitimate devices that have wrong configuration or bugs.

- **VoIP protocol stack**—Security factors are not much considered when most VoIP protocols (for example, SIP and H.323) are designed. For example, the initial version of SIP (RFC 2543) allows clear-text–based credentials; that is, anyone can see the password as long as they can sniff the packets. The latest version of SIP (RFC 3261) supports the digest format of password (that is, hashed password), but it is still vulnerable to brute-force or dictionary attack. Quite a large number of current threats abuse this kind of security weakness on the protocol. Therefore, these protocols recommend combining with other security protocols (for example, Transport Layer Security [TLS], Secure/Multipurpose Internet Mail Extensions [S/MIME]) when implementing them.

Now that you are aware of the vulnerable components in VoIP, the next section explains some misunderstandings about the vulnerability.

Myths Versus Reality

Certain misunderstandings related to VoIP's vulnerability and protection are common. The following sections describe typical myths and the contrasting reality.

Legacy Versus VoIP Systems

Myth #1: A legacy phone system is more secure than VoIP system.

Reality: Most ordinary people are concerned about privacy issues (typically, wiretapping) when using VoIP devices (such as an IP phone) that are mostly connected to the open or public Internet. It sounds easy for a hacker to sniff the packets and eavesdrop the conversation, but in reality, it is not that easy. The hacker has to have a sniffing tool located in the same broadcasting domain as the IP phone (using switched Ethernet), or on the same media path in order to eavesdrop, which means that it is almost impossible for an external hacker to sniff the packets. Moreover, if the media packets are encrypted, even sniffed packets are useless.

However, wiretapping the legacy phone line is much easier in fact. Even from outside a building, an eavesdropper can physically wiretap the phone line because the phone and the telephone company's equipment do not have any intelligent mechanism of security.

Of course, VoIP has many vulnerable factors, as described in previous sections, but comparing those directly with legacy phone systems is not reasonable because the scope of VoIP service is far more than that of legacy phone service providing voice and fax service only. As mentioned before, today's VoIP provides not only rich media service (such as voice, video, text, presence, and fax) but also integrated services with other applications (such as email, web, and messenger). The complexity creates more vulnerability issues by nature.

When you focus on only voice and fax service, you will see that VoIP is more secure than legacy phone systems as long as it has a basic level of security infrastructure, which is discussed in Part II, "VoIP Security Best Practices."

Protecting Networks Using Strict Authentication and Encryption

Myth #2: Strict authentication and encryption are enough to protect network and end-users against threats.

Reality: Many people, even some network administrators, believe that strict authentication and encryption mechanisms make VoIP service secure enough. Those are important features, but the reality is that those are not enough to mitigate today's sophisticated threats. The typical type of threat is that malicious users or spammers impersonate their endpoints or infect legitimate internal devices with malware (such as viruses or zombies), so that they become authorized users that easily pass the authentication and encryption process. Therefore, they need a comprehensive solution covering multiple aspects of threats.

Protecting Networks Using a Data Security Infrastructure

Myth #3: Data security infrastructure can protect VoIP network.

Reality: Some people believe that secure data networks can protect VoIP as well because VoIP packets flow through IP networks anyway like other real-time data. That's partially right from the network-layer perspective, but there are so many application-layer–specific attacks that typical data security devices (such as firewalls, IDS/IPS) or architecture cannot detect or prevent them. For example, malformed SIP or H.323 messages could threaten the target server when parsing them, but provide no clue to data security devices unless they are looking into the messages in the application-layer. Therefore, additional VoIP security modules, devices, or architecture are necessary on top of the data security infrastructure.

Summary

VoIP has been prevailing in the telecommunication world since its emergence in the late 90s, as a new technology transporting multimedia over the IP network. The reason for its prevalence is that VoIP gives significant benefits compared to legacy phone systems. The key benefits are cost savings, rich media service, phone portability, service portability, integration with other applications, lack of geographical boundary, and rich features.

The benefits of VoIP do not come without cost. There are significant disadvantages for using VoIP, such as complicated service architecture, interoperability issues, QoS issues, power outages, and legal and security issues. Among these disadvantages, VoIP security issues are becoming more serious because traditional security devices (for example, firewalls, IDS/IPS), protocols (for example, encryption), and architectures do not adequately protect VoIP service or network from recent intelligent threats.

There are two types of vulnerability in VoIP. One is the inherited vulnerability coming from an existing infrastructure such as network, operating system, or web server that VoIP applications are running on. The other is its own vulnerability coming from VoIP protocol and devices, such as IP phone, voice gateway, media server, signaling controller, and so on.

These vulnerabilities are derived from the characteristics of VoIP, which uses IP-based network infrastructure, public (or open) networks, standard protocol, exposed interface to the public, real-time communications, mobility, and integration with data.

All components involved in VoIP service have vulnerable elements that affect it directly or indirectly. The main components of vulnerability are the operating system of the VoIP application, the VoIP application itself, the management interface, TFTP server, web client/ server, access device (switch, router), network, and VoIP protocol stack.

There are some misunderstandings related to VoIP's vulnerability and protection. The reality is that a VoIP system is more secure than a legacy phone system as long as it maintains a basic level of security infrastructure. Strict authentication and encryption are not enough to protect network and end users against today's sophisticated threats. Secure infrastructure of the data network can help to make VoIP network secure but not enough to protect application-specific attacks.

End Notes

1 Security Considerations for VoIP Systems, NIST (National Institute of Standards and Technology), January 2000.

2 Comparison of Voice over IP with circuit switching techniques, R. Sinden (Southampton University, UK), January 2002.

References

"A Security Blueprint of Enterprise Networks," Cisco Systems, http://www.cisco.com/warp/public/cc/so/cuso/epso/sqfr/safe_wp.pdf.

"Comprehensive VoIP Security for the Enterprise," Sipera Systems, http://www.sipera.com/assets/Documents/whitepapers/Sipera_Enterprise_VoIP_Security_WP.pdf.

Hersent, O., J. P. Petit, and D. Gurle. *IP Telephony (Deploying Voice-over-IP Protocols).* Wiley, 2005.

RFC 3261, "SIP (Session Initiation Protocol)," J. Rosenberg, H. Schulzrinne, G. Camarillo, A. Johnston, J. Peterson, R. Sparks, M. Handley, and E. Schooler, June 2002.

This chapter covers the taxonomy of VoIP threats based on the following categories:

- Threats against availability
- Threats against confidentiality
- Threats against integrity
- Threats against social context

CHAPTER 2

VoIP Threat Taxonomy

The VoIP vulnerabilities that were introduced in Chapter 1, "Working with VoIP," can be exploited to create many different kinds of threats. Attackers may disrupt media service by flooding traffic, collect privacy information by intercepting call signaling or call content, hijack calls by impersonating servers or impersonating users, make fraudulent calls by spoofing identities, and so on.

Spammers may utilize VoIP networks to deliver spam calls, instant messages, or presence information, which are more effective than email spams because it is very difficult to filter VoIP spam.

This chapter is not intended to provide exhaustive lists of current and potential threats, but to define the taxonomy for the following purposes:

- To identify the threat in the first place
- To measure the current impact and potential future impact of the threat
- To help develop the protection method and design a secure service architecture

NOTE   For an exhaustive list of all current and potential threats, go to www.voipsa.org (Voice over IP Security Alliance).

There are many possible ways to categorize the threats. This book uses the following four categories that most VoIP threats can belong to:

- Threats against availability
- Threats against confidentiality
- Threats against integrity
- Threats against social context

Each section in this chapter covers each category with typical threat examples. To give you a better understanding, each section uses figures and protocol examples with Session Initiation Protocol (SIP).

NOTE   This chapter approaches these threats at a high level, focusing on the taxonomy. If you want to see a detailed analysis with simulation, refer to Chapter 6, "Analysis and Simulation of Current Threats."

The following section introduces the most critical threats that impact service availability.

Threats Against Availability

Threats against availability are actually a group of threats against service availability that is supposed to be running 24/7 (24 hours, 7 days a week). That is, these threats aim at VoIP service interruption, typically in the form of Denial of Service (DoS).

The typical threats against availability are as follows:

- Call flooding
- Malformed messages (protocol fuzzing)
- Spoofed messages (call teardown, toll fraud)
- Call hijacking (registration or media session hijacking)
- Server impersonating
- Quality of Service (QoS) abuse

The following subsections describe the threats with examples, which show you how they impact service availability.

Call Flooding

The typical example of DoS is intentional call flooding; an attacker floods valid or invalid heavy traffic (signals or media) to a target system (for example, VoIP server, client, and underlying infrastructure), and drops the performance significantly or breaks down the system. The typical methods of flooding are as follows:

- **Valid or invalid registration flooding**—An attacker uses this method commonly because most registration servers accept the request from any endpoints in the public Internet as an initial step of authentication. Regardless of whether the messages are valid or invalid, the large number of request messages in a short period of time (for example, 10,000 SIP REGISTER messages per second) severely impacts the performance of the server.

- **Valid or invalid call request flooding**—Most VoIP servers have a security feature that blocks flooded call requests from unregistered endpoints. So, an attacker registers first after spoofing a legitimate user, and then sends flooded call requests in a short period of time (for example, 10,000 SIP INVITE messages per second). This impacts the performance or functionality of the server regardless of whether the request message is valid or not.

- **Call control flooding after call setup**—An attacker may flood valid or invalid call control messages (for example, SIP INFO, NOTIFY, Re-INVITE) after call setup. Most proxy servers are vulnerable because they do not have a security feature to ignore and drop those messages.

- **Ping flooding**—Like Internet Control Message Protocol (ICMP) ping, VoIP protocols use ping messages in the application layer to check out the availability of a server or keep the pinhole open in the local Network Address Translation (NAT) server, such as SIP OPTIONS message. Most IP network devices (for example, a router or firewall) in the production network do not allow ICMP pings for security reasons. However, many VoIP servers should allow the application-layer ping for proper serviceability, which could be a critical security hole.

Figure 2-1 illustrates the example of distributed flooding with zombies; an attacker compromises other computers with malware (for example, a virus) and uses them as zombies flooding registration messages. Each zombie sends 1,000 SIP REGISTER messages per second with different credentials that are randomly generated.

Figure 2-1 *Call Flooding Example*

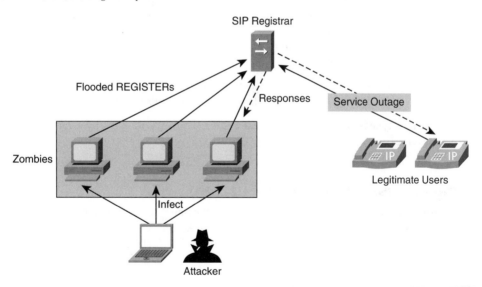

In Figure 2-1, the flooded messages will impact the registration server (SIP Registrar) severely as long as the server processes and replies with any error codes, such as "401 Unauthorized," "404 Not Found," "400 Bad Request," and so on. The impact can be high resource consumption (for example, CPU, memory, network bandwidth), system malfunction, or service outage. Whether the server responds or not, flooding the SIP registrar with sufficient registration messages will result in the degradation of service to the legitimate endpoints.

Not only the intentional flooding just mentioned, but also unintentional flooding exists in VoIP networks, so-called "self-attack," because of incorrect configuration of devices, architectural service design problems, or unique circumstances. Here are some examples:

- **Regional power outage and restoration**—When the power is backed up after a regional outage, all endpoints (for example, 10,000 IP phones) will boot up and send registration messages to the server almost at the same time, which are unintentional flooded messages. Because those phones are legitimate and distributed over a wide area, it is hard to control the flooding traffic proactively.

- **Incorrect configuration of device**—The most common incorrect configuration is setting endpoint devices (for example, IP phones) to send too many unnecessary messages, such as a registration interval that is too short.

- **Misbehaving endpoints**—Problematic software (firmware) or hardware could create unexpected flooding, especially when multiple or anonymous types of endpoints are involved in the VoIP service network.

- **Legitimate call flooding**—There are unusual days or moments when many legitimate calls are made almost at the same time. One example is Mother's Day, when a lot of calls are placed in the United States. Another example is natural disasters (for example, earthquakes), when people within the area make a lot of calls to emergency numbers (for example, 911) and their family and friends make calls to the affected area at the same time.

Those types of intentional and unintentional call flooding are common and most critical threats to VoIP service providers, who have to maintain service availability continually.

The next type is another form of threat against service availability, by means of malformed messages.

Malformed Messages (Protocol Fuzzing)

An attacker may create and send malformed messages to the target server or client for the purpose of service interruption. A *malformed message* is a protocol message with wrong syntax. Example 2-1 shows an example with a SIP INVITE message.

NOTE   Protocol fuzzing is another name for malformed messages. A small difference is that protocol fuzzing includes malicious messages that have correct syntax but break the sequence of messages, which may cause system error by making the state machine confused.

Example 2-1   *Malformed SIP INVITE Message*

```
Request-URI: aaaaaaaaa sip:1001@192.168.10.10 SIP/2.0
Message Header
    Via: SIP/2.0/UDP CAL-D600-5814.cc-
ntd1.example.com:5060;branch=z9hG4bK00002000005
    From::::::::: 2 <sip:user@CAL-D600-5814.cc-ntd1.example.com>;tag=2
    To: Receiver <sip:1001@192.168.10.10>
    Call-Id: 555555555555555555555-55555555555555555555555555-5555555555555555-
            5555555-555555555555555555555-5555555555555-55555555555555555-555555555-
            555555555@CAL-D600-5814.cc-ntd1.example.com
    CSeq: 1 INVITE
    Contact: 2 <sip:user@CAL-D600-5814.cc-ntd1.example.com>
    Expires: 1200
    Max-Forwards: 70
    Content-Type: application/sdp
    Content-Length: 143

Message body
Session Description Protocol
    Session Description Protocol Version (v): = = = = = = 0
    Owner/Creator, Session Id (o): 2 2 2 IN IP4 CAL-D600-5814.cc-ntd1.example.com
    Session Name (s): Session SDP
    Connection Information (c): IN IP4 192.168.10.10
    Time Description, active time (t): 0 0
    Media Description, name and address (m): audio 9876 RTP/AVP 0
    Media Attribute (a): rtpmap:0 PCMU/8000
```

Note that the comments (bold letters) in Example 2-1 are not shown in the actual SIP INVITE message. You can find something wrong in the example of an INVITE message. Three SIP headers (Request-URI, From, and Call-Id) and one version in Session Description Protocol (SDP) have the wrong format.

The server receiving this kind of unexpected message could be confused (fuzzed) and react in many different ways depending on the implementation. The typical impacts are as follows:

- Infinite loop of parsing
- Buffer overflow, which may permit execution of arbitrary code
- Break state machine
- Unable to process other normal messages
- System crash

This vulnerability comes from the following sources in general:

1 Weakness of protocol specification

Most VoIP protcols are open to the public and don't strictly define every single line. Attackers could find where the weakness of syntax is. Additionally, there are many customizable fields or tags.

2 Ease of creating the malformed message

Creating a message like that in Example 2-1 is easy for regular programmers. Even for nonprogrammers, many tools are available to make customized messages.

3 Lack of exception handling in the implementation

Because of time restrictions, most implementers are apt to focus on product features and interfaces, rather than create exception handling for massive negative cases.

4 Difficulty of testing all malformed cases

It is very difficult to test all the negative cases, even though sophisticated testing tools covering more cases are coming out these days.

The threat of malformed messages should be preventable as long as the parsing algorithm handles them properly.

The next threat is spoofed messages that are not malformed but still impact service availability.

Spoofed Messages

An attacker may insert fake (spoofed) messages into a certain VoIP session to interrupt the service, or insert them to steal the session. The typical examples are "call teardown" and "toll fraud."

Call Teardown

The method of malicious call teardown is that an attacker monitors a SIP dialog and obtains session information (Call-ID, From tag, and To tag), and sends a call termination message (for example, SIP BYE) to the communication device while the users are talking. The device receiving the termination message will close the call session immediately. Figure 2-2 illustrates the example with SIP messages.

Figure 2-2   *Malicious Call Teardown*

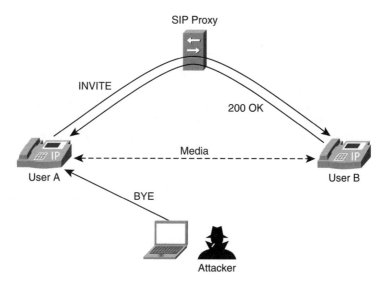

Figure 2-2 assumes that the attacker already monitored call signals between User A and B, and knew the session information (SIP dialog). The attacker injects the session information to the BYE message. The IP phone of user A receives the BYE and disconnects the media channel.

Another method of attack is that an attacker sends the termination messages to random devices (especially, proxy server) without knowing session information, which may affect current call sessions.

Compared to previous threats in this section, the malicious call teardown is not a common attack because the attacker should monitor the target call session before sending a termination message (BYE).

The next type of attack, toll fraud, also requires preliminary information like credentials before making fraud calls, but it happens commonly because of monetary benefit.

Toll Fraud

A fraudulent toll call is one of the common threats these days, especially for long distance or international calls. Because most mediation devices (for example, public switched telephone network [PSTN] media gateway, proxy server) require valid credentials (for example, ID and password) before setting up the toll call, an attacker collects the credentials first in many different ways. Typically, an attacker creates spoofed messages for brute-force password assault on the server until he receives authorization. If the clients use default passwords or easy-to-guess passwords, it is much easier to find them, especially when an attacker uses a password dictionary (see Note).

NOTE   A *password dictionary* is a file that contains millions of frequently used passwords.

Most passwords are manually created by humans (rather than by computers), so it's highly likely that they will be simple and easy to remember. No one really wants to have to remember random passwords that are longer than 10 digits, except perhaps system administrators. For example, a user named John Kim is apt to have passwords such as "jkim," "iamjohn," "johnkim," "john2kim," "john4me," and so on. Therefore, an attacker using a password dictionary containing millions of commonly used passwords would not need much time to crack most user-created passwords.

In some cases, the server does not require the credentials, but checks out the source IP address or subnet of the client to control the access. Especially when call trunking (for example, SIP trunking) is set up between a VoIP service provider and an enterprise customer, access control based on the source IP or subnet is commonly used. An attacker may be able to access the server by spoofing the source IP address.

Call Hijacking

Hijacking occurs when some transactions between a VoIP endpoint and the network are taken over by an attacker.

The transactions can be registration, call setup, media flow, and so on. This hijacking can make serious service interruption by disabling legitimate users to use the VoIP service. It is similar to call teardown in terms of stealing session information as a preliminary, but the actual form of attack and impact are different.

The typical cases are registration hijacking, media session hijacking, and server impersonating. The next few sections describe each of these cases.

Registration Hijacking

The registration process allows an endpoint to identify itself to the server (for example, SIP Registrar) as a device that a user is located.

An attacker monitors this transaction and sends spoofed messages to the server in order to hijack the session. When a legitimate user has been compromised, that user cannot receive inbound calls. Figure 2-3 illustrates the example with SIP messages.

Figure 2-3 *Registration Hijacking*

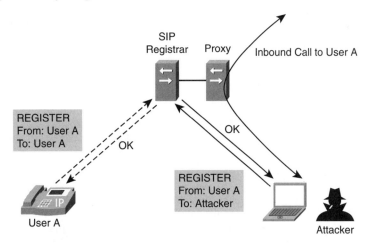

In Figure 2-3, an attacker impersonates a user agent by modifying the "From" header and adding the attacker's address to the "To" header when it sends a REGISTER message, which updates the address-of-record of the target user. All inbound calls to User A will be routed to the attacker.

This threat happens when the user agent server (Registrar) is relying on only SIP headers to identify the user agent.

Media Session Hijacking

When a media session is being negotiated between VoIP endpoints, an attacker may send spoofed messages to either one of them to redirect the media to another endpoint such as the attacker's phone or voicemail box. The victim will only be able to talk with the attacker's endpoint. Figure 2-4 illustrates the example with SIP messages.

Figure 2-4   *Media Session Hijacking*

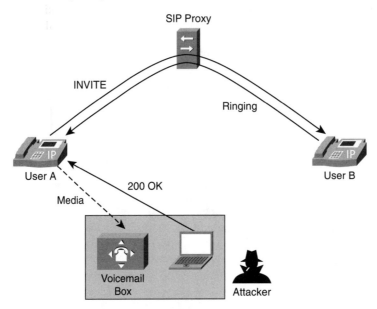

In Figure 2-4, User A tries to make a call to User B and the IP phone of User B is ringing. Having monitored call requests to User B, an attacker detects the call and sends 200 OK messages to User A with the IP/port address of the attacker's voicemail server. User A leaves a voice message for User B in the attacker's voicemail box. This hijacking happens before the media session is established between User A and (the intended) user B.

Even after the media session is established between A and B, an attacker can still hijack an active session by sending a Re-Invite message to User A.

Server Impersonating

A VoIP client sends a request message to a server in the target domain for registration, call setup or routing, and so on. It is possible for an attacker to impersonate the server, receive the request message, and then manipulate it for malicious purposes.

The typical method of impersonating a server is attacking the local TFTP server or Domain Name Service (DNS) server as the initial step. An attacker may intrude into the TFTP server and replace the configuration file for IP phones with his file having an IP address of a malicious server (for example, SIP Registrar).

The IP phones downloading the malicious file will send a request message to the wrong server.

An attacker may also compromise the DNS server and replace the entry of current VoIP server with an IP address of a malicious server. The IP phones looking up the server IP will receive a wrong one. Figure 2-5 illustrates an example based on SIP transactions with a Redirect server.

Figure 2-5 *Server Impersonating*

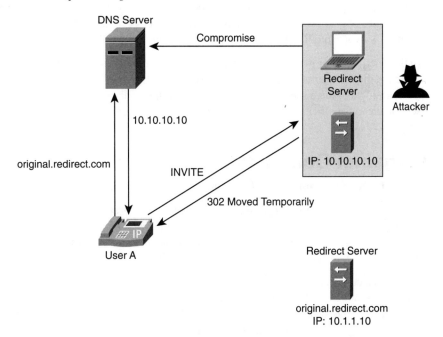

In Figure 2-5, the attacker compromised the local DNS server first by replacing the IP address (10.1.1.10) of original.redirect.com with 10.10.10.10, which is the attacker's redirect server.

When User A tries to make a call to User B, the IP phone looks up the IP address of the redirect server (original.redirect.com) and receives the IP (10.10.10.10) of the impersonated server. The INVITE message is sent to the impersonated server, and it replies "302 Moved Temporarily" with wrong contact information that could be a dummy address or attacker's proxy server for further threat. The original redirect server (10.1.1.10) cannot receive any call request in this situation.

QoS Abuse

The elements of a media session are negotiated between VoIP endpoints during call setup time, such as media type, coder-decoder (codec) bit rate, and payload type. For example, it may be necessary or desirable to use G.729 when leaving a network (to conserve bandwidth) but to use G.711 when calls are staying inside a network (to keep call quality higher). An attacker may intervene in this negotiation and abuse the Quality of Service (QoS), by replacing, deleting, or modifying codecs or payload type.

Another method of QoS abuse is exhausting the limited bandwidth with a malicious tool so that legitimate users cannot use bandwidth for their service. Some VoIP service providers or hosting companies limit the bandwidth for certain groups of hosts to protect the network. An attacker may know the rate limit and generate excessive media traffic through the channel, so voice quality between users may be degraded.

In this section so far, you have learned about threats against availability, such as call flooding, malformed messages, spoofed messages (call teardown, toll fraud), call hijacking (registration and media session hijacking, server impersonating), and QoS abuse. The next section covers another type of threat: attacks against call data and media confidentiality.

Threats Against Confidentiality

Another category of VoIP threat is the threat against confidentiality.

Unlike the service interruptions in the previous section, threats against confidentiality do not impact current communications generally, but provide an unauthorized means of capturing media, identities, patterns, and credentials that are used for subsequent unauthorized connections or other deceptive practices.

VoIP transactions are mostly exposed to the confidentiality threat because most VoIP service does not provide full confidentiality (both signal and media) end-to-end. In fact, full encryption of message headers is not possible because intermediary servers (for example, SIP proxy server) have to look at the headers to route the call. In some cases, the servers have to insert some information into the header (for example, Via header in SIP) as the protocol is designed.

This section introduces the most popular types of confidentiality threats: eavesdropping media, call pattern tracking, data mining, and reconstruction.

Eavesdropping Media

Eavesdropping on someone's conversation has been a popular threat since telecommunication service started a long time ago, even though the methods of eavesdropping are different between legacy phone systems and VoIP systems.

In VoIP, an attacker uses two methods typically. One is sniffing media packets in the same broadcasting domain as a target user's, or on the same path as the media. The other is compromising an access device (for example, Layer 2 switch) and forwarding (duplicating) the target media to an attacker's device.

The media can be voice-only or integrated with video, text, fax, or image. Figure 2-6 illustrates these cases.

Figure 2-6   *Eavesdropping Media*

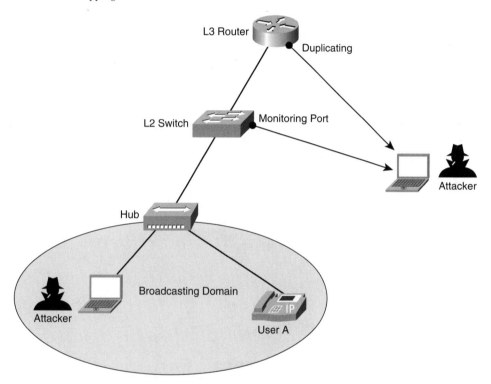

In Figure 2-6, the attacker's device that is in the same broadcasting domain as the IP phone of User A can capture all signals and media through the hub. This figure also shows the possibility that the attacker intrudes in a switch or router, and configures a monitoring port for voice VLAN, and forwards (duplicates) the media to the attacker's capturing device.

Another possible way of eavesdropping media is that an attacker taps the same path as the media itself, which is similar to legacy tapping technique on PSTN. For example, the attacker has access to the T1 itself and physically splits the T1 into two signals.

Although this technique is targeting media, the next method (call pattern tracking) is targeting signal information.

Call Pattern Tracking

Call pattern tracking is the unauthorized analysis of VoIP traffic from or to any specific nodes or network so that an attacker may find a potential target device, access information (IP/port), protocol, or vulnerability of network. It could also be useful for traffic analysis—knowing who called who, and when. For example, knowing that a company's CEO and CFO have been calling the CEO and CFO of another company could indicate that an acquisition is under way. For another example, knowing that a CEO called her stockbroker immediately after meeting with someone with insider stock knowledge is useful. That is, this is useful for learning about people and information.

To show an example of unauthorized analysis, sample messages that an attacker may capture in the middle of a network are illustrated in Example 2-2. It shows simple SIP request (INVITE) and response (200 OK) messages, but an attacker can extract a great deal of information from them by analyzing the protocol (key fields are highlighted).

Example 2-2 *Exposed Information from SIP Messages*

```
INVITE sip:9252226543@192.168.10.10:5060 SIP/2.0
Via: SIP/2.0/UDP 10.10.10.10:5060;branch=z9hG4bK00002000005
From: Alice <sip:4085251111@10.10.10.10:5060>;tag=2345
To: Bob <sip:9252226543@192.168.10.10>
Call-Id: 9252226543-0001
CSeq: 1 INVITE
Contact: <sip:4085251111@10.10.10.10>
Expires: 1200
Max-Forwards: 70
Content-Type: application/sdp
Content-Length: 143

Session Description Protocol Version (v): = 0
Owner/Creator, Session Id (o): 2 2 2 IN IP4 10.10.10.10
Session Name (s): Session SDP
Connection Information (c): IN IP4 10.10.10.10
Media Description, name and address (m): audio 9876 RTP/AVP 0 8 18
Media Attribute (a): rtpmap:0 PCMU/8000
Media Attribute (a): rtpmap:8 PCMA/8000
Media Attribute (a): rtpmap:18 G729a/8000


============================================================
SIP/2.0 200 OK
Via: SIP/2.0/UDP 10.10.10.10:5060;branch=z9hG4bK00002000005
From: Alice <sip:4085251111@10.10.10.10:5060>;tag=2345
To: Bob <sip:9252226543@192.168.10.10>;tag=4567
Call-Id: 9252226543-0001
CSeq: 1 INVITE
Contact: <sip:9252226543@172.26.10.10>
Content-Type: application/sdp
Content-Length: 131
```

Example 2-2   *Exposed Information from SIP Messages (Continued)*

```
Session Description Protocol Version (v): = 0
Owner/Creator, Session Id (o): 2 2 2 IN IP4 172.26.10.10
Session Name (s): Session SDP
Connection Information (c): IN IP4 172.26.10.10
Media Description, name and address (m): audio 20000 RTP/AVP 18
Media Attribute (a): rtpmap:18 G729a/8000
```

The following list shows sample information that the attacker may extract from Example 2-2:

- The IP address of the SIP proxy server is 192.168.10.10, and the listening port is 5060.

- They use User Datagram Protocol (UDP) packets for signaling without any encryption, such as Transport Layer Security (TLS) or Secure Multipurpose Internet Mail Extension (S/MIME).

- The proxy server does not require authentication for a call request.

- The caller (Alice), who has a phone number 4085251111, makes a call to Bob at 9252226543.

- The IP address of Alice's phone is 10.10.10.10 and a media gateway is 172.26.10.10 (supposing that the call goes to PSTN).

- The media gateway opens a UDP port, 20000, to receive Real-time Transport Protocol (RTP) stream from Alice's phone.

- The media gateway accepts only G.729a codec (Alice's phone offered G.711a, G.711u, and G.729a initially).

The information just presented can be used for future attacks, such as DoS attack on the proxy server or the media gateway.

Data Mining

Like email spammers who collect email addresses from various sources like web pages or address books, VoIP spammers also collect user information like phone numbers from intercepted messages, which is one example of data mining.

The general meaning of data mining in VoIP is the unauthorized collection of identifiers that could be user name, phone number, password, URL, email address, strings or any other identifiers that represent phones, server nodes, parties, or organizations on the network. In Example 2-2, you can see that kind of information from the messages.

An attacker utilizes the information for subsequent unauthorized connections such as:

- Toll fraud calls

- Spam calls (for example, voice, Instant Messaging [IM], presence spam)

- Service interruptions (for example, call flooding, call hijacking, and call teardown)
- Phishing (identity fraud; see the section "Threats Against Social Context" for more information)

With valid identities, attackers could have a better chance to interrupt service by sending many different types of malicious messages. Many servers reject all messages, except registration, unless the endpoint is registered.

Reconstruction

Reconstruction means any unauthorized reconstruction of voice, video, fax, text, or presence information after capturing the signals or media between parties. The reconstruction includes monitoring, recording, interpretation, recognition, and extraction of any type of communications without the consent of all parties. A few examples are as follows:

- Decode credentials encrypted by a particular protocol.
- Extract dual-tone multifrequency (DTMF) tones from recorded conversations.
- Extract fax images from converged communications (voice and fax).
- Interpret the mechanism of assigning session keys between parties.

These reconstructions do not affect current communications, but they are utilized for future attacks or other deceptive practices.

In this section so far, you have learned about threats against confidentiality such as eavesdropping media, call pattern tracking, data mining, and reconstruction. The next section covers another type of threats: breaking message and media integrity.

Threats Against Integrity

Another category of VoIP threat is the threat against integrity, which impacts current service severely in most cases.

The basic method of the integrity threat is altering messages (signals) or media after intercepting them in the middle of the network. That is, an attacker can see the entire signaling and media stream between endpoints as an intermediary. The alteration can consist of deleting, injecting, or replacing certain information in the VoIP message or media.

This section is divided into two types of threat at a high level:

- Threats against message integrity (message alteration)
- Threats against media integrity (media alteration)

The next section describes and gives examples of each type of threat.

Message Alteration

Message alteration is the threat that an attacker intercepts messages in the middle of communication entities and alters certain information to reroute the call, change information, interrupt the service, and so on. The typical examples are call rerouting and black holing.

Call Rerouting

Call rerouting is any unauthorized change of call direction by altering the routing information in the protocol message. The result of call rerouting is either to exclude legitimate entities or to include illegitimate entities in the path of call signal or media.

Figure 2-7 illustrates the example of including a malicious entity during call setup.

Figure 2-7   *Call Rerouting*

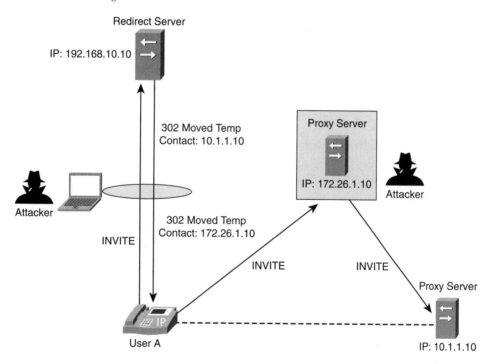

In Figure 2-7, an attacker keeps monitoring the call request message (for example, SIP INVITE) from User A to a redirect server. When User A initiates a call, the IP phone sends an INVITE message to the redirect server, as shown in Example 2-3.

Example 2-3 *IP Phone Sends an INVITE Message to the Redirect Server*

```
INVITE sip:Bob@192.168.10.10:5060 SIP/2.0
Via: SIP/2.0/UDP 10.10.10.10:5060;branch=z9hG4bK00002000005
From: UserA <sip:UserA@10.10.10.10:5060>;tag=2345
To: Bob <sip:Bob@192.168.10.10>
Call-Id: 9252226543-0001
CSeq: 1 INVITE
Contact: <sip:UserA@10.10.10.10>
Max-Forwards: 70
Content-Length: 0
```

The attacker detects the INVITE and intercepts the response message (that is, "302 Moved Temporarily") from the redirect server, as shown in the continuation of Example 2-3.

```
SIP/2.0 302 Moved Temporarily
From: UserA <sip:UserA@10.10.10.10:5060>;tag=2345
To: Bob <sip:Bob@192.168.10.10>;tag=6789
Call-Id: 9252226543-0001
CSeq: 1 INVITE
Contact: <sip:Bob@10.1.1.10>
Content-Length: 0
```

The attacker replaces the IP address of the proxy server (10.1.1.10) in the Contact header with his proxy server (172.26.1.10), and sends to the IP phone, as shown in the continuation of Example 2-3.

```
SIP/2.0 302 Moved Temporarily
From: UserA <sip:UserA@10.10.10.10:5060>;tag=2345
To: Bob <sip:Bob@192.168.10.10>;tag=6789
Call-Id: 9252226543-0001
CSeq: 1 INVITE
Contact: <sip:Bob@172.26.1.10>
Content-Length: 0
```

The IP phone sends a new INVITE to attacker's proxy server rather than the legitimate server, and his server relays the message as shown in the picture. From now on, the attacker in the middle can see all signals between the endpoints and modify for any malicious purpose.

Call Black Holing

Call black holing is any unauthorized method of deleting or refusing to pass any essential elements of protocol messages, in the middle of communication entities. The consequence of call black holing is to delay call setup, refuse subsequent messages, make errors on applications, drop call connections, and so on. Here are a few examples with SIP:

1   An attacker as an intermediary drops only ACK messages between call entities so that the SIP dialog cannot be completed, even though there could be early media between them.

2   An attacker as an intermediary deletes media session information (SDP) in the INVITE message, which could result in one-way audio or call disconnection.

3   An attacker as an intermediary refuses to pass all messages to a specific user (victim) so that the user cannot receive any inbound calls.

The call rerouting and black holing belong to message alteration as previously described. The next section covers media alteration as part of the threat against integrity.

Media Alteration

Media alteration is the threat that an attacker intercepts media in the middle of communication entities and alters media information to inject unauthorized media, degrade the QoS, delete certain information, and so on. The media can be voice-only or integrated with video, text, fax, or image. The typical examples are media injection and degrading.

Media Injection

Media injection is an unauthorized method in which an attacker injects new media into an active media channel or replaces media in an active media channel. The consequence of media injection is that the end user (victim) may hear advertisement, noise, or silence in the middle of conversation. Figure 2-8 illustrates the example with voice stream.

Figure 2-8   *Media Injection*

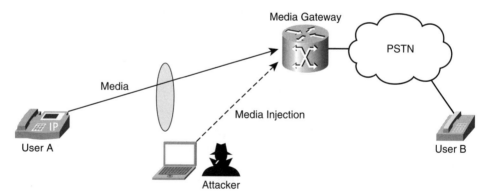

In Figure 2-8, User A with an IP phone makes a call to User B who has a PSTN phone through a media gateway. After the call setup, the IP phone sends voice (RTP) packets to the media gateway. An attacker in the middle monitors the RTP sequence number of the voice packets, and adjusts the sequence number of illegitimate packets (for example, advertisements), and injects them into the voice channel so that they will arrive before the legitimate packets. User B in PSTN hears the injected voice.

Media Degrading

Media degrading is an unauthorized method in which an attacker manipulates media or media control (for example, Real-Time Control Protocol [RTCP]) packets and reduces the QoS of any communication. Here are a couple of examples:

1 An attacker intercepts RTCP packets in the middle, and changes (or erases) the statistic values of media traffic (packet loss, delay, and jitter) so that the endpoint devices may not control the media properly.

2 An attacker intercepts RTCP packets in the middle, and changes the sequence number of the packets so that the endpoint device may play the media with wrong sequence, which degrades the quality.

In this section so far, you have learned about VoIP threats against integrity such as message alteration (call rerouting, call black holing) and media alteration (media injection, media degrading). The next section covers another type of threats: social threats.

Threats Against Social Context

A threat against social context (as known as "social threat") is somewhat different from other technical threats against availability, confidentiality, or integrity, as previously discussed, in terms of the intention and methodology. It focuses on how to manipulate the social context between communication parties so that an attacker can misrepresent himself as a trusted entity and convey false information to the target user (victim).

The typical threats against social context are as follows:

- Misrepresentation of identity, authority, rights, and content
- Spam of call (voice), IM, and presence
- Phishing

NOTE   A call with misrepresentation is initiated by an attacker who is a communication entity, which is different from the threats in the "Threats Against Integrity" section, which are based on interception and then modification.

The general meaning of spam is unsolicited bulk email that you may see every day. It wastes network bandwidth and system resources, as well as annoying email users. The spam exists in VoIP space as well, so-called VoIP spam, in the form of voice, IM, and presence spam. This section looks into each type of VoIP spam with SIP protocol. The content refers to RFC 5039.[1]

Phishing is becoming popular in the VoIP world these days as a method of getting somebody's personal information by deceiving the identity of an attacker.

The following sections give more details about these social threats.

NOTE   These same types of attacks are equally available in today's PSTN environment.

Misrepresentation

Misrepresentation is the intentional presentation of a false identity, authority, rights, or content as if it were true so that the target user (victim) or system may be deceived by the false information. These misrepresentations are common elements of a multistage attack, such as phishing.

Identity misrepresentation is the typical threat that an attacker presents his identity with false information, such as false caller name, number, domain, organization, email address, or presence information.

Authority or rights misrepresentation is the method of presenting false information to an authentication system to obtain the access permit, or bypassing an authentication system by inserting the appearance of authentication when there was none. It includes presentation of password, key, certificate, and so on. The consequence of this threat could be improper access to toll calls, toll calling features, call logs, configuration files, presence information of others, and so on.

Content misrepresentation is the method of presenting false content as if it came from a trusted source of origin. It includes false impersonation of voice, video, text, or image of a caller.

Call Spam (SPIT)

Call (or voice) spam is defined as a bulk unsolicited set of session initiation attempts (for example, INVITE requests), attempting to establish a voice or video communications session. If the user should answer, the spammer proceeds to relay their message over real-time media. This is the classic telemarketer spam, applied to VoIP, such as SIP. This is often called SPam over IP Telephony, or SPIT.

The main reason SPIT is becoming popular is that it is cost-effective for spammers. As you know, legacy PSTN-call spam already exists in the form of telemarketer calls. Although these calls are annoying, they do not arrive in the same kind of volume as email spam. The difference is cost; it costs more for the spammer to make a phone call than it does to send email. This cost manifests itself in terms of the cost for systems that can perform telemarketer calls, and in cost per call. However, the cost is dramatically dropped when switching to

SPIT for many reasons: low hardware cost, low line cost, ease of writing a spam application, no boundary for international calls, and so on. Additionally, in some countries, such telemarketing calls over the PSTN are regulated.

In some cases, spammers utilize computational and bandwidth resources provided by others, by infecting their machines with viruses that turn them into "zombies" that can be used to generate call spam.

Another reason SPIT is getting popular is its effectiveness, compared to email spams. For email spams, you may already realize that there is a big difference between turning on and off a spam filter for your email account. In fact, most spam filters for email today work very well (filter more than 90 percent of spams) because of the nature of email; store and forward. All emails can be stored and examined in one place before forwarding to users. Even though users may still receive a small percentage of email spams, they usually look at profiles (for example, sender name and subject) and delete most of them without seeing the contents. However, the method of filtering emails does not work for SPIT because voice is real-time media. Only after listening to some information initially can users recognize whether it is a spam or not. So, spammers try to put main information in the initial announcement so that users may listen to it before hanging up the phone. There is a way to block those call attempts based on a blacklist (spammers' IP address or caller ID), but it is useless if spammers spoof the source information.

You can find more information on SPIT and mitigation methods in Chapter 6, "Analysis and Simulation of Current Threats."

The next topic is a different type of VoIP spam, IM spam.

IM Spam (SPIM)

IM spam is similar to email. It is defined as a bulk unsolicited set of instant messages, whose content contains the message that the spammer is seeking to convey. This is often called Spam over Instant Messaging, or SPIM.

SPIM is usually sent in the form of request messages that cause content to automatically appear on the user's display. The typical request messages in SIP are as follows:

- SIP MESSAGE request (most common)
- INVITE request with large Subject headers (since the Subject is sometimes rendered to the user)
- INVITE request with text or HTML bodies

Example 2-4 shows examples with SIP INVITE and MESSAGE.

Example 2-4   *IM Spam*

```
INVITE sip:Bob1@192.168.10.10:5060 SIP/2.0
Via: SIP/2.0/UDP 10.10.10.10:5060;branch=z9hG4bK00002000005
From: Spammer <sip:spammer1@10.10.10.10:5060>;tag=2345
To: Bob <sip:Bob1@192.168.10.10>
Call-Id: 9252226543-0001
CSeq: 1 INVITE
Subject: Hi there, buy a cool stuff in our website www.spam-example.com
Contact: <sip:spammer1@10.10.10.10>
Expires: 1200
Max-Forwards: 70
Content-Type: application/sdp
Content-Length: 143


======================================================================
MESSAGE sip:Bob1@192.168.10.10:5060 SIP/2.0
Via: SIP/2.0/UDP 10.10.10.10:5060;branch=z9hG4bK00002000005
From: Spammer <sip:spammer1@10.10.10.10:5060>;tag=2345
To: Bob <sip:Bob1@192.168.10.10>
Call-Id: 9252226543-0001
CSeq: 1 MESSAGE
Max-Forwards: 70
Content-Type: test/plain
Content-Length: 25

Hi there, buy a cool stuff in our website www.spam-example.com
```

SPIM is very much like email, but much more intrusive than email. In today's systems, IMs automatically pop up and present themselves to the user. Email, of course, must be deliberately selected and displayed.

Presence Spam (SPPP)

Presence spam is similar to SPIM. It is defined as a bulk unsolicited set of presence requests (for example, SIP SUBSCRIBE requests) in an attempt to get on the "buddy list" or "white list" of a user to subsequently send them IM or INVITEs. This is occasionally called SPam over Presence Protocol, or SPPP.

The cost of SPPP is within a small constant factor of IM spam, so the same cost estimates can be used here. What would be the effect of such spam? Most presence systems provide some kind of consent framework. A watcher that has not been granted permission to see the user's presence will not gain access to their presence. However, the presence request is usually noted and conveyed to the user, allowing them to approve or deny the request. This request itself can be spam, as shown in Example 2-5.

In SIP, this is done using the watcherinfo event package. This package allows a user to learn the identity of the watcher, in order to make an authorization decision. This could provide a vehicle for conveying information to a user; Example 2-5 shows the example with SIP SUBSCRIBE.

Example 2-5 *Presence Spam*

```
SUBSCRIBE sip:bob@example.com SIP/2.0
Event: presence
To: sip:bob@example.com
From: sip:buy-cool-dvds-and-games@spam-example.com
Contact: sip:buy-cool-dvds-and-games@spam-example.com
Call-ID: knsd08alas9dy@3.4.5.6
CSeq: 1 SUBSCRIBE
Expires: 3600
Content-Length: 0
```

A spammer in Example 2-5 generates the SUBSCRIBE request from the identity (sip:buy-cool-dvds-and-games@spam-example.com), and this brief message can be conveyed to the user, even though the spammer does not have permission to access presence. As such, presence spam can be viewed as a form of IM spam, where the amount of content to be conveyed is limited. The limit is equal to the amount of information generated by the watcher that gets conveyed to the user through the permission system.

Phishing

The general meaning of *phishing* is an illegal attempt to obtain somebody's personal information (for example, ID, password, bank account number, credit card information) by posing as a trust entity in the communication. In VoIP, phishing is typically happening through voice or IM communication, and voice phishing is sometimes called "vishing."

The typical sequence is that a phisher picks target users and creates request messages (for example, SIP INVITE) with spoofed identities, pretending to be a trusted party. When the target user accepts the call request, either voice or IM, the phisher provides fake information (for example, bank policy announcement) and asks for personal information. Some information like user name and password may not be directly valuable to the phisher, but it may be used to access more information useful in identity theft.

Here are a couple of phishing examples:

 1 A phisher makes a call to a target user and leaves a voice message like: "This is an important message from ABC Bank. Because our system has changed, you need to change your password. Please call back at this number: 1-800-123-4567." When the target user calls the number back, the phisher's Interactive Voice Response (IVR) system picks up the call and acquires the user's password by asking "Please enter your current password for validation purposes . . .."

2 A phisher sends an instant text message to a smart phone (for example, PDA phone) or softphone (for example, Skype client) users, saying "This message is from ABC Bank. Your credit card rate has been increased. Please check it out on our website: http://www.abcbank.example.com." When the users click the URL, it goes to a phisher's website (example.com) that appears to have exactly the same web page that ABC Bank has. The fake website collects IDs and passwords that the users type in.

In this section, you have learned about VoIP threats in a social context, such as misrepresentation, call spamming, IM spamming, presence spamming and phishing. For more detailed information about VoIP spamming, refer to Chapter 6, "Analysis and Simulation of Current Threats."

Summary

VoIP vulnerabilities can be exploited to create many different kinds of threats. The threats can be categorized as four different types: threats against availability, confidentiality, integrity, and social context.

A threat against availability is a threat against service availability that is supposed to be running 24/7. That is, the threat is aiming at VoIP service interruption, typically, in the form of DoS. The examples are call flooding, malformed messages (protocol fuzzing), spoofed messages (call teardown, toll fraud), call hijacking (registration or media session hijacking), server impersonating, and QoS abuse.

A threat against confidentiality does not impact current communications generally, but provides an unauthorized means of capturing conversations, identities, patterns, and credentials that are used for the subsequent unauthorized connections or other deceptive practices. VoIP transactions are mostly exposed to the confidentiality threat because most VoIP service does not provide full confidentiality (both signal and media) end-to-end. The threat examples are eavesdropping media, call pattern tracking, data mining, and reconstruction.

A threat against integrity is altering messages (signals) or media after intercepting them in the middle of the network. That is, an attacker can see the entire signaling and media stream between endpoints as an intermediary. The alteration can consist of deleting, injecting, or replacing certain information in the VoIP message or media. The typical examples are call rerouting, call black holing, media injection, and media degrading.

A threat against social context focuses on how to manipulate the social context between communication parties so that an attacker can misrepresent himself as a trusted entity and convey false information to the target user. The typical examples are misrepresentation (identity, authority, rights, and content), voice spam, instant message spam, presence spam, and phishing.

End Notes

1 RFC 5039, "SIP and Spam," J. Rosenberg, C. Jennings, http://www.ietf.org/rfc/rfc5039.txt, January 2008.

References

"Phishing," Wikipedia, http://en.wikipedia.org/wiki/Phishing.

RFC 3261, "SIP (Session Initiation Protocol)," J. Rosenberg, H. Schulzrinne, G. Camarillo, A. Johnston, J. Peterson, R. Sparks, M. Handley, and E. Schooler, June 2002.

RFC 3428, "Session Initiation Protocol (SIP) Extension for Instant Messaging," B. Campbell, J. Rosenberg, H. Schulzrinne, C. Huitema, D. Gurle, December 2002.

Trammell, Dustin D. "VoIP Attacks," http://www.dustintrammell.com/presentations/.

"VoIP Security Threat Taxonomy," VOIPSA, http://www.voipsa.org/Activities/taxonomy-wiki.php.

This chapter covers the security profiles in the following VoIP protocols:

- H.323
- Session Initiation Protocol (SIP)
- Media Gateway Control Protocol (MGCP)

CHAPTER 3

Security Profiles in VoIP Protocols

Three protocols are dominating in VoIP network today: H.323, Session Initiation Protocol (SIP), and Media Gateway Control Protocol (MGCP). SIP and H.323 are peer-to-peer session protocols that are necessary for global VoIP service, especially interconnecting heterogeneous service networks. MGCP is a device control protocol that provides a simple and centralized mechanism of controlling media gateways. Similar control protocols are H.248 (Megaco), Network-based Call Signaling Protocol Specification (NCS), and Skinny Call Control Protocol (SCCP).

These protocols define specific security mechanisms as part of the protocols, or recommend a combined solution with other security protocols, such as IP Security (IPSec), Transport Layer Security (TLS), or Secure Real-time Transport Protocol (SRTP).

This chapter looks into the security profiles of the following protocols at a high level, as well as an overview of protocols:

- H.323
  - Overview
  - Security Profiles
    H.235 Annex D (Baseline Security)
    H.235 Annex E (Signature Security)
    H.235 Annex F (Hybrid Security)
- SIP
  - Overview
  - Security Profiles
    Digest Authentication
    Identity Authentication
    S/MIME
    SRTP
    TLS
    IPSec

- MGCP
    - Overview
    - Security Profiles

Even though these security profiles are not enough to make the whole VoIP service secure, they are essential elements as part of a comprehensive solution.

NOTE   The detailed usage of SIP security is demonstrated in Chapter 7, "Protection with VoIP Protocol."

H.323

H.323[1] is the International Telecommunication Union (ITU) specification describing the complete architecture and operations of audio and video communications across packetized networks. H.323 is the first VoIP standard that is publicly used and adopts Real-Time Transport Protocol (RTP) to transport voice and video over the IP network. Since H.323 was released for the first time in 1996, it has been updated with many enhancements and the latest one was released in 2006, commonly referred to as H.323v6.

Before looking into the security profiles, this section briefly summarizes H.323 as follows.

Overview

H.323 is an umbrella specification that encompasses many other protocols; in particular, the following protocols are key components:

- **H.225 (Q.931)**—Defines call setup messages and procedures used to establish a call, request changes in bandwidth of the call, get status of the endpoints in the call, and disconnect the call. It also defines Registration, Admission, and Status (RAS) messages and procedures.
- **H.245**—Defines control messages and procedures used to exchange capabilities (for example, coder-decoder [codec]) and open the media channels.
- **RTP/RTCP**—Real-Time Transport Protocol (RTP) provides end-to-end network transport functions suitable for applications transmitting real-time data, such as voice and video. Real-Time Transport Control Protocol (RTCP) provides statistical information on Quality of Service (QoS), such as packet loss, delay, and jitter.
- **H.235**—Defines security profiles for H.323, such as authentication, message integrity, signature security, and voice encryption.

The contents in this section refer to the H.323 specification, and the first topic is its components.

Components

The H.323 service network consists of several components: terminal, gateway (GW), gatekeeper (GK), Multipoint Controller (MC), and Multipoint Control Unit (MCU). Each component has different roles and functions to establish communications between end users.

A *terminal* (endpoint) is a user device, such as an IP phone. It contains a protocol stack implementing the basic functionality of real-time communications, such as H.225, H.245, and RTP. This endpoint communicates with a gatekeeper to send or receive a call.

A *gatekeeper* is a key component that provides call control services to endpoints. More than one gatekeeper may be present and they may communicate with each other in an unspecified fashion. The gatekeeper is logically separate from the endpoints; however, its physical implementation may coexist with a terminal, MCU, gateway, MC, or other non-H.323 network device. When it is present in a system, the gatekeeper shall provide the following services:

- **Address Translation**—Translate H.323 alias address to transport address. This should be done using a translation table, which is updated using the registration messages.

- **Admissions Control**—Authorize network access using H.225 messages (admission request, confirm or reject). This may be based on call authorization, bandwidth, or some other criteria that is left to the manufacturer. It may also be a null function, which admits all requests.

- **Bandwidth Control**—Support bandwidth control messages (bandwidth request, confirm or reject). It may also be a null function that accepts all requests.

- **Zone Management**—Provides the other three functions in this list for terminals, MCUs, and gateways that have registered with it.

The gatekeeper may also perform other optional functions such as:

- **Call Control Signaling**—Process the call signaling with endpoints.

- **Call Authorization**—Authorize call attempts. Through the use of H.225 signaling, the gatekeeper may reject calls from a terminal due to authorization failure. The reasons for rejection may include restricted access to/from particular terminals or gateways and restricted access during certain periods of time.

- **Bandwidth Management**—Control the number of H.323 terminals permitted simultaneous access to the network. Through the use of the H.225.0 signaling, the gatekeeper may reject calls from a terminal due to bandwidth limitations.

- **Alias Address Modification**—May return a modified alias address in an admission confirm (ACF) so that the endpoint may use the alias address in establishing the connection.

- **Dialed Digit Translation**—May translate dialed digits into an E.164 number or a private network number.

The gatekeeper with these functions receives a call request from an endpoint and terminates the call according to the routing and security policy. One of the common termination points is a gateway, especially for a PSTN call.

A *gateway* is a translation device between an H.323 network and other networks, such as ISDN or a mobile network. The typical usage of the gateway is enabling terminal users to make calls to public switched telephone network (PSTN) users, and the reverse. It may also be possible for an endpoint on one segment of the network to call out through one gateway and back onto the network through another gateway in order to bypass a router or a low-bandwidth link.

A Multipoint Controller (MC) is a control device supporting conferences between three or more endpoints in a multipoint conference. The MC carries out the capabilities exchange with each endpoint in a multipoint conference. The MC sends a capability set to the endpoints in the conference indicating the operating modes in which they may transmit. The MC may revise the capability set that it sends to the terminals as a result of terminals joining or leaving the conference or for other reasons.

A Multipoint Control Unit (MCU) is an endpoint that provides support for multipoint conferences. It uses H.245 messages and procedures to implement features. A gatekeeper or gateway may also include the MCU as a separate module.

Now that you have learned about the functions of each component in H.323, the next section takes a look at the basic call flow.

Basic Call Flow

The provision of an H.323 call is made in the following steps:

Step 1   Call setup (H.225)

Step 2   Initial communication and capability exchange (H.245)

Step 3   Establishment of audiovisual communication (H.245)

Step 4   Call services (RTP/RTCP)

Step 5   Call termination (H.225)

The method of implementing the steps varies depending on the service architecture, type of service, and call scenarios. One of the typical call flows with a gatekeeper is shown in Figure 3-1; Endpoint A makes a call to Endpoint B through Gatekeeper.

Figure 3-1 *H.323 Basic Call Flow*

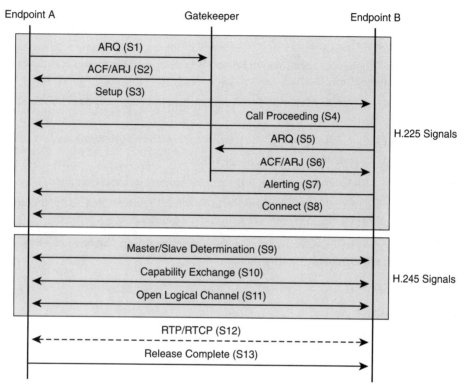

In the scenario shown in Figure 3-1, both endpoints are registered to the same gatekeeper, and the gatekeeper has chosen direct call signaling. Here is the description of each signal:

- **S1**—Endpoint A (calling endpoint) initiates the ARQ (admission request) to Gatekeeper.
- **S2**—Gatekeeper responds ACF (admission confirm) with the Call Signaling Channel Transport Address of Endpoint B (called endpoint).
- **S3**—Endpoint A then sends the Setup message directly to Endpoint B using that Transport Address.
- **S4**—Endpoint B responds Call Proceeding to notify its processing.
- **S5 and S6**—If Endpoint B wants to accept the call, it initiates an ARQ/ACF exchange with Gatekeeper. It is possible that an ARJ (admission reject) is received by Endpoint B, in which case it sends Release Complete (disconnection) to Endpoint A.

- **S7**—When Endpoint B is ringing, it responds Alerting.
- **S8**—When a user picks up the call, Endpoint B responds with a Connect message, which contains an H.245 Control Channel Transport Address for use in H.245 signaling.
- **S9**—Signals between Endpoint A and B to determine the master and slave of the call to avoid conflicts.
- **S10**—Signals to exchange the media capability of each endpoint (for example, codec negotiation).
- **S11**—Signals to open logical channels for transferring multimedia data.
- **S12**—RTP/RTCP channel is opened.
- **S13**—Endpoint A disconnects the call by sending Release Complete.

Not only is direct call signaling possible, as shown in Figure 3-1, but also gatekeeper-routed call signaling; all H.225 signals are relayed by a gatekeeper.

In this section so far, you have learned about the components and basic call flow of H.323. The next section covers security profiles.

Security Profiles

H.235[2] describes security enhancements within the framework of H.323 to incorporate security services such as authentication and privacy. The proposed scenario is applicable to both simple point-to-point and multipoint conferences for any terminals that utilize H.245 as a control protocol.

NOTE   This section uses many terms related to cryptography. For more detailed information, refer to Chapter 4, "Cryptography."

The latest version (3) of H.235 was released in 2003, featuring a procedure for encrypted dual-tone multifrequency (DTMF) signals, object identifiers for the Advanced Encryption Standard (AES) encryption algorithm for media payload encryption, the enhanced OFB (EOFB; see the following Note) stream-cipher encryption mode for encryption of media streams, and an authentication-only (see Note) option for Network Address Translation (NAT)/firewall traversal, and so on.

NOTE

Output Feedback Mode (OFB) defines an operation mode that deploys a stream cipher using block encryption algorithms. The OFB mode provides:

- Improved performance through reduced encryption processing delay

- Easier and less complex handling of incomplete blocks

- Good error resiliency against bit errors

Enhanced OFB (EOFB) is a slightly modified OFB mode, which deploys the same features as OFB but in addition to that:

- Uses a salting key (KS) in addition to the encryption key (KE)

- Introduces an implicit packet index

NOTE

H.235 uses the following terms for provisioning the security services:

- **Authentication and integrity**—This is a combined security service part of the baseline profile that supports message integrity in conjunction with user authentication. The user may ensure authentication by correctly applying a shared secret key procedure. Both security services are provided by the same security mechanism.

- **Authentication-only**—This security service offered by the baseline security profile as an option supports authentication of selected fields only, but does not provide full message integrity. The authentication-only security profile is applicable for signaling messages traversing NAT/firewall devices. The user may ensure authentication by correctly applying a shared secret key procedure.

H.235 includes several annexes that each hold security profiles of H.235. A security profile specifies specific usage of H.235 or a subset of H.235 functionality for well-defined environments with scoped applicability.

Depending on the environment and application, security profiles may be implemented either selectively or all together. Typically, H.235-enabled systems indicate within object identifiers as part of signaling messages which security profiles they deploy. H.235-enabled systems should select the security profile according to their needs.

The following sections describe the security profiles of H.235 that this section refers to.

H.235 Annex D (Baseline Security)

H.235 Annex D defines a simple, baseline security profile. The profile provides basic security by simple means, using secure password-based cryptographic techniques. It may use the voice-encryption security profile for achieving voice confidentiality, if necessary. Note that this media encryption is incompatible with SRTP.

The baseline security profile is applicable in an environment where subscribed passwords/symmetric keys can be assigned to the secured H.323 entities (terminals) and network elements (GKs, proxies). It provides authentication and integrity, or authentication-only for H.225 RAS protocol and call signaling, H.225 and tunneled H.245 using password-based HMAC-SHA1-96 hash. H.225 call establishment using FastStart (GK-to-GK or terminal-to-terminal) includes integrated key management with Diffie-Hellman. Refer to Chapter 4, "Cryptography," for those cryptographic information.

Table 3-1 represents the baseline security profile.

Table 3-1   *Baseline Security Profile*

Security Services	Call Functions			
	RAS	**H.225**	**H.245**	**RTP**
Authentication and integrity	Password HMAC-SHA1-96	Password HMAC-SHA1-96	Password HMAC-SHA1-96	–
Nonrepudiation	–	–	–	–
Confidentiality	–	–	–	–
Access control	–	–	–	–
Key management	Subscription-based password assignment	Subscription-based password assignment	–	–

Optionally, the voice-encryption security profile can be combined smoothly with the baseline security profile. Audio streams may be encrypted using the voice-encryption security profile deploying Data Encryption Standard (DES), RC2-compatible or triple-DES, and using the authenticated Diffie-Hellman key-exchange procedure.

The baseline security profile mandates the fast connect procedure with integrated key management elements. Signaling means are provided also for tunneled H.245 key-update and synchronization. For long-duration calls, these messages require tunneling of H.245 within H.225.0 messages.

That was a brief summary of baseline security. The next topic, Annex E, covers signature security.

H.235 Annex E (Signature Security)

H.235 Annex E describes a security profile deploying digital signatures that is suggested as an option. Security entities (terminals, gatekeepers, gateways, MCUs, and so on) may implement this signature security profile for improved security or whenever required. Typically, it is applicable in environments with potentially many terminals where password/symmetric key assignment is not feasible, for example, in large-scale or global-scale scenarios.

The signature security profile mandates the GK-routed model and is based on H.245 tunneling techniques; support for non-GK-routed models is for further study.

The signature security profile is applicable for scaleable IP telephony; this security profile overcomes the limitations of the simple, baseline security profile of Annex D. For example, the signature security profile does not depend on the administration of mutual shared secrets in different domains. It provides tunneling of H.245 messages for H.245 message integrity and also provisions for nonrepudiation (see Note) of messages.

NOTE   *Nonrepudiation* is the concept of ensuring that a communication party cannot deny the validity of a message. In a digital signature, the private key is only accessible by its holder; the signature proves that the message was signed "only" by the holder, which offers nonrepudiation. For more detailed information about digital signatures, refer to Chapter 4, "Cryptography."

The signature security profile supports hop-by-hop security as well as true end-to-end authentication with simultaneous use of H.235 proxies or intermediate gatekeepers.

The features provided by these profiles include, for RAS, H.225.0 and H.245 messages:

- User authentication to a desired entity irrespective of the number of application-level hops that the message traverses.

- Integrity of all or critical portions (fields) of messages arriving at an entity irrespective of the number of application-level hops that the message traverses. Integrity of the message itself using a strongly generated random number is also optional.

- Application-level hop-by-hop message authentication, integrity, and nonrepudiation provide these security services for the entire message.

- Nonrepudiation of messages exchanged between two entities irrespective of the number of application-level hops that the message traverses can also be provided. Specifically, the nonrepudiation is provided for critical portions (fields) of the message. For instance, this may be the case when an endpoint sends a SETUP message to its gatekeeper and the two (endpoint and gatekeeper) are separated by one or more proxies.

Table 3-2 shows the scope of signature security profile. An option within the profile is to select between RSA-SHA1 or RAS-MD5 digital signatures.

Table 3-2 *Signature Security Profile*

Security Services	Call Functions			
	RAS	**H.225**	**H.245**	**RTP**
Authentication	SHA1/MD5 Digital signature	SHA1/MD5 Digital signature	SHA1/MD5 Digital signature	–
Non-repudiation	SHA1/MD5 Digital signature	SHA1/MD5 Digital signature	SHA1/MD5 Digital signature	–
Integrity	SHA1/MD5 Digital signature	SHA1/MD5 Digital signature	SHA1/MD5 Digital signature	–
Confidentiality	–	–	–	–
Access control	–	–	–	–
Key management	Certificate Allocation	Certificate Allocation	–	–

That was a brief summary of signature security. The next topic, Annex F, covers hybrid security.

H.235 Annex F (Hybrid Security)

H.235 Annex F describes an efficient and scalable, public key infrastructure (PKI)-based hybrid security profile deploying digital signatures from Annex E and deploying the baseline security profile from Annex D. This annex is suggested as an option. H.323 security entities (terminals, gatekeepers, gateways, MCUs, and so on) may implement this hybrid security profile for improved security or whenever required.

The notion of "hybrid" in this text means that security procedures from the signature profile in Annex E are actually applied in a lightweight sense and the digital signatures still conform to Rivest, Shamir, Adleman (RSA) procedures. However, digital signatures are deployed only where absolutely necessary, and highly efficient symmetric security techniques from the baseline security profile in Annex D are used otherwise.

The hybrid security profile is applicable for scalable "global" IP telephony. This security profile overcomes the limitations of the simple, baseline security profile of Annex D when strictly applied. Furthermore, this security profile overcomes certain drawbacks of Annex E, such as the need for higher bandwidth and increased performance needs for processing, when strictly applied. For example, the hybrid security profile does not depend on the (static) administration of mutual shared secrets of the hops in different domains. Thus, users can more easily choose their VoIP provider. This security profile supports a certain kind of user mobility as well. It applies asymmetric cryptography with signatures and certificates only where necessary and otherwise uses simpler and more efficient symmetric techniques. It provides tunneling of H.245 messages for H.245 message integrity and also implements some provisions for nonrepudiation of messages.

The hybrid security profile mandates the GK-routed model and is based on the H.245 tunneling techniques. Support for non GK-routed models is for further study.

Table 3-3 shows an overview of hybrid security with security mechanisms.

Table 3-3   *Hybrid Security Profile*

Security Services	Call Functions			
	RAS	**H.225**	**H.245**	**RTP**
Authentication	RSA Digital Signature (SHA1)	RSA Digital Signature (SHA1)	RSA Digital Signature (SHA1)	–
	HMAC-SHA1-96	HMAC-SHA1-96	HMAC-SHA1-96	
Nonrepudiation	(possible only on first message)	(possible only on first message)	RSA Digital Signature (SHA1)	–
Integrity	RSA Digital Signature (SHA1)	RSA Digital Signature (SHA1)	HMAC-SHA1-96	
	HMAC-SHA1-96	HMAC-SHA1-96		
Confidentiality	–	–	–	–
Access control	Certificate Allocation	Certificate Allocation	–	–
Key management	(authenticated Diffie-Hellman key-exchange)	(authenticated Diffie-Hellman key-exchange)	–	–

The preceding sections were a brief summary of hybrid security. So far, you have learned about the components, basic call flow, and security profiles of H.323. The next section covers those same points with SIP.

SIP

SIP (RFC 3261[3]) is an application-layer control protocol that can establish, modify, and terminate multimedia sessions such as Internet telephony (VoIP) calls. SIP can also invite participants to already existing sessions, such as multicast conferences. Media can be added to (and removed from) an existing session. SIP transparently supports name mapping and redirection services, which supports personal mobility—users can maintain a single externally visible identifier regardless of their network location.

In this section, you learn about the security profiles of SIP, as well as the components, basic call flow, and session setup examples, based on RFC 3261.

Overview

SIP is not a vertically integrated communications system. SIP is rather a component that can be used with other protocols to build a complete multimedia architecture.

Typically, these architectures will include protocols such as RTP for transporting real-time data and providing QoS feedback, Real-Time Streaming Protocol (RTSP) for controlling delivery of streaming media, MGCP for controlling gateways to the STN, and Session Description Protocol (SDP) for describing multimedia sessions. Therefore, SIP should be used in conjunction with other protocols to provide complete services to the users. However, the basic functionality and operation of SIP does not depend on any of these protocols.

SIP also provides a suite of security services, which include Denial-of-Service (DoS) prevention, authentication (both user-to-user and proxy-to-user), integrity protection, and encryption and privacy services.

SIP supports five facets of establishing and terminating multimedia communications:

1 **User location**—Determination of the end system to be used for communication.

2 **User availability**—Determination of the willingness of the called party to engage in communications.

3 **User capabilities**—Determination of the media and media parameters to be used.

4 **Session setup**—Establishment of session parameters at both called and calling party.

5 **Session management**—Including transfer and termination of sessions, modifying session parameters, and invoking services.

The next section describes the SIP components.

Components

In SIP, there are two logical entities: User Agent Client (UAC) and User Agent Server (UAS), often just called User Agents.

A *UAC* is a logical entity that creates a new request, and then uses the client transaction state machinery to send it. The role of UAC lasts only for the duration of that transaction. In other words, if a piece of software initiates a request, it acts as a UAC for the duration of that transaction. If it receives a request later, it assumes the role of a user agent server for the processing of that transaction.

On the other hand, a *UAS* is a logical entity that receives a request and generates a response to that SIP request. The UAS accepts, rejects, or redirects the request. This role lasts only for the duration of that transaction. In other words, if a piece of software responds to a request, it acts as a UAS for the duration of that transaction. If it generates a request later, it assumes the role of a user agent client for the processing of that transaction.

Therefore, all IP phones supporting the SIP protocol can be either UAC or UAS depending on the direction of the call request.

It is possible to make a call directly between endpoints (that is, end-to-end call setup), but in most cases, servers are involved in the communication for authentication, call routing, advanced feature services, and so on. There are four servers in SIP: registrar, redirect, and proxy servers, and a Back-to-Back User Agent (B2BUA). Here is the description of each server.

1 **Registrar**—A registration server that accepts REGISTER requests and places the information it receives in those requests into the location service for the domain it handles. It maintains a list of bindings that are accessible to proxy servers and redirect servers within its administrative domain.

2 **Redirect server**—A redirect server that generates 3xx responses to requests it receives, directing the client to contact an alternate set of uniform resource identifiers (URIs).

3 **Proxy server**—An intermediary entity that acts as both a server and a client for the purpose of making requests on behalf of other clients. A proxy server primarily plays the role of routing, which means its job is to ensure that a request is sent to another entity "closer" to the targeted user. A proxy server is also useful for enforcing policy (for example, making sure a user is allowed to make a call). It interprets, and, if necessary, rewrites specific parts of a request message before forwarding it.

4 **Back-to-Back User Agent**—A logical entity that receives a request and processes it as a UAS. To determine how the request should be answered, it acts as a UAC and generates requests. Unlike a proxy server, it maintains dialog state and must participate in all requests sent on the dialogs it has established. Because it is a concatenation of a UAC and UAS, no explicit definitions are needed for its behavior.

These servers could be separate entities physically, or integrated in a single machine, for example, a softswitch. An example of the relationship between a server and a client (UAC) is shown in Figure 3-2.

Now that you are aware of the components of SIP, the next section takes a look at the basic call flow to understand more about SIP.

Basic Call Flow

The call flows between SIP clients and servers are various depending on the service architecture. One of the common call flows is shown in Figure 3-2, assuming that servers share the registration information of users, and clients have to send INVITE to a redirect server first when initiating a call.

Figure 3-2 *Basic Call Flow with Servers*

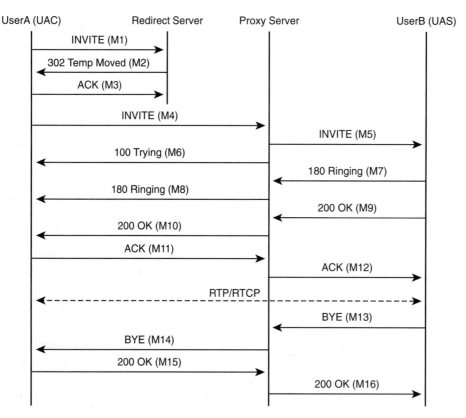

Here is a brief comment for each message in Figure 3-2:

- **M1**—UserA (UAC) sends INVITE message to a Redirect server first to make a call to UserB (UAS).

- **M2**—The Redirect server returns 302 Moved Temporarily response containing a Contact header with UserB's current SIP address.

- **M3**—Acknowledgment.

- **M4 and M5**—UserA then generates a new INVITE with SDP and sends to UserB via a proxy server.

- **M6**—Notifies that the proxy server received the request and continues to process it.
- **M7 and M8**—UserB sends 180 Ringing when the phone is ringing.
- **M9 and M10**—UserB sends 200 OK with SDP when picking up the phone.
- **M11 and M12**—Acknowledgment. After this, the media channel (RTP/RTCP) is opened.
- **M13 and M14**—UserB sends BYE when hanging up the phone.
- **M15 and M16**—Confirmation of disconnecting.

This is a typical example of call flow to set up and disconnect a SIP dialog among a UAC, a UAS, and a proxy server.

The following section shows examples of actual messages with detailed information.

Session Setup Example

This section introduces how a call session between endpoints is established through a proxy server, explaining the content of SIP messages. The reason for adding this section is to give you a deeper understanding of SIP because most protocol examples in this book use the SIP protocol.

Figure 3-3 illustrates a typical example of SIP message exchange between two users (UserA and UserB), assuming that they are in the same domain (example.com) and a single proxy server facilitates the session establishment. Each message is shown in the following examples with comments.

Figure 3-3 *Session Establishment*

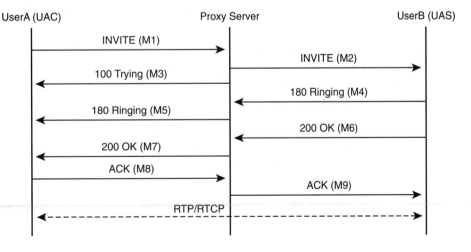

Example 3-1 shows the initial INVITE (M1) from UserA to proxy server.

Example 3-1 *M1*

```
INVITE sip:UserB@example.com SIP/2.0
   Via  SIP/2.0/UDP userAclient.example.com:5060;branch=z9hG4bK74bf9
   Max-Forwards: 70
   From  UserA <sip:UserA@example.com>;tag=9fxced76sl
   To  UserB <sip:UserB@example.com>
   Call-ID: 2xTb9vxSit55XU7p8@example.com
   CSeq: 1 INVITE
   Contact: <sip:UserA@userAclient.example.com>
   Content-Type: application/sdp
   Content-Length: 151

   v=0
   o=UserA 2890844526 2890844526 IN IP4 userAclient.example.com
   s=-
   c=IN IP4 192.0.2.101
   t=0 0
   m=audio 49172 RTP/AVP 0
   a=rtpmap:0 PCMU/8000
```

UserA calls UserB using his SIP identity, a type of URI called a SIP URI. In this case, it is sip:UserB@example.com, where example.com is the domain of UserB's SIP service provider. UserA has a SIP URI of sip:UserA@example.com.

SIP also provides a secure URI, called a SIPS URI. An example would be sips:UserB@ example.com. A call made to a SIPS URI guarantees that secure, encrypted transport (namely TLS) is used to carry all SIP messages from the caller to the domain of the callee. From there, the request is sent securely to the callee, but with security mechanisms that depend on the policy of the domain of the callee.

SIP is based on an HTTP-like request/response transaction model. Each transaction consists of a request that invokes a particular method, or function, on the server and at least one response. In this example, the transaction begins with UserA's IP phone sending an INVITE request addressed to UserB's SIP URI. INVITE is an example of a SIP method that specifies the action that the requestor (UserA) wants the server (UserB) to take. The INVITE request contains a number of header fields. Header fields are named attributes that provide additional information about a message. The ones present in an INVITE include a unique identifier for the call, the destination address, UserA's address, and information about the type of session that UserA wishes to establish with UserB.

The first line of the text-encoded message contains the method name (INVITE). The lines that follow are a list of header fields. This example contains a minimum required set; the following six headers are mandatory. The header fields are briefly described in the following list:

- **Via**—Contains the address (userAclient.example.com) at which UserA is expecting to receive responses to this request. It also contains a branch parameter that identifies this transaction.

- **Max-Forwards**—Serves to limit the number of hops a request can make on the way to its destination. It consists of an integer that is decremented by one at each hop.

- **From**—Contains a display name (UserA) and a SIP or SIPS URI (sip:UserA@example.com) that indicate the originator of the request. This header field also has a tag parameter containing a random string (9fxced76sl) that was added to the URI by the UAC. It is used for identification purposes.

- **To**—Contains a display name (UserB) and a SIP or SIPS URI (sip:UserB@example.com) toward which the request was originally directed.

- **Call-ID**—Contains a globally unique identifier for this call, generated by the combination of a random string and the IP phone's host name or IP address. The combination of the To tag, From tag, and Call-ID completely defines a peer-to-peer SIP relationship between UserA and UserB and is referred to as a dialog.

- **CSeq or Command Sequence**—Contains an integer and a method name. The CSeq number is incremented for each new request within a dialog and is a traditional sequence number.

The following three headers also can be used for specific purposes, even though they are not mandatory.

- **Contact**—Contains a SIP or SIPS URI that represents a direct route to contact UserA, usually composed of a username at a fully qualified domain name (FQDN). The Via header field tells other elements where to send the response, and the Contact header field tells other elements where to send future requests.

- **Content-Type**—Contains a description of the message body, which is typically application/sdp (described next).

- **Content-Length**—Contains an octet (byte) count of the message body.

The remaining portion is the body of a SIP message, typically SDP (RFC 4566), which contains the description of the session, such as the type of media, codec, and port ("m=" line), IP address ("c=" line), and sampling rate ("a=" line).

Example 3-2 shows INVITE (M2) from proxy server to UserB in Figure 3-3.

Example 3-2 *M2*

```
INVITE sip:UserB@userBclient.example.com SIP/2.0
   Via: SIP/2.0/UDP ss2.example.com:5060;branch=z9hG4bK2d4790.1
   Via: SIP/2.0/UDP
     userAclient.example.com:5060;branch=z9hG4bK74bf9;received=192.0.2.101
   Max-Forwards: 69
   From: UserA <sip:UserA@example.com>;tag=9fxced76sl
   To: UserB <sip:UserB@example.com>
   Call-ID: 2xTb9vxSit55XU7p8@example.com
   CSeq: 1 INVITE
   Contact: <sip:UserA@userAclient.example.com>
   Content-Type: application/sdp
   Content-Length: 151

   v=0
   o=UserA 2890844526 2890844526 IN IP4 userAclient.example.com
   s=-
   c=IN IP4 192.0.2.101
   t=0 0
   m=audio 49172 RTP/AVP 0
   a=rtpmap:0 PCMU/8000
```

Example 3-3 shows 100 Trying (M3) from proxy server to UserA in Figure 3-3.

Example 3-3 *M3*

```
SIP/2.0 100 Trying
   Via: SIP/2.0/UDP userAclient.example.com:5060;branch=z9hG4bK74bf9
    ;received=192.0.2.101
   From: UserA <sip:UserA@example.com>;tag=9fxced76sl
   To: UserB <sip:UserB@example.com>
   Call-ID: 2xTb9vxSit55XU7p8@example.com
   CSeq: 1 INVITE
   Content-Length: 0
```

The proxy server receives SIP requests and forwards them on behalf of the requestor. In this example, the proxy server receives the INVITE request and sends a 100 Trying response back to UserA's IP phone. The 100 Trying response indicates that the INVITE has been received and that the proxy is working on UserA's behalf to route the INVITE to the destination. Responses in SIP use a three-digit code followed by a descriptive phrase. This response contains the same To, From, Call-ID, CSeq, and branch parameter in the Via as in the INVITE, which allows UserA's IP phone to correlate this response to the sent INVITE.

Before forwarding the request, the proxy server adds an additional Via header field value that contains its own address (the INVITE already contains UserA's address in the first Via).

The proxy server consults a database, generically called a location service, which contains the current IP address of UserB.

Example 3-4 shows 180 Ringing (M4) from UserB to proxy server in Figure 3-3.

Example 3-4   *M4*

```
SIP/2.0 180 Ringing
    Via: SIP/2.0/UDP ss2.example.com:5060;branch=z9hG4bK2d4790.1
    ;received=192.0.2.222
    Via: SIP/2.0/UDP userAclient.example.com:5060;branch=z9hG4bK74bf9
    ;received=192.0.2.101
    From: UserA <sip:UserA@example.com>;tag=9fxced76sl
    To: UserB <sip:UserB@example.com>;tag=314159
    Call-ID: 2xTb9vxSit55XU7p8@example.com
    CSeq: 1 INVITE
    Contact: <sip:UserB@userBclient.example.com>
    Content-Length: 0
```

Example 3-5 shows 180 Ringing (M5) from proxy server to UserA in Figure 3-3.

Example 3-5   *M5*

```
SIP/2.0 180 Ringing
    Via: SIP/2.0/UDP userAclient.example.com:5060;branch=z9hG4bK74bf9
    ;received=192.0.2.101
    From: UserA <sip:UserA@example.com>;tag=9fxced76sl
    To: UserB <sip:UserB@example.com>;tag=314159
    Call-ID: 2xTb9vxSit55XU7p8@example.com
    CSeq: 1 INVITE
    Contact: <sip:UserB@userBclient.example.com>
    Content-Length: 0
```

UserB's SIP phone receives the INVITE and alerts UserB to the incoming call from UserA so that UserB can decide whether to answer the call, that is, UserB's phone rings. UserB's SIP phone indicates this in a 180 Ringing response, which is routed back through the proxy in the reverse direction. The proxy uses the Via header field to determine where to send the response and removes its own address from the top.

When UserA's IP phone receives the 180 Ringing response, it passes this information to UserA, perhaps using an audio ringback tone or by displaying a message on UserA's screen.

Example 3-6 shows 200 OK (M6) from UserB to proxy server in Figure 3-3.

Example 3-6 *M6*

```
SIP/2.0 200 OK
    Via: SIP/2.0/UDP ss2.example.com:5060;branch=z9hG4bK2d4790.1
     ;received=192.0.2.222
    Via: SIP/2.0/UDP userAclient.example.com:5060;branch=z9hG4bK74bf9
     ;received=192.0.2.101
    From: UserA <sip:UserA@example.com>;tag=9fxced76sl
    To: UserB <sip:UserB@example.com>;tag=314159
    Call-ID: 2xTb9vxSit55XU7p8@example.com
    CSeq: 1 INVITE
    Contact: <sip:UserB@userBclient.example.com>
    Content-Type: application/sdp
    Content-Length: 147

    v=0
    o=UserB 2890844527 2890844527 IN IP4 userBclient.example.com
    s=-
    c=IN IP4 192.0.2.201
    t=0 0
    m=audio 3456 RTP/AVP 0
    a=rtpmap:0 PCMU/8000
```

Example 3-7 shows 200 OK (M7) from proxy server to UserA in Figure 3-3.

Example 3-7 *M7*

```
SIP/2.0 200 OK
    Via: SIP/2.0/UDP userAclient.example.com:5060;branch=z9hG4bK74bf9
     ;received=192.0.2.101
    From: UserA <sip:UserA@example.com>;tag=9fxced76sl
    To: UserB <sip:UserB@example.com>;tag=314159
    Call-ID: 2xTb9vxSit55XU7p8@example.com
    CSeq: 1 INVITE
    Contact: <sip:UserB@userBclient.example.com>
    Content-Type: application/sdp
    Content-Length: 147

    v=0
    o=UserB 2890844527 2890844527 IN IP4 userBclient.example.com
    s=-
    c=IN IP4 192.0.2.201
    t=0 0
    m=audio 3456 RTP/AVP 0
    a=rtpmap:0 PCMU/8000
```

In this example, UserB decides to answer the call. When he picks up the handset, his SIP phone sends a 200 OK response to indicate that the call has been answered. The 200 OK contains a message body with the SDP media description of the type of session that UserB is willing to establish with UserA. As a result, there is a two-phase exchange of SDP messages: UserA sent one to UserB, and UserB sent one back to UserA. This two-phase exchange provides basic negotiation capabilities and is based on a simple offer/answer model of SDP exchange based on RFC 3264. If UserB did not want to answer the call or was busy on another call, an error response would have been sent instead of the 200 OK, which would have resulted in no media session being established.

UserB's SIP phone has added a tag parameter to the To header field (UserA's phone has added a tag to the From header in the initial INVITE). This tag will be incorporated by both endpoints into the dialog and will be included in all future requests and responses in this call.

The Contact header field contains a URI at which UserB can be directly reached at his SIP phone.

Example 3-8 shows ACK (M8) from UserA to proxy server in Figure 3-3.

Example 3-8   *M8*

```
ACK sip:UserB@userBclient.example.com SIP/2.0
    Via: SIP/2.0/UDP userAclient.example.com:5060;branch=z9hG4bK74b7b
    Max-Forwards: 70
    From: UserA <sip:UserA@example.com>;tag=9fxced76sl
    To: UserB <sip:UserB@example.com>;tag=314159
    Call-ID: 2xTb9vxSit55XU7p8@example.com
    CSeq: 1 ACK
    Content-Length: 0
```

Finally, UserA's phone sends an acknowledgment message, ACK, to UserB's phone to confirm the reception of the final response (200 [OK]).

UserA and UserB's media session has now begun, and they send media packets using the format to which they agreed in the exchange of SDP. In general, the end-to-end media packets take a different path from the SIP signaling messages.

Now that you are aware of basic call setup with SIP messages, the next section looks into security profiles.

Security Profiles

The SIP protocol describes several security features and their usage guidelines. The main features are as follows:

- Digest authentication
- Identity authentication
- Message encryption (S/MIME)

- Media encryption (SRTP)
- Transport layer security (TLS)
- Network layer security (IPSec)

Only the authentication mechanism is defined within the SIP protocol, and the others are adapted from other security protocols.

This section introduces the features at a high level, referring to RFC 3261.[3] For more detailed information, refer to each protocol specification. Chapter 7, "Protection with VoIP Protocol," shows the usage examples.

Digest Authentication

SIP provides challenge-based Digest authentication that is derived from HTTP authentication. It challenges one-direction between UAC and UAS including Registrar, or between user agent (UA) and proxy server.

When UAS, proxy, or registrar receives a request, it may challenge the request to provide the assurance of identity of the originator. The originator can reply with its credential with encryption (for example, MD5), or reject the challenge. When the credential is received, the server verifies and sends back respective response codes like 401 (Unauthorized) or 200 (OK).

The high-level mechanism is shown in Figure 3-4.

Figure 3-4 *Authentication and Authorization Mechanism*

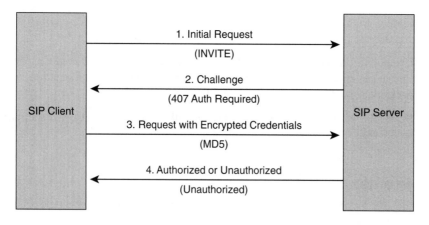

Because of the security issue, the previous method of Basic authentication (RFC 2543) is not acceptable anymore: It is supposed to be rejected or ignored.

NOTE   This section uses many cryptographic terms and methods. For more detailed information, refer to Chapter 4, "Cryptography."

Identity Authentication

In general, the "From" header in a SIP request message contains the identity of an originator (address-of-record; see the following Note), and the originator may manipulate or spoof the identity when making a call. This type of identity issues and authentication mechanism for SIP is defined in RFC 4474.[4]

NOTE   An address-of-record (AoR) is a SIP or SIPS URI that points to a domain with a location service that can map the URI to another URI where the user might be available. Typically, the location service is populated through registrations. An AoR is frequently thought of as the "public address" of the user.

RFC 3261 itself does not define the solid mechanism for securely identifying originators of SIP requests. Instead, it recommends the way in which a user agent authenticates itself to a local proxy server, which in turn authenticates itself to a remote proxy server via mutual TLS, creating a two-link chain of transitive authentication between the originator and the remote domain. This transitive trust is inherently weaker than an assertion that can be validated end-to-end. It is possible for SIP requests to cross multiple intermediaries in separate administrative domains, in which case transitive trust becomes even less compelling.

One solution to this problem is to use "trusted" SIP intermediaries that assert an identity for users in the form of a privileged SIP header. A mechanism for doing so (with the P-Asserted-Identity header) is given in RFC 3325. However, this solution allows only hop-by-hop trust between intermediaries, not end-to-end cryptographic authentication, and it assumes a managed network of nodes with strict mutual trust relationships, an assumption that is incompatible with widespread Internet deployment.

Accordingly, RFC 4474 specifies a means of sharing a cryptographic assurance of end-user SIP identity in an interdomain or intradomain context that is based on the concept of an "authentication service" and a new SIP header, the Identity header.

The RFC 4474 specification allows either a user agent or a proxy server to provide identity services and to verify identities. To maximize end-to-end security, it is obviously preferable for end users to acquire their own certificates and corresponding private keys; if they do, they can act as an authentication service. However, end-user certificates may be neither practical nor affordable, given the difficulties of establishing a Public Key Infrastructure (PKI) that extends to end users. Accordingly, in the initial use of this mechanism, it is likely that intermediaries will instantiate the authentication service role.

Here is a usage example: Imagine the case of Alice, who has the home proxy of example.com and the address-of-record (AoR) sip:alice@example.com, wants to communicate with Bob, sip:bob@example.org.

Alice generates an INVITE and places her identity in the From header field of the request. She then sends an INVITE over TLS to an authentication service proxy for her domain. The authentication service authenticates Alice (possibly by sending a Digest authentication challenge) and validates that she is authorized to assert the identity that is populated in the From header field. This value may be Alice's AoR, or it may be some other value that the policy of the proxy server permits her to use. It then computes a hash over some particular headers, including the From header field and the body of the message (which usually contains SDP). This hash is signed with the certificate for the domain (example.com, in Alice's case) and inserted in a new header field in the SIP message, the "Identity" header.

The authentication service, as the holder of the private key of its domain, is asserting that the originator of this request has been authenticated and that she is authorized to claim the identity (the SIP address-of-record) that appears in the From header field. The proxy also inserts a companion header field, Identity-Info, that tells Bob how to acquire its certificate, if he does not already have it.

When Bob's domain receives the request, it verifies the signature provided in the Identity header, and thus can validate that the domain indicated by the host portion of the AoR in the From header field authenticated the user, and permitted the user to assert that From header field value. This same validation operation may be performed by Bob's UAS.

Secure/Multipurpose Internet Mail Extensions (S/MIME)

End-to-end full encryption is the most common way to provide message confidentiality and integrity between communication endpoints. The SIP standard (RFC 3261) also recommends encryption for the purpose, but there are some limitations on providing the full encryption.

It is almost impossible, or we might say not practical, to encrypt all SIP requests and responses end-to-end because intermediaries like proxy servers have to look at the message fields to route properly. In particular, "Request-URI", "Route", and "Via" headers should be visible to the proxy server to route the call. Furthermore, the proxy server needs to modify some message field like the "Via" header by adding its own IP address.

If there is a limitation on end-to-end full encryption, what is the alternative? Two parts of the SIP transaction can be encrypted: message body and media. Message body encryption with S/MIME is recommended in SIP.

Secure/Multipurpose Internet Mail Extensions (S/MIME) is, as the name implies, a combination of MIME format plus security specification. MIME was developed by the Internet Engineering Task Force (IETF) to define the format of email messages, supporting characters beyond US-ASCII, non-test attachment, multipurpose message bodies, and header information in non-ASCII characters.

This MIME format is also adapted by other protocols like HTTP as a supplement (SIP is derived from HTTP). The security specification was originally defined in the de facto standard PKCS #7 by RSA Laboratories, showing how to encrypt messages with a public key. IETF adapted PKCS #7 and documented it in RFC 2315 (Cryptographic Message Syntax [CMS]).

S/MIME allows SIP UAs to encrypt MIME bodies within SIP and secure the bodies end-to-end without affecting message headers. The typical MIME types securing the contents are 'multipart/signed' and 'application/pkcs7-mime'.

However, there could be an issue if some of the network intermediaries rely on the message body (SDP) and modifying it. Typical proxy servers do not do this, but some servers like B2BUA (Back-to-Back User Agent) do.

Secure RTP

Secure RTP (SRTP) is an extension of RTP, which provides security features, such as encryption and authentication.

The method of securing RTP packets was not defined when SIP (RFC 3261) was released. In 2004, researchers from Cisco and Ericsson proposed the specification and IETF listed in RFC 3711. It provides a framework for encryption and message authentication of RTP and RTCP streams (note that SRTP includes SRTCP in this context).

SRTP has not been widely deployed yet for VoIP services because of some issues like performance, complexity of implementation, and interoperability. However, it is critical technology that you can provide to ensure the confidentiality and integrity of media streams.

It uses a common security mechanism in which, between communication parties, they share keys and encrypt/decrypt RTP packets. Chapter 7 demonstrates the usage of SRTP.

TLS

Because the full encryption of a message is almost impossible within public service networks because of intermediary servers, as mentioned before, we need a low-layer security mechanism that encrypts entire SIP requests and responses on the wire for providing the confidentiality and integrity of messages.

The main role of TLS is to provide transport-layer security over connection-oriented protocols (that is, TCP) as defined in its RFC 4346.[5] Figure 3-5 illustrates the typical example of the TLS handshake protocol to negotiate a secure session between client and server; in particular, it shows how the client verifies and creates a session with the server.

Figure 3-5   *TLS Handshake*

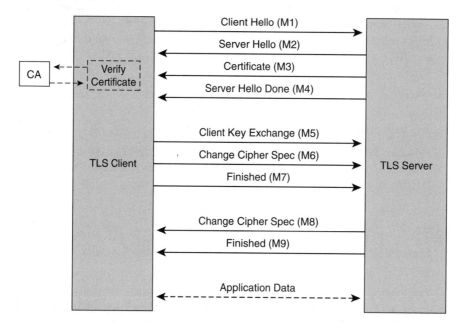

- **M1** and **M2**—The client hello and server hello are used to establish security capabilities between client and server, such as protocol version, session ID, cipher suite, and compression method.

- **M3**—Following the hello messages, the server will send its certificate containing the server's public key, name, and Certificate Authority (CA), for example, VeriSign. The client may contact the CA to confirm that the certificate is authentic.

- **M4**—Hello done message, indicating that the hello-message phase of the handshake is complete. The server will then wait for a client response.

- **M5**—With client key exchange message, the pre-master secret is set; the client encrypts a random number with the server's public key to generate session keys for the connection.

- **M6**—Change cipher spec message is sent by the client, and the client copies the pending Cipher Spec into the current Cipher Spec.

- **M7**—The client then immediately sends the finished message under the new algorithms, keys, and secrets.

- **M8** and **M9**—In response, the server will send its own change cipher spec message, transfer the pending to the current Cipher Spec, and send its finished message under the new Cipher Spec. At this point, the handshake is complete, and the client and server may begin to exchange application layer data.

Typically, SIP uses TLS to provide hop-by-hop security in the service network and eventually give end-to-end security between UAs. For example, think about this kind of common situation: User agent A tries to make a call to user agent B through A's proxy server and B's proxy server. Also, there is no trust between A and B, but A trusts A's proxy server and B trusts B's proxy server through TLS (or another way like IPSec). In this case, we can provide end-to-end security by exchanging certificates between A's and B's proxy server through TLS.

NOTE   Transport mechanisms are specified on a hop-by-hop basis in SIP, so a user agent that sends requests over TLS to a proxy server has no assurance that TLS will be used end-to-end.

The following section describes another lower-layer security mechanism, IPSec, which SIP also recommends.

IPSec

IPSec is a suite of network-layer protocols securing IP network communications by encrypting and authenticating data. It is generally used for Virtual Private Network (VPN) connection.

Basically, the IPSec protocol (network layer) is independent of the SIP protocol (application layer) and there is no required integration between them. Unlike the integration with TLS, SIP does not provide any indication of IPSec in the messages. However, practically speaking, IPSec is very useful to provide security between SIP entities, especially between a UA and a proxy server. UAs that have a preshared keying relationship with their first-hop proxy server are good candidates to use IPSec.

Implementers should consider a separate security mechanism from SIP protocol because IPSec is usually deployed at the operating system level in a host, or on a security gateway (for example, a VPN server) that provides confidentiality and integrity for all traffic that it receives from a particular interface.

In this section, you have learned about the security profiles of SIP, such as Digest authentication, identity authentication, S/MIME, SRTP, TLS, and IPSec. The next section covers another VoIP protocol, MGCP.

MGCP

MGCP was initially defined in RFC 2705 as a control protocol of media gateway, and updated in year 2003 as RFC 3435. RFC 3435 is still MGCP version 1 because it updates only minor things with error fixes. As a variant, the organization PacketCable adapted this protocol and released NCS, which is available on the PacketCable website. The content in this section refers to RFC 3435.[6]

Overview

As the name Media Gateway Control Protocol (MGCP) implies, it is a protocol based on a master-slave relation between entities. The master is called Call Agent, which controls the slave, called Media Gateway. Figure 3-6 illustrates the transaction between the elements; the call agent initiates transactions (commands) to manage or configure the media gateway. The protocol is text-based and offers a set of simple primitives.

Figure 3-6 *MGCP Transaction*

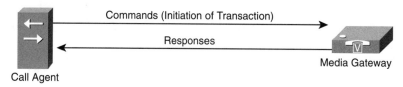

A *media gateway* is a network element that provides conversion between the audio signals carried on telephone circuits and data packets carried over the Internet or over other packet networks. Some examples of media gateways are:

- **Trunking gateways**—Interface between the telephone network and a VoIP network. Such gateways typically manage a large number of digital circuits.

- **Residential gateways**—Provide a traditional analog (RJ11) interface to a VoIP network. Examples of residential gateways include cable modem/cable set-top boxes, DSL devices, and broadband wireless devices.

- **Access gateways**—Provide a traditional analog (RJ11) or digital PBX interface to a VoIP network. Examples of access gateways include small-scale VoIP gateways.

MGCP assumes a call control architecture where the call control "intelligence" is outside the gateways and handled by external call control elements. The MGCP assumes that these call control elements (call agents) will synchronize with each other to send coherent commands to the gateways under their control. MGCP does not define a mechanism for synchronizing call agents.

Basic Call Flow

MGCP defines nine commands for the service that consist of connection handing and endpoint handling. The nine commands are as follows:

- **NotificationRequest (RQNT)**—The call agent can issue a command to a gateway, instructing the gateway to watch for specific events such as hook actions or DTMF tones on a specified endpoint.

- **Notify (NTFY)**—The gateway will then use this command to inform the call agent when the requested events occur.

- **CreateConnection (CRCX)**—The call agent can use this command to create a connection that terminates in an "endpoint" inside the gateway.

- **ModifyConnection (MDCX)**—The call agent can use this command to change the parameters associated with a previously established connection.

- **DeleteConnection (DLCX)**—The call agent can use this command to delete an existing connection. This command may also be used by a gateway to indicate that a connection can no longer be sustained.

- **AuditEndpoint (AUEP)** and **AuditConnection (AUCX)**—The call agent can use these commands to audit the status of an "endpoint" and any connections associated with it.

- **RestartInProgress (RSIP)**—The gateway can use the command to notify the call agent that a group of endpoints managed by the gateway is being taken out of service or is being placed back in service.

- **EndpointConfiguration (EPCF)**—The call agent can issue this command to a gateway, instructing the gateway about the coding characteristics.

As an example of call flow, Figure 3-7 illustrates the call setup procedure between two residential gateways controlled by a call agent; User A (using Gateway A) makes a call to User B (using Gateway B) through Call Agent.

Figure 3-7 shows many different commands among Gateway A, Call Agent, and Gateway B, while User A picks up the phone (off-hook), hears a dial tone, presses digits, hears ringback, and so on. For the details of each command, refer to RFC 3435.

The next subsection discusses the security profiles of MGCP.

Security Profiles

MGCP does not define any specification of security profile, but refers to lower-layer security protocols. It recommends that MGCP messages always be carried over secure Internet connections, as defined in IPSec using either the IP Authentication Header (AH) or the IP Encapsulation Security Payload (ESP). The complete MGCP protocol stack would thus include the layers in Figure 3-8.

Figure 3-7 *MGCP Call Setup*

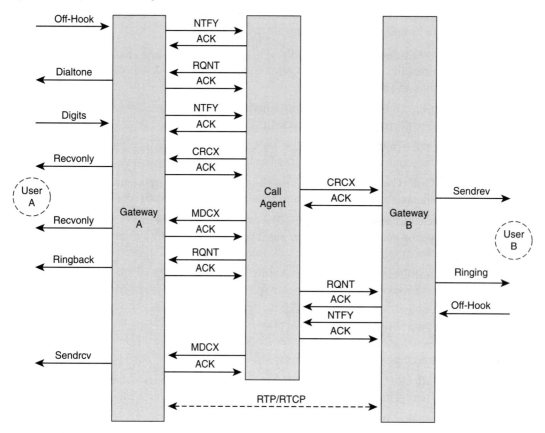

Figure 3-8 *MGCP Protocol Stack*

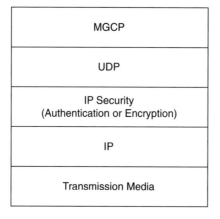

Adequate protection of the connections will be achieved if the gateways and the call agents only accept messages for which IP security provided an authentication service. An encryption service will provide additional protection against eavesdropping or traffic analysis, thus preventing third parties from monitoring the connections set up by a given endpoint.

The encryption service will also be useful if the session descriptions are used to carry session keys, as defined in SDP.

These procedures do not necessarily protect against Denial-of-Service attacks by misbehaving gateways or misbehaving call agents. However, they will provide an identification of these misbehaving entities, which should then be deprived of their authorization through maintenance procedures.

For the protection of media connections, MGCP allows the call agent to provide gateways with "session keys" that can be used to encrypt the audio messages, protecting against eavesdropping, based on RFC 4568.

A specific problem of packet networks is "uncontrolled barge-in." This attack can be performed by directing media packets to the IP address and UDP port used by a connection. If no protection of the media is implemented, the packets will be decoded and played to the user. A basic protection against this attack is to only accept packets from communication parties; however, this tends to conflict with RTP principles. This also has two issues:

- **It slows down connection establishment**—To enable the address-based protection, the call agent must obtain the source address of the egress gateway and pass it to the ingress gateway (see Note). This requires at least one network round trip, and leaves us with a dilemma: either allow the call to proceed without waiting for the round trip to complete, and risk for example "clipping" a remote announcement; or wait for the full round trip and settle for slower call setup procedures.

NOTE   Such IP address validation requires the far-end user-symmetric RTP/RTCP, based on RFC 4961. Although the symmetric RTP/RTCP is commonly used, it is not required by MGCP, SIP, or H.323.

- **It can be fooled by source spoofing**—Source spoofing is only effective if the attacker can obtain valid pairs of source and destination addresses and ports, for example by listening to a fraction of the traffic. To fight source spoofing, one could try to control all access points to the network. But in practice, this is very hard to achieve.

An alternative to checking the source address is to encrypt and authenticate the packets, using a secret key that is conveyed during the call setup procedure. This will provide strong protection against address spoofing.

In this section, you have learned about the components, basic call flow, and security profiles of MGCP.

Summary

VoIP protocols (SIP, H.323, and MGCP) define specific security mechanisms as part of the protocols, or recommend combined solution with other security protocols. Even though these security profiles are not enough to make the whole VoIP service secure, they are essential elements as part of the comprehensive solution.

H.323 is the ITU specification describing the complete architecture and operations of audio and video communications across packetized networks. It is an umbrella specification that encompasses many other protocols, such as H.225, H.235, H.245, and RTP/RTCP. The main components are terminal, gateway, gatekeeper, MC, and MCU.

H.235 describes security enhancements within the framework of H.323 to incorporate security services such as authentication and privacy. The proposed scheme is applicable to both simple point-to-point and multipoint conferences for any terminals that utilize H.245 as a control protocol.

H.235 includes several annexes that each hold security profiles of H.235. Annex D defines a simple, baseline security profile that provides security mechanism by simple means using secure password-based cryptographic techniques. Annex E describes a security profile deploying digital signatures. Annex F describes an efficient and scalable, PKI-based hybrid security profile deploying digital signatures from Annex E and deploying the baseline security profile from Annex D.

SIP (RFC 3261) is an application-layer control protocol that can establish, modify, and terminate multimedia sessions such as VoIP calls. It is not a vertically integrated communications system, but a component that can be used with other protocols to build a complete multimedia architecture. Typically, these architectures will include protocols such as RTP/RTCP, RTSP, and SDP.

SIP describes several security features and their usage guidelines. The main features are digest authentication, identity authentication, message encryption (S/MIME), media encryption (SRTP), TLS, and network layer security (IPSec).

Digest authentication means that, when a server receives a request, it may challenge the request to provide the assurance the originator's identity. The originator can reply with its credential with encryption, and the server verifies it and sends back respective response codes.

Identity authentication is defined in RFC 4474, which specifies a means of sharing a cryptographic assurance of end-user SIP identity in an interdomain or intradomain context that is based on the concept of an "authentication service" and a new SIP header, the Identity header.

S/MIME allows SIP UAs to encrypt MIME bodies within SIP and secure the bodies end-to-end without affecting message headers.

SRTP is an extension of RTP, which provides a framework for encryption and message authentication of RTP and RTCP stream between SIP endpoints.

TLS is to provide transport-layer security over connection-oriented protocols (TCP). Typically, SIP uses TLS to provide hop-by-hop security in the service network and eventually give end-to-end security between UAs.

IPSec is a suite of network-layer protocols securing IP network communications by encrypting and authenticating data. It is independent of the SIP protocol and there is no required integration between them. However, IPSec is very useful to provide security between SIP entities, especially between UA and a proxy server.

MGCP is a device control protocol that provides a simple and centralized mechanism of controlling media gateways, based on a master-slave relation between call agent and media gateway. The protocol is text-based and offers a set of simple primitives.

MGCP does not define any specification of security profile, but refers to lower-layer security protocols. It recommends that MGCP messages always be carried over secure Internet connections, as defined in IPSec using either the IP AH or the IP ESP.

End Notes

1 H.323, "Packet-based multimedia communications systems," ITU-T, June 2006.

2 H.235, "Security and encryption for H-series (H.323 and other H.245-based) multimedia terminals," ITU-T, August 2003.

3 RFC 3261, "SIP (Session Initiation Protocol)," J. Rosenberg, H. Schulzrinne, G. Camarillo, A. Johnston, J. Peterson, R. Sparks, M. Handley, and E. Schooler, June 2002.

4 RFC 4474, "Enhancements for Authenticated Identity Management in the SIP," J. Peterson, C. Jennings, August 2006.

5 RFC 4346, "Transport Layer Security (TLS) Protocol," T. Dierks, E. Rescorla, April 2006.

6 RFC 3435, "Media Gateway Control Protocol (MGCP) Version 1.0," F. Andreasen, B. Foster, January 2003.

References

"Security Considerations for VoIP Systems," NIST (National Institute of Standards and Technology), January 2005.

RFC 2617, "HTTP Authentication: Basic and Digest Access Authentication," J. Franks, P. Hallam-Baker, J. Hostetler, S. Lawrence, P. Leach, A. Luotonen, L. Stewart, June 1999.

RFC 3264, "An Offer/Answer Model with the Session Description Protocol (SDP)," J. Rosenberg, H. Schulzrinne, June 2002.

RFC 3711, "Secure Real-time Transport Protocol (SRTP)," M. Baugher, D. McGrew, M. Naslund, E. Carrara, K. Norrman, March 2004.

RFC 4566, "Session Description Protocol," M. Handley, V. Jacobson, C. Perkins, July 2006.

RFC 4568, "Session Description Protocol (SDP) Security Descriptions for Media Streams," F. Andreasen, M. Baugher, D. Wing, July 2006.

RFC 4961, "Symmetric RTP/RTP Control Protocol," D. Wing, July 2007.

This chapter covers the basic concept and practice of the following topics in cryptography:

- Symmetric (Private) Key Cryptography
  - DES
  - 3DES
  - AES
- Asymmetric (Public) Key Cryptography
  - RSA
  - Digital Signature (DSA)
- Hashing
  - MD5
  - SHA
  - Message Authentication Code (MAC)
- Key Management

CHAPTER 4

Cryptography

The topic of "VoIP security" includes many aspects. One of the key aspects is the methodology of information hiding; that is, how to conceal the signals and media in real-time communications from unauthorized entities. Cryptography is the main solution for this aspect.

NOTE The purpose of this chapter is to give a high-level understanding of each technique with comprehensible figures, rather than looking into the mathematical detail of cryptographic algorithms.

As an introduction, here are some explanations of the terminology related to this topic.

Cryptography is that part of cryptology that is derived from the Greek *cryptos* (meaning hidden) and *logos* (meaning science), which literally means the science of hiding information. Cryptology consists of two areas: cryptography and cryptanalysis.

Cryptography is the practice and study of hiding information based on a secret key. Only people who have access to the key can encrypt or decrypt the information.

Cryptanalysis (also known as "hacking") is the practice and study of deciphering encrypted information without any information about the keys that are used. In a positive way, cryptanalysis helps cryptologists evaluate certain cryptography and create better algorithms. In a negative way, it is illegally used for cracking encrypted information.

This chapter briefly covers cryptanalysis, but mainly focuses on cryptography in terms of basic concept and high-level algorithms.

Cryptography is divided into two categories according to the usage of keys: *symmetric* and *asymmetric* key cryptography.

Symmetric key cryptography is based on a single key that both the sender and the receiver use for encrypting and decrypting the information. Asymmetric key cryptography is based on two keys: one for encrypting and the other for decrypting. Their implementation is various, and this chapter covers the well-known cryptographic methods as follows:

- Symmetric (Private) Key Cryptography
  — DES (Data Encryption Standard)
  — 3DES
  — AES (Advanced Encryption Standard)
- Asymmetric (Public) Key Cryptography
  — RSA
  — Digital Signature Algorithm (DSA)

Additionally, this chapter covers cryptographic hashing functions such as Message-Digest Algorithm 5 (MD5), Secure Hash Algorithm (SHA), and Message Authentication Code (MAC), which provide message integrity or authenticity.

Besides these cryptographic methods focusing on the protection of information, key management is another important aspect in cryptography. Key management includes key generation, distribution, storage, replacement, and final destruction. The last section of this chapter discusses this topic, mainly focusing on key distribution.

The first section introduces symmetric key cryptography.

Symmetric (Private) Key Cryptography

The most common way of hiding a message is encrypting it with a key, supposing that decrypting without the key is virtually impossible. The communication parties share the key only between themselves before sending their messages. This kind of shared single key is called a *private* or *symmetric* key.

Figure 4-1 illustrates the basic mechanism of symmetric (private) key cryptography; when User A sends a message to User B, A encrypts it with a private key, and B decrypts with the same private key. An attacker in the middle may intercept the encrypted message, but it is almost impossible to decrypt it without the private key.

There are many standards defining private key cryptography. This section describes three popular algorithms at a high level: DES, 3DES, and AES.

Figure 4-1 *Symmetric (Private) Key Cryptography*

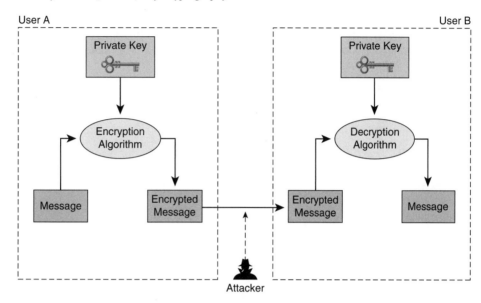

Data Encryption Standard (DES) was approved as an official Federal Information Processing Standard (FIPS 46) in 1976, and subsequently has been reaffirmed many times. It has been popular since then, but it is considered to be insecure because of the relatively short length of the key (56 bits). Therefore, the latest version (FIPS-46-6) released in 1999 recommends using Triple DES (3DES), which runs the DES algorithm three times. DES was superseded by Advanced Encryption Standard (AES) in 2002. Even though DES was superseded, it remains in widespread use. The National Institute of Standard Technology (NIST) has approved 3DES through the year 2030 for sensitive government information.

The following three sections give the details of each algorithm.

DES

DES is the most well-known cryptographic algorithm that specifies the method of encrypting and decrypting data with a secret key.

The algorithm is designed to encrypt and decrypt blocks of data consisting of 64 bits under control of a 64-bit key. Only 56 bits of the key are used and the remaining 8 bits are used for parity check. Decrypting must be accomplished by using the same key as for encrypting, but with the schedule of addressing the key bits altered so that the deciphering process is the reverse of the enciphering process.

Figure 4-2 illustrates the general diagram of the DES algorithm where the following notation is used:

The 64-bit input data can be denoted LR. L is 32 left-hand bits and R is 32 right-hand bits. K1–K16 are DES subkeys that are derived from the 64-bit original key K.

Figure 4-2 *DES Algorithm*

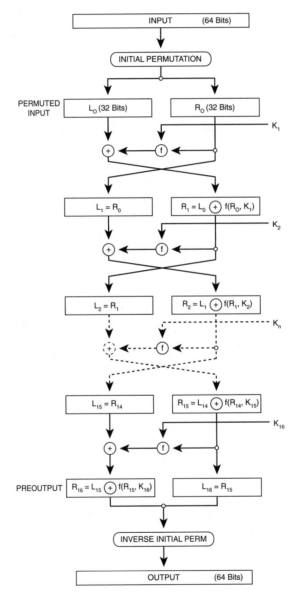

The 64-bit input data is divided into 32 L bits and 32 R bits when passing through the initial permutation. After this, 16 operations (called DES rounds) are performed, and inverse permutation of the two blocks of data is calculated at the last step. The output is 64-bit encrypted data.

Regarding the 16 operations, every step exchanges L bits with R bits, and the original L bits are first processed in some manner that consists of binary addition to the function F. The function F depends on the R bits and a subkey. Assuming that the output of each step is denoted by L'R' and the input is LR, the operation can be defined as follows:

L' = R

R' = L + F(R,K)

The next algorithm, 3DES, uses this DES three times to add more complexity.

3DES

DES has been used internationally for a long time since its public release, but it is considered to be insecure because of the short length of its private key, 56 bits. In 1999, two non-profit organizations (Distributed.net and Electronic Frontier Foundation) collaborated to publicly break a DES key in 22 hours and 15 minutes to demonstrate its weakness. Besides this event, there are some analytical papers showing theoretical vulnerability in the DES.

NOTE   For more information on the vulnerability in the DES, go to your favorite search engine and search for "DES Challenges."

Therefore, the latest version of DES (FIPS-46-6) recommends using 3DES, which runs DES three times, which is a practical means of providing a more secure mechanism. Figure 4-3 illustrates the algorithm; each block is same as that of DES in Figure 4-2.

Now that you are aware of the basic cryptographic mechanism of DES and 3DES, the next section takes a look at the latest algorithm, AES.

Figure 4-3 *3DES Algorithm*

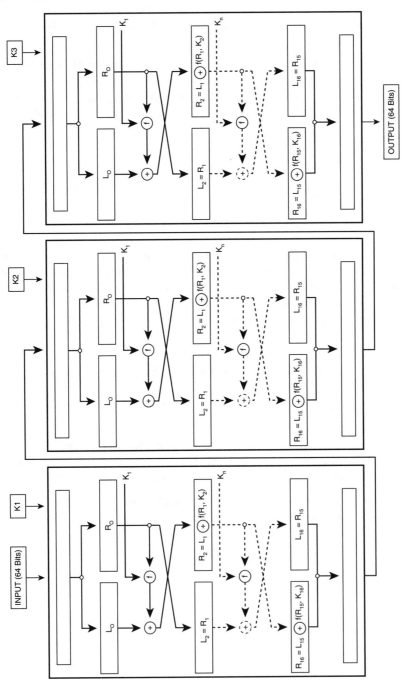

AES

AES,[1] superseding DES, is a symmetric block cipher that can process data blocks of 128 bits, using cipher keys with lengths of 128, 192, and 256 bits. Based on the fixed block size of 128 bits, AES operates on a 4x4 array of bytes, called the State.

At the start of the encryption, the input data is copied to the State array and processed by the following sequence:

Step 1   Initial round

— AddRoundKey

Step 2   Rounds (being executed multiple times)

— SubBytes

— ShiftRows

— MixColumns

— AddRoundKey

Step 3   Final round

— SubBytes

— ShiftRows

— AddRoundKey

The first step is adding round keys that are values derived from the private key using the key expansion routine; they are applied to the State.

The second step is main rounds that consist of four round functions: SubBytes, ShiftRows, MixColumns, and AddRoundKey. The functions are executed multiple times (depending on the key length) to the State array.

The third step is the final round, which executes the three functions once. The final State is then copied to the output. Here is the brief description of four main functions.

SubBytes

The SubBytes() function is a non-linear byte substitution that operates independently on each byte of the State using a substitution table (S-box). This S-box takes input value (bits) and transforms them into some number of output value (bits), implemented as a lookup table. For example, if a State array (1,1) has a value {32}, the substitution value would be determined by the intersection of the row with index '3' and the column with index '2' in Table 4-1. This would result in a new value {4b}.

Table 4-1   *Substitution Table*

	0	1	2	3	4
0	ab	11	3d	e2	C1
1	24	bf	ca	bc	19
2	e8	a7	12	7e	f7
3	17	ee	4b	5d	16
4	99	2d	0f	bn	54

Figure 4-4 illustrates the effect of the SubBytes() function on the State.

Figure 4-4   *SubBytes() Function*

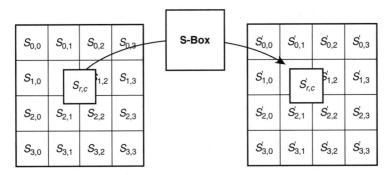

ShiftRows

In the ShiftRows() function, the bytes in the last three rows of the State are cyclically shifted over different numbers of bytes (offsets). The first row, r = 0, is not shifted.

This has the effect of moving bytes to "lower" positions in the row, while the "lowest" bytes wrap around into the "top" of the row. This transformation provides diffusion in the cipher. Figure 4-5 illustrates the ShiftRows() function.

Figure 4-5 *ShiftRows() Function*

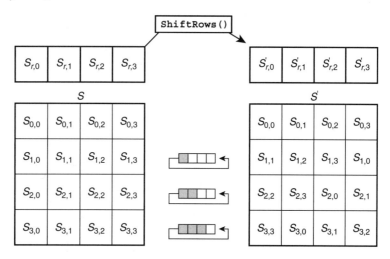

MixColumns

The MixColumns() function operates on the State column by column, treating each column as a four-term polynomial. The four bytes of each column of the State are combined using an invertible linear transformation. The MixColumns function takes four bytes as input and outputs four bytes, where each input byte affects all four output bytes. Like ShiftRows, MixColumns provides diffusion in the cipher. Figure 4-6 illustrates the MixColumns() function.

Figure 4-6 *MixColumns() Function*

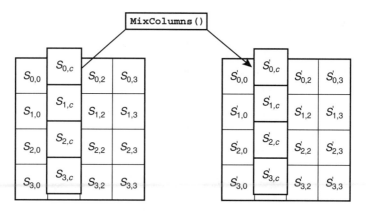

AddRoundKey

In the AddRoundKey() function, a round key is added to the State by a simple bitwise XOR operation. Each round key consists of Nb words from the key schedule (Rijndael's key schedule); each key is the same size as the State. Those Nb words are each added into the columns of the State. The action of this transformation is shown in Figure 4-7, where l = round * Nb.

Figure 4-7   *AddRoundKey() Function*

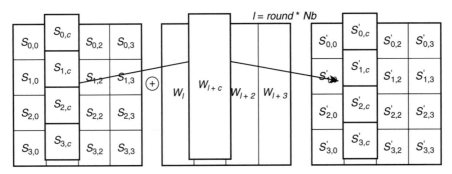

Now that you are aware of the basic algorithm of AES, the next section covers public-key based asymmetric cryptography.

Asymmetric (Public) Key Cryptography

Symmetric key cryptography, as described in the previous section, uses a single (private) key for encryption and decryption, which is relatively simple and secure. However, there is one serious issue in key management, especially on key distribution.

How do you make sure that only the communication parties have the same private key? The classic way is that a reliable courier passes the key physically to the communication parties, which is not realistic in today's networks.

Another way is using a separate key channel that is securely designed only for passing a key, which is not practical either between large numbers of communication parties. An asymmetric (public) key system can resolve this kind of problem.

Asymmetric key cryptography uses two keys: one for encryption and the other for decryption.

The most common usage is for message hiding where a public key is used for encrypting and a private key for decrypting. A message receiver maintains both keys and exposes only a public key to the public. A sender encrypts the sender's own message with the public key whenever sending to the receiver. It is virtually impossible to crack the encrypted message without the private key.

NOTE   Many asymmetric key systems use the public/private keys to securely exchange a symmetric key. The symmetric key is then used to send/receive the actual data between the two endpoints. This is done because symmetric cryptography uses fewer CPU resources than public key cryptography. TLS, for example, does this.

The section "Key Management" in this chapter shows the detailed information.

Another popular usage of asymmetric key cryptography is Digital Signature (DS), which is an electronic analogue of a written signature, which proves the message was signed by the originator.

In other words, the receiver can verify the identity of the originator (that is, authenticity) through the signature. Additionally, the digital signature provides a mechanism to verify that the message has not been altered in transit (that is, message integrity).

This section introduces two commonly used standards: Rivest, Shamir, and Adleman (RSA) and Digital Signature Algorithm (DSA). RSA can be used for both message encryption and digital signature. DSA can be used only for digital signature.

NOTE   Keep in mind that the purpose of this section is not looking into the mathematical detail of cryptographic algorithms, but giving a high-level understanding of each technique with comprehensible figures.

RSA

Since RSA was publicly released in 1977, it has been the most popular type of public key cryptography. The name RSA is the surname initials of the inventors (Rivest, Shamir, and Adleman) at Massachusetts Institute of Technology (MIT).

RAS uses two keys: one key for encrypting and the other key for decrypting data. For message privacy (hiding), the public key is for encryption and the private key for decryption. For digital signature, the private key is for encryption and the public key for decryption (authentication). Figures 4-8 and 4-9 show the difference.

The public key can be and often is shared with other parties. However, the private key remains a secret of the device (or user), and is never shared.

It is relatively easy for communication parties to calculate the public/private pair of keys. However, it is almost impossible for an attacker in the middle to determine the private key even if the attacker knows the public key and the cryptographic algorithm.

RSA can be used for both message privacy and digital signature. Figure 4-8 illustrates the usage of message privacy, and Figure 4-9 the usage of digital signature.

Figure 4-8 *RSA for Message Privacy*

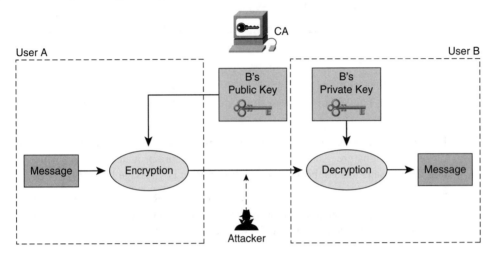

Figure 4-8 shows how to protect the privacy of User A's message with User B's public key. When User A sends a message to User B, User A encrypts it with User B's public key. User B receives the encrypted message and decrypts it with User B's private key based on the RSA algorithm. An attacker in the middle may already know User B's public key and intercept the encrypted User A's message, but there is no reverse algorithm that retrieves the original message or the private key.

Figure 4-9 *RSA for Digital Signature*

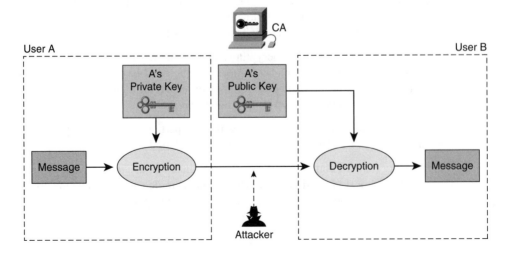

Figure 4-9 shows the mechanism of a digital signature that provides two things; only User A sent the message (authenticity), and the message was not changed while being transferred (integrity). When User A sends a message, A encrypts it with User A's private key, which is never exposed to the public. User B receives the message and decrypts it with User A's public key to verify its authenticity and integrity.

There could be many different ways to pass the User A's public key. The popular one is that User A includes his own certificate (includes User A's public key) in the message, which is signed by a Certificate Authority (CA; see Note). When User B receives the message (including the certificate), User B validates the certificate by the public key of the CA, and then uses User A's public key.

An attacker in the middle may intercept the message and change some information, but User B can detect the attack while authenticating the message with User A's public key.

NOTE   Certificate Authority (CA) is an organization or network entity that issues a digital certificate, which contains a public key and the owner's identity information according to the request. Because of security issues, a CA is supposed to be a trusted entity (for example, a trusted third party) that both applicants and communication parties can rely on.

There are many third-party commercial CAs, such as VeriSign or Comodo, as well as free CAs. Some organizations, such as governments, use their own CA.

Digital Signature

The purpose of a digital signature is verifying two things, as mentioned previously: the authenticity of the originator and the integrity of the message.

The well-known standard of digital signature is DSA, which was proposed by NIST in 1991, specified in FIPS 186. Figure 4-10 illustrates the DSA mechanism, which is how the digital signature is created, transferred, and verified at a high level.

In Figure 4-10, User A sends a message to User B, along with User A's signature. The steps of the process can be summarized as follows:

Step 1   User A generates a hash value from User A's original message. (Refer to the next section for hash functions.)

Step 2   User A creates a digital signature with the hash value and User A's private key, by DSA algorithm.

Step 3   User A attaches the signature to the original message.

Step 4   User A sends the combined message to User B.

Step 5   User B divides the combined message into the original message and signature.

Step 6 User B generates a hash value from the message.

Step 7 User B uses the hash value and User A's public key, and generates a value by DSA.

Step 8 User B compares the value with the signature, and determines the authenticity of User A and message integrity.

Figure 4-10 *DSA Mechanism*

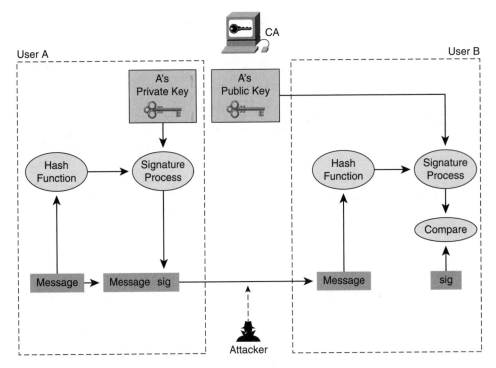

In this section so far, you have learned about asymmetric cryptography, which uses two keys (private and public key) for message privacy and digital signature. The next section covers hashing algorithms, which are often used as part of other cryptographies.

Hashing

This section covers well-known hashing algorithms that are employed by many applications, such as transport layer security (TLS), secure shell (SSH), secure multipurpose Internet mail extensions (S/MIME), and IP security (IPSec). This section introduces three well-known hashing algorithms; message digest algorithm 5 (MD5), SHA, and MAC.

The first algorithm is MD5 as described in the following section.

Hash Function (MD5)

A cryptographic hash function converts various lengths of data (input) into fixed-length data (output) without using a key, which is different from regular key-based cryptographic algorithms. Generally, the hash function is used as part of other cryptographies, such as DSA. It also used by CAs when the CA signs a certificate.

Calculating the output is simple and quick, but there is no reverse algorithm that retrieves the original message.

Figure 4-11 illustrates a hash function that transforms two different input messages into same fixed-sized outputs (hash value). An attacker may intercept the hash value, but it is virtually impossible to produce the original message because there is no reverse algorithm.

Figure 4-11   *Hash Function*

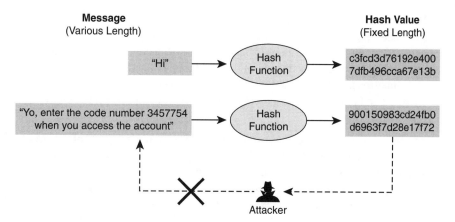

The most popular hash function is Message-Digest algorithm 5 (MD5), defined in RFC 1321.[2] The MD5 algorithm takes a message of arbitrary length as input and produces a 128-bit "fingerprint" or "message digest" as output. It is conjecture that it is computationally infeasible to produce two output messages having the same input, or to produce the same output having two different input messages.

The MD5 algorithm is intended for digital signature applications, where a large file must be "compressed" in a secure manner before being encrypted with a private (secret) key under a public-key cryptosystem, such as RSA.

The MD5 algorithm is designed to be quite fast on 32-bit machines. In addition, the MD5 algorithm does not require any large substitution tables; the algorithm can be coded quite compactly.

The next hashing algorithm, Secure Hash Algorithm (SHA), provides a more secure mechanism, and is considered to be the successor to MD5.

SHA

Secure Hash Standard (SHS) specifies, as defined in FIPS 180-2,[3] four Secure Hash Algorithms; SHA-1, SHA-256, SHA-384, and SHA-512. All four of the algorithms are iterative, one-way hash functions that can process a message to produce a condensed representation called a message digest. These algorithms enable the determination of a message's integrity: any change to the message will, with a very high probability, result in a different message digest. This property is useful in the generation and verification of digital signatures and message authentication codes, and in the generation of random numbers (bits).

Each algorithm can be described in two stages: preprocessing and hash computation. Preprocessing involves padding a message, parsing the padded message into m-bit blocks, and setting initialization values to be used in the hash computation. The hash computation generates a message schedule from the padded message and uses that schedule, along with functions, constants, and word operations, to iteratively generate a series of hash values. The final hash value generated by the hash computation is used to determine the message digest.

The four algorithms differ most significantly in the number of bits of security that are provided for the data being hashed—this is directly related to the message digest length. When a secure hash algorithm is used in conjunction with another algorithm, there may be requirements specified elsewhere that require the use of a secure hash algorithm with a certain number of bits of security. For example, if a message is being signed with a digital signature algorithm that provides 128 bits of security, that signature algorithm may require the use of a secure hash algorithm that also provides 128 bits of security (for example, SHA-256).

Additionally, the four algorithms differ in terms of the size of the blocks and words of data that are used during hashing. Table 4-2 presents the basic properties of all four secure hash algorithms.

Table 4-2 *SHA Properties*

Algorithm	Message Size (bits)	Block Size (bits)	Word Size (bits)	Message Digest Size (bits)
SHA-1	$< 2^{64}$	512	32	160
SHA-256	$< 2^{64}$	512	32	256
SHA-386	$< 2^{128}$	1024	64	384
SHA-512	$< 2^{128}$	1024	64	512

The next algorithm, Message Authentication Code (MAC), is different from MD5 or SHA in terms of using a shared private key, as follows.

Message Authentication Code

When User A sends a message to User B, how can User B make sure that the message has never been altered in transit? That is, how can User B be sure of the message integrity? Of course, DES or AES could be the solution, which encrypts the entire message with a shared private key. However, DES or AES would not be the proper solution if some proxies (for example, SIP proxy) between the endpoints need to look at the part of message for routing or applying a different policy.

Also, encrypting and decrypting the entire message with DES or AES takes time and consumes relatively high resources. For the purpose of message integrity, MAC can be one of the solutions, without encrypting the message.

MAC is a small amount of data generated from an original message and a shared private key. Figure 4-12 illustrates the usage of MAC when sending and receiving a message.

Figure 4-12 *MAC Usage*

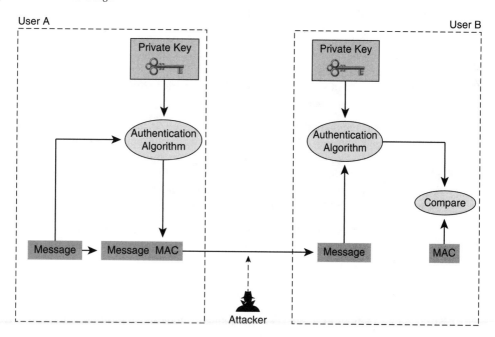

In Figure 4-12, when User A sends a message to User B, User A generates MAC first with the original message and the private key by the authentication algorithm. User A attaches the MAC to the original message and sends to User B. When User B receives it, she extracts the original message only and generates the output (MAC) by the same algorithm. User B compares the output with the MAC that User A sent, and verifies message integrity. If User A and B fully trust each other and the private key is shared only between them, this verification includes the authenticity of originator as well.

An attacker in the middle may intercept and modify the message, but the attacker's modification will be discovered by User B comparing the MAC.

MAC algorithms also can be constructed with cryptographic hash functions like MD5 or SHA-1, in combination with a shared secret key. This MAC algorithm is called Keyed-Hashing Message Authentication Code (HMAC), which is defined in RFC 2104. The cryptographic strength of HMAC depends on the properties of the underlying hash function.

MAC Versus Digital Signature

MAC looks similar to digital signatures in terms of supporting message integrity and authenticity, but there are two main differences between them.

The first one is the keys that are used. MAC values are generated and verified using the same secret key, which implies that both communication parties have to agree on the key before the communication, as is the case of symmetric cryptography. However, digital signature uses a pair of keys; a private key for encryption and a public key for decryption, as described in the previous section.

The second one is nonrepudiation. MAC does not provide the property of nonrepudiation offered by digital signature. The nonrepudiation is the concept of ensuring that a communication part cannot deny the validity of a message. In digital signature, the private key is only accessible to its holder; the signature proves that the message was signed "only" by the holder, which offers nonrepudiation. In contrast, any user who can verify MAC is also capable of generating MAC for other messages, which does not offer nonrepudiation.

Now that you are aware of cryptographic hashing algorithms, the next section takes a look at key management, especially key distribution.

Key Management

The previous sections examined cryptographic methods and algorithms with symmetric or asymmetric keys, which focus on how to provide message integrity, confidentiality, and authenticity with the keys. The remaining topic in this cryptography is key management, which focuses on how to securely maintain those keys from creation to final destruction.

Key management includes the following aspects: key generation, distribution, storage, replacement, and final destruction.

The key generation must be unpredictable, even for the key users. If certain keys have a higher possibility of being generated, it would be easier for attackers to find the key. So, the key must be generated randomly by machine, with enough complexity. If the system of key generation requires the user's input, it should combine multiple users' input so that a single user cannot predict the source of key generation.

The key distribution is most critical because the key in transit could be exposed to attackers. The key distribution system should assume that all keys could be modified in transit and prepare a secure mechanism for the case.

One of the desirable system capabilities is detecting any modification of a key while being transferred and discarding the key immediately.

Using additional keys for distribution (named transportation keys) is also a desirable solution. The following subsection shows how to use asymmetric keys (a private and public key) to distribute another key (a symmetric key).

The session keys should be stored in a secure format (for example, encrypted format) that requires a storage key. The key storage protects the key even if an intruder obtains the encrypted key. The storage keys and transportation keys are often called meta keys.

The key replacement is closely related to the security level of the system, depending on how frequently the system changes the keys. Even though an attacker intercepts and cracks an encrypted key with sophisticated tools, which takes time usually, the cracked key is useless if the system already changed the key. The frequency of replacement could be determined by the importance of data, strength of the cryptographic algorithm, security level of the network, and so on.

Key destruction means to completely erase used keys. If an attacker could find used keys, even though they are not used now, they might give a clue of a pattern for generating keys in the system.

Key Distribution

The most significant aspect of key management is key distribution that could be exposed to potential attackers in transit. There are many ways to distribute keys securely based on either symmetric or asymmetric cryptography. One of the popular ways is, based on the RSA algorithm, using asymmetric keys (a private and public key) to distribute another key (a symmetric key), as shown in Figure 4-13.

Figure 4-13 *Key Distribution Based on RSA*

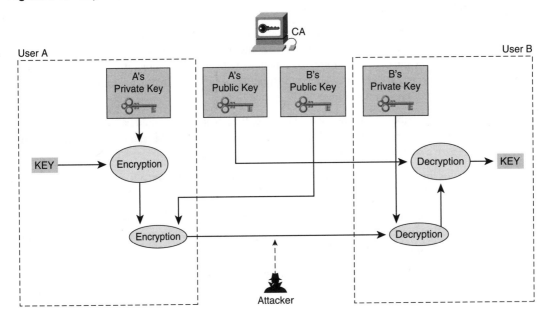

In Figure 4-13, User A sends a KEY (symmetric key) to User B, by using their given asymmetric keys. The steps of key distribution from User A to User B are summarized as follows:

Step 1 User A encrypts a key with User A's private key.

— It proves that User A sent the message.

Step 2 User A encrypts the output (from Step 1) with User B's public key.

— It encrypts the message so that only User B can decrypt it.

Step 3 User A sends the output (from Step 2) to User B.

Step 4 User B receives and decrypts it with User B's private key.

— Only User B can decrypt this message.

Step 5 User B decrypts the output (from Step 4) with User A's public key.

— It validates that User A created the message.

Step 6 User B gets the KEY (the output from Step 5).

— Now User B has the symmetric key used for the data sent by User A and B.

As long as the private keys (A's and B's) are maintained securely, it is virtually impossible for an attacker in the middle to extract the key from the encrypted message, even when the attacker knows User A's and User B's public key.

Summary

The purpose of cryptography is to provide message integrity, confidentiality, and authenticity between communication parties, by means of shared keys. It is divided into two categories according to the type of key used: symmetric and asymmetric key cryptography.

Symmetric key cryptography is based on a single key that both the sender and the receiver use for encrypting and decrypting the message. The well-known standards are DES, 3DES, AES, and MAC.

DES is designed to encrypt and decrypt blocks of data consisting of 64 bits under control of a 64-bit key. Only 56 bits of the key are used and the remaining 8 bits are used for parity checks. DES was considered to be insecure because of the relatively short length of the key (56 bits). Therefore, the latest version (FIPS-46-6) released in 1999 recommends using 3DES, which runs the DES algorithm three times.

AES, superseding DES, is a symmetric block cipher that can process data blocks of 128 bits, using cipher keys with lengths of 128, 192, and 256 bits. Based on the fixed block size of 128 bits, AES operates on a 4x4 array of bytes called the State. At the start of the encryption, the input data is copied to the State array and processed by three steps; each step executes its own round functions.

Asymmetric key cryptography use two keys; one for encryption and the other for decryption. The most common usage (RSA algorithm) is for message encryption in which a public key is used for encrypting and a private key for decrypting. A message receiver maintains both keys and exposes only a public key to the public. A sender encrypts his own message with the private key whenever sending to the receiver. It is virtually impossible to crack the encrypted message without the private key.

Another popular usage of asymmetric key cryptography is the digital signature, which is an electronic analogue of a written signature, which proves the message was signed by the originator. In other words, the receiver can verify the identity of the originator (that is, authenticity) through the signature. Additionally, the digital signature provides a mechanism to verify that the message has not been altered in transit (that is, message integrity).

A cryptographic hash function converts various lengths of data (input) into fixed-length data (output) without using a key, which is different from regular key-based cryptographic algorithms. Calculating the output is simple and quick, but there is no reverse algorithm that retrieves the original message. Generally, the hash function is used as part of other cryptographies, such as DSA. The well-known hashing algorithms are MD5, SHA, and HMAC.

Besides the cryptographic methods described in this chapter, which focus on the protection of information, key management is another important aspect in cryptography. It focuses on how to securely maintain those keys from generation to distribution, storage, replacement, and final destruction. The key distribution is most critical because the key in transit could be exposed to men in the middle. The key distribution system should assume that all keys could be modified in transit, and prepare a secure mechanism for the case.

End Notes

1   Advanced Encryption Standard (FIPS 197), NIST (National Institute of Standards and Technology), November, 2001.

2   RFC 1321, "MD5 Message-Digest Algorithm," R. Rivest, April, 1992.

3   Secure Hash Standard (FIPS 180-2), NIST (National Institute of Standards and Technology), August, 2002.

References

"Certificate Authority," Wikipedia, http://en.wikipedia.org/wiki/Certificate_authority.

"Cryptography Basics," Tech-invite, http://www.tech-invite.com/Ti-crypto.html.

"Data Encryption Standard," Wikipedia, http://en.wikipedia.org/wiki/Data_Encryption_Standard.

Data Encryption Standard (FIPS 46-6), NIST (National Institute of Standards and Technology), October 1999.

Digital Signature Algorithm (FIPS 186-2), NIST (National Institute of Standards and Technology), January 2000.

"SHA hash functions," Wikipedia, http://en.wikipedia.org/wiki/SHA.

"Message authentication code," Wikipedia, http://en.wikipedia.org/wiki/Message_authentication_code.

RFC 2104, "Keyed-Hashing for Message Authentication (HMAC)," H. Krawczyk, M. Bellare, C. Canetti, February 1997.

van der Lubbe, J.C.A. *Basic Methods of Cryptography*. Cambridge, UK: Cambridge University Press, 1998.

This chapter covers fundamental information about the following VoIP network elements from a security perspective:

- Security devices
  - VoIP-aware firewall
  - Network Address Translation (NAT)
  - Session Border Controller
  - Lawful Interception Server
- Service devices
  - Customer Premise Equipment (CPE)
- Call processing servers

CHAPTER 5

VoIP Network Elements

The network architecture of VoIP security consists of two groups of devices: service devices and security devices.

The service devices are primarily designed for providing VoIP services such as call setup, media control, protocol conversion, voicemail access, user interaction, and so on. As a secondary purpose, most service devices provide limited security features.

The security devices are primarily designed for providing security services such as access control, intrusion detection, Denial-of-Service protection, lawful interception, and so on. Some examples of those devices are as follows:

- VoIP security devices
  - VoIP-aware firewall
  - Network Address Translation (NAT) device
  - Session Border Controller
  - Lawful Interception server
- VoIP service devices
  - Customer Premise Equipment (CPE): IP phone, softphone, Analog Telephone Adapter (ATA), and Integrated Access Device (IAD)
  - Call processing servers: Softswitch, protocol proxy, Back-to-Back User Agent (B2BUA), IP PBX, rich media server, and media gateway

There is no magic bullet—a single device or architecture that can protect the whole VoIP service network securely. The best practice is analyzing current vulnerability and applying a "consolidated" solution that includes all possible network devices.

The purpose of this chapter is to introduce these devices from a high-level security perspective, rather than looking into detailed usages, which are shown in Part II, "VoIP Security Best Practices," in this book. If you already have basic knowledge of these devices, you may move on to the next chapter.

Security Devices

The security devices are primarily designed for providing security itself. There are two types of VoIP security devices. One originated from legacy data security, such as firewalls and NAT. The other was invented for VoIP service, such as Session Border Controller and Lawful Interception server. The following section gives a brief description of these devices.

VoIP-Aware Firewall

A *firewall* is a primary device for security in an IP network that protects the internal network and devices from external attacks. The general function is blocking certain types of traffic based on a policy that an administrator preconfigured. This policy consists of the range of IP addresses, port numbers, protocols, traffic directions, bandwidth consumption, and so on.

There are two types of firewall in terms of capability of recognizing VoIP protocols: legacy and VoIP-aware firewalls.

The legacy firewall handles packets only in the network and transport layer, and does not care what protocol is going through into the application layer. However, the VoIP-aware firewall has additional capability to inspect and manipulate VoIP packets in the application layer for secure service.

Next, you will learn about the VoIP-aware firewall.

An Access Control List (ACL) is a primary method used by a firewall to protect VoIP servers, media gateways, and CPEs from external devices that are not supposed to communicate with them. Using ACL for VoIP traffic is not simple because the ports used by VoIP entities change dynamically based on the call setup. You may use a static configuration, such as a certain range being always opened or blocked, but that creates potential vulnerability.

In general, an endpoint and a server (for example, SIP proxy) are using the client/server model for signaling for call setup, and the media channel between endpoints is established directly, that is, end-to-end. If the call signaling message does not go through a firewall, the media stream cannot pass through it because the firewall does not know which ports need to be opened.

Besides the dynamic port assignment, an advanced VoIP-aware firewall has the following capabilities:

- **Protocol message inspection**—An advanced VoIP-aware firewall checks out the integrity of protocol messages (for example, Session Initiation Protocol), and blocks the originator if it detects any malformed messages. If those malformed messages pass through without being blocked, the receiver (VoIP server, IP phone, and so on) may have system error.

- **Denial-of-Service (DoS) protection**—It detects any flooded messages and blocks the originator for a certain amount of time, based on the policy. The policy may include number of call attempts per second, number of messages per second, number of invalid messages, and so on.

- **Bandwidth control**—It can assign maximum bandwidth for each endpoint (or group), and block any overused endpoint.

Because a firewall handles a large amount of traffic by nature, capabilities and performance need to be taken into account. Performance includes the amount of latency, which the firewall can increase if it is under high load or even under attack. The general rule in VoIP deployment is to keep the CPU usage less than 60 percent for normal usage. If the CPU usage goes up more than 60 percent, especially in sustained high usage, the quality of service (QoS) will degrade and phones will start to unregister. When this happens, the phones will attempt to reregister with a VoIP server, which increases the load on the firewall even more.

NAT

Network Address Translation (NAT), as defined in RFC 2663,[1] is a method by which IP addresses are mapped from one realm to another, in an attempt to provide transparent routing to hosts. Traditionally, NAT devices are used to connect an isolated address realm with private unregistered addresses to an external realm with public unique registered addresses. There are four different types of NAT based on RFC 3489[2] as follows, even though these well-known names are inadequate for describing real-life NAT behavior (see the following Note):

1 Full cone NAT

   In full cone NAT, all requests from the same internal IP address and port are mapped to the same external IP address and port. Furthermore, any external host can send a packet to the internal host, by sending a packet to the mapped external address.

2 Restricted cone NAT

   In restricted cone NAT, all requests from the same internal IP address and port are mapped to the same external IP address and port. Unlike a full cone NAT, an external host (with IP address X) can send a packet to the internal host only if the internal host had previously sent a packet to IP address X.

3 Port restricted cone NAT

   Port restricted cone NAT is like a restricted cone NAT, but the restriction includes port numbers. Specifically, an external host can send a packet, with source IP address X and source port P, to the internal host only if the internal host had previously sent a packet to IP address X and port P.

4 Symmetric NAT

In symmetric NAT, all requests from the same internal IP address and port, to a specific destination IP address and port, are mapped to the same external IP address and port. If the same host sends a packet with the same source address and port, but to a different destination, a different mapping is used. Furthermore, only the external host that receives a packet can send a User Datagram Protocol (UDP) packet back to the internal host.

Determining the type of NAT is important in many cases. Depending on what the application wants to do, it may need to take the particular behavior into account.

NOTE   RFC 3489 used the terms "full cone," "restricted cone," "port restricted cone," and "symmetric" to refer to different variations of NATs applicable to UDP only. Unfortunately, this terminology has been the source of much confusion, as it has proven inadequate for describing real-life NAT behavior. Therefore, RFC 4787 refers to specific individual NAT behaviors instead of using the cone/symmetric terminology.

One of the benefits of NAT is reducing the usage of public IP addresses.

NOTE   In the rest of this section, *NAT* means Network Address and Port Translation (NAPT).

Multiple internal hosts use only private addresses when communicating with each other, and share the single public IP when communicating with external hosts.

The other benefit of NAT is providing access security, much like a firewall that blocks incoming unsolicited packets. The access from internal to external hosts is relatively simple depending on the type of NAT. However, the access from external to internal hosts is almost impossible because the addresses of internal hosts are not publicly routable. The only way to make it work is that the internal host makes a mapping first on the NAT and the external host sends packets through the pinhole, which provides strict access security. However, this benefit has serious side effects on VoIP.

NAT devices are application-unaware in that the translations are limited to IP, TCP, UDP, Internet Control Message Protocol (ICMP) headers, and ICMP error messages only.

NAT devices do not change the payload of the packets, as payloads tend to be application-specific. For this reason, there are serious issues with VoIP protocols, such as SIP/Session Definition Protocol (SDP). Figure 5-1 illustrates the NAT traversal issue with the SIP/SDP protocol. User A (IP phone user) makes a call to User B (public switched telephone network [PSTN] phone user) through NAT and media gateway.

Figure 5-1 *NAT Traversal Issue with SIP/SDP*

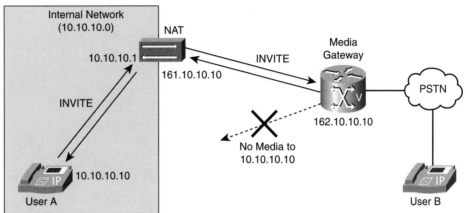

The IP phone uses a private IP address (10.10.10.10) and the NAT device maps it to the public address (161.10.10.10) whenever sending outbound packets. The media gateway has a public IP address (162.10.10.10) and works as an endpoint on behalf of User B's phone. (Note that this example does not consider port numbers, just to simplify.)

The SIP INVITE message in Figure 5-1 is shown in Example 5-1.

Example 5-1 *SIP/SDP Messages Through NAT*

```
(From IP phone to NAT device):
 INVITE sip:UserB@162.10.10.10 SIP/2.0
    Via: SIP/2.0/UDP 10.10.10.10:5060;branch=z9hG4bK74bf9
    From: UserA <sip:UserA@10.10.10.10>;tag=9fxced76sl
    To: UserB <sip:UserB@162.10.10.10>
    Max-Forwards: 70
    Contact: <sip:UserA@10.10.10.10>
    Call-ID: 2xTb9vxSit55XU7p8
    CSeq: 1 INVITE
    Content-Type: application/sdp
    Content-Length: 151

    v=0
    o=UserA 2890844526 2890844526 IN IP4 10.10.10.10
    s=-
    c=IN IP4 10.10.10.10
    t=0 0
    m=audio 49172 RTP/AVP 0
    a=rtpmap:0 PCMU/8000
```

continues

Example 5-1 *SIP/SDP Messages Through NAT (Continued)*

```
(From NAT device to Media Gateway):
 INVITE sip:UserB@162.10.10.10 SIP/2.0
    Via: SIP/2.0/UDP 161.10.10.10:5060;branch=z9hG4bK74bf9
    From: UserA <sip:UserA@161.10.10.10>;tag=9fxced76sl
    To: UserB <sip:UserB@162.10.10.10>
    Max-Forwards: 70
    Contact: <sip:UserA@10.10.10.10>
    Call-ID: 2xTb9vxSit55XU7p8
    CSeq: 1 INVITE
    Content-Type: application/sdp
    Content-Length: 151

    v=0
    o=UserA 2890844526 2890844526 IN IP4 10.10.10.10
    s=-
    c=IN IP4 10.10.10.10
    t=0 0
    m=audio 49172 RTP/AVP 0
    a=rtpmap:0 PCMU/8000
```

When the media gateway receives the INVITE message, it looks at the "c=" line in the SDP to find out where it will send media. After establishing a SIP dialog, the media gateway tries to send User B's voice to IP phone, but it fails because the private IP (10.10.10.10) is not publicly routable. This is a typical problem when NATed endpoints try to communicate with other external endpoints.

There are some sophisticated NAT devices that know the application protocols and replace all IP/port information in the layer, but those devices are not commonly deployed yet.

Another typical problem happens when making inbound calls, supposing that the IP phone of User A is registered to the media gateway. When User B makes a call to User A, the media gateway sends an initial INVITE message to the IP phone based on the address-of-record (IP phone's mapped IP and port). That is, the registration process is very critical because that is the only way for the media gateway to know the actual mapped IP/port address of the IP phone. The problem happens when the registration interval is not short enough (for example, the IP phone registers every 30 minutes), as the following three examples show:

- If the NAT device refreshes the mapping table, the media gateway cannot reach the IP phone until the next registration message comes in.

- If the internal address of the IP phone is changed, the media gateway cannot reach the phone until the next registration message comes in.

- If the media gateway is rebooted (for example, because of system error) and loses the registration information, it cannot reach the phone until the next registration message comes in.

Of course, you can minimize the impact as long as you make the registration interval very short, but doing that consumes more bandwidth and resources.

The next topic is Session Border Controller, which is another important element for secure VoIP service.

Session Border Controller

Session Border Controller (SBC) is, as the name implies, a controlling device located in a border of two network sessions. The session is a logical boundary of the VoIP network, which may be called *domain* or *realm*. Figure 5-2 illustrates the location of session borders among different VoIP networks.

Figure 5-2   *Session Borders in a VoIP Network*

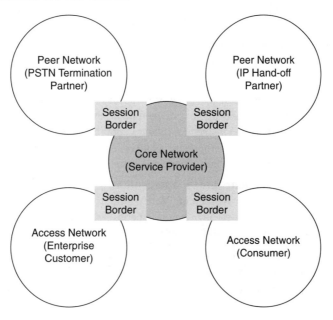

There are typically two network borders from a VoIP service provider's perspective. One is between the customer's access network and the service provider's network (core network). The other is between the core network and the other service provider's network (peer network).

The customer's access network is most likely that of the local Internet service provider (ISP) who provides Internet access service, which is generally different from the telephony service provider's network. (Note that it is possible for the telephony service provider to provide the access network, especially for enterprise customers.) The peer network is typically a call-termination network, such as a PSTN termination or IP hand-off.

The role of SBC is, simply speaking, resolving border issues that include interoperability and security issues as described in the following list:

- **DoS (intentional flooding)**—Malicious traffic from a large number of infected devices around public networks (Distributed Denial-of-Service [DDoS]), or from an attacker's machine generating massive call requests. Most VoIP servers are vulnerable to this type of attack because it's very difficult to implement sophisticated access control.

- **DoS (unintentional flooding)**—This is not malicious traffic, but the impact is almost same as intentional flooding. An example is a large number of registration requests issued at the same time after a global power outage followed by a power backup.

- **Exposed topology of core network**—Most IP addresses and port numbers of VoIP servers are exposed for public service, which means that attackers may send probe messages to learn the characteristics of the servers and then generate many types of malicious calls, such as spoofed or malformed messages.

- **Traversing firewall or NAT**—Most enterprise customers use firewall or NAT for security purposes, but this may cause a one-way or no-audio issue when traversing two different networks. The SBC can resolve this issue.

- **Protocol conflict**—Each service provider has its own VoIP protocol and there are always interoperability issues between them, even if they use the same standard protocol, such as coder-decoder (codec) conflict. Most issues are not directly related to security, but some of them are related. For example, one requires Transport Layer Security (TLS) connection when sending SIP messages, but the other does not.

- **Regulatory mandate (lawful interception)**—There is a complicated governmental security issue when intercepting VoIP traffic in this border because of many different types of call routing through heterogeneous networks. The details of lawful interception are discussed in Part III, "Lawful Interception (CALEA)," in this book.

- **Ensuring quality of service**—This is a generic issue when VoIP traffic goes through heterogeneous networks (not directly related to border security).

For details about SBC, refer to Chapter 8, "Protection with Session Border Controller."

Lawful Interception Server

Lawful Interception (LI) is a quite different aspect of VoIP security that is defined from the government's perspective. The general consensus is that LI belongs to the category of VoIP security even though some people may not agree.

LI, also known as *wiretapping*, is the lawfully authorized interception of communications (for example, call content) and call-identifying information (for example, call data) for a particular telecommunication subscriber (target subscriber), requested by a law enforcement agency (LEA).

The call content is, for example, voice or video. The call data is a dialed number, call direction, call duration or signaling information, and so on. The target subscriber is identified generally by a phone number. The LEA could be any agency that is able to request the lawful interception. For example, in the United States, the FBI or a police officer requests it with a corresponding warrant.

LI in PSTN networks has been executed for a long time in most developed countries. The scope of LI in this context is a VoIP network, managed by telecommunication service providers (TSPs) who are being asked to meet legal and regulatory requirements for the interception of voice and data communications in IP networks in a variety of countries worldwide. Almost every developed country has its own LI requirements and has adopted global standards (or proposals) fully or partially, developed by standard organizations.

The LI servers are performing multiple functions to provide LI service. The functions are broadly categorized as access, delivery, collection, service provider administration, and law enforcement administration functions. Each function could be performed by each logical server. The relationship between these functional categories is shown in Figure 5-3.

Figure 5-3 *Lawful Interception Reference Model*

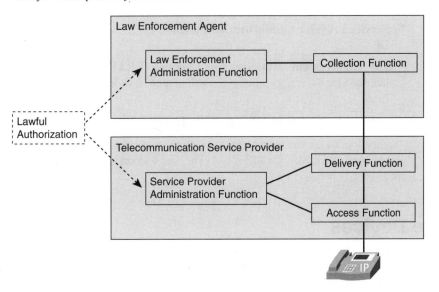

In Figure 5-3, the Access Function, Delivery Function, and Service Provider Administration Function are the responsibility of the TSP, and the Collection Function and Law Enforcement Administration Function are the responsibility of the LEA.

NOTE   All LI functions begin with an initial capital letter for each function's name followed by the letter "F," such as "AF" for "Access Function," because these names are defined by LI specifications and not as general terms.

The use of these functions to perform an interception is initiated by receipt of a specific lawful authorization. Here is a brief description of each function:

- **Access Function (AF)**—Consists of one or more Intercept Access Points (IAPs), and accesses and intercepts the target subscriber's call data and content confidentially. An IAP may be an existing device that has intercept capability or it could be a special device that is provided for that purpose; for example, an SBC.

- **Delivery Function (DF)**—Delivers intercepted communications to one or more Collection Functions. The DF delivers intercepted communications in the form of call content and data.

- **Collection Function (CF)**—Collects and analyzes the call content and data received from the DF.

- **Service Provider Administration Function (SPAF)**—Controls the TSP's AF and DF.

- **Law Enforcement Administration Function (LEAF)**—Provides the provisioning interface for the interception as a result of a court order or warrant delivered by the LEA.

For more details on LI, refer to Chapter 10, "Lawful Interception Fundamentals."

In this section, so far you have learned basic information about security devices: VoIP-aware firewall, NAT, SBC, and LI server. The next section introduces VoIP service devices from a security perspective.

Service Devices

The service devices are primarily designed for providing VoIP services like call setup, media control, protocol conversion, voicemail access, user interaction, and so on. They also have some security features in order to provide access control or protect service features. The following sections give a brief description of service devices that are commonly used in VoIP service.

Customer Premise Equipment

Customer Premise Equipment (CPE) consists of devices that provide a service interface to users directly or indirectly. IP phone, softphone, IAD, and ATA belong to this category.

- **IP phone**—An IP-based phone that converts digital signals to analog tones, and vice versa. It communicates with a VoIP server (for example, Softswitch) to send and receive calls. An example is the Cisco 7960 series.

  Most IP phones are password-protected and provide an interface (for example, HTTP) to enable or disable communication ports or security features (for example, media encryption).

- **Softphone**—A software-based phone that runs on a computer. It relies on computer resources (for example, sound cards, CPU, and memory) to process calls, which makes it relatively easy to implement phone functions. An example is the Skype client program.

  Most softphones provide an interface to enable or disable communication ports or security features, similar to IP phones. They also rely on the security features from the operating system (for example, the Windows firewall).

- **Analog Telephone Adapter (ATA)**—An access device that has Foreign Exchange Stations (FXS) and Ethernet interfaces. Regular analog phones are connected to the FXS ports and send/receive calls through an IP network. An example is Cisco ATA 188. The security features are almost the same as those of IP phones. Generally, ATA provides an interface to apply different security policy to each port.

- **Integrated Access Device (IAD)**—An access device that provides multiple types of interfaces to users, such as analog (FXS, FXO) and digital (T1/E1) interfaces. Different types of phones (analog or IP phones) are connected to the interfaces and send/receive calls through an IP trunk. Typically, it has proxy functions (for example, SIP proxy) that negotiate call setup with external servers.

  One of the well-known IADs is the Cisco IAD 2400 series. An IAD provides relatively rich security features because of multiple interfaces, high volume of traffic, and different types of call control. The features might include access control for administration, user credential management, encryption, session key control, and ACL for signal or media.

Besides these CPE, the following call processing servers are also essential service devices.

Call Processing Servers

Call processing servers facilitate call setup in the middle of communication endpoints. These devices also have security features, and play an important role for providing secure services by means of enforcing policies. The policy is decided according to type of service (for example, voice vs. instant message), type of endpoints (for example, IP phone vs. softphone), type of network (for example, managed vs. unmanaged), and so on.

There are many different kinds of call processing servers, and the typical ones are as follows:

- **Protocol proxy**—An intermediary entity that sets up call connections between clients. It acts as both a receiver and sender for the purpose of making requests on behalf of other clients.

  A protocol proxy server mainly plays the role of routing, which means its job is to ensure that a request is sent to another entity closer to the target user. It is also useful for enforcing policy, such as applying call permissions depending on source or destination numbers. It may interpret and rewrite specific parts of a request message before forwarding it. Some examples of protocol proxies are SIP proxy, H.323 gatekeeper, and Media Gateway Control Protocol (MGCP) call agent.

  The basic security mechanism is that protocol proxies rely on authentication of each endpoint before setting up the call. The endpoints are generally authenticated based on user ID, password, IP address, or credentials.

- **Back-to-Back User Agent (B2BUA)**—A logical SIP entity that receives a request and processes it as a user agent server, and regenerates the request as a user agent client to the target user agent. Unlike a SIP proxy, it maintains dialog state and participates in all requests sent on the dialogs it has established. So, it has full control of all messages.

  B2BUA also relies on the authentication of each endpoint before processing the call, as protocol proxies do.

- **IP PBX**—An IP-based PBX that manages internal calls within the domain and terminates external calls through an IP trunk or PSTN media gateway. It has features of legacy PBX plus advanced ones, such as call forward, call transfer, call routing, call waiting, call parking, interactive voice response (IVR), music on hold, FMFM (Find Me Follow Me), VoIP protocol conversion, SIP trunking, and so on. An example of IP PBX is Asterisk.

  Generally, IP PBX authenticates each phone based on phone number, MAC address, IP address, user ID, or password.

- **Softswitch**—Works like a legacy Class 4 or 5 switch in the central office, providing Class 4 features (for example, routing) and Class 5 features (for example, call transfer and forward). However, the difference is that it is a program running on regular operating systems (for example, Linux), and it is located in an IP network; that is, all in and out traffic consists of IP packets. It typically has multiple VoIP protocol interfaces (for example, SIP, H.323, and MGCP) and converts them when passing through, as a B2BUA. An example of Softswitch is Sylantro Softswitch.

  Most Softswitches have rich security features like user authentication, message encryption, media encryption, TLS (transport layer security), CAC (call admission control), Denial-of-Service protection, and ACL (access control list).

- **Rich media server**—A controlling device that provides rich media communications like voice, video, instant messaging(IM), presence, web collaboration, and multimedia conference. An example is Cisco Unified Communication Manager. The security features are almost the same as what Softswitch has.

- **Media gateway**—A gateway device located in between different types of networks, such as Time-Division Multiplexing (TDM), IP, and Next Generation Network (NGN). Typically, it converts media packets (IP network) to digitized signals (TDM network), and vice versa. An example of a media gateway is the Cisco AS5400 series.

  The security features of media gateway include

  — User authentication (for example, Password Authentication Protocol [PAP])

  — Challenge Handshake Authentication Protocol (CHAP; see the "PAP Versus CHAP" section)

  — Multilevel password protection

  — ACL

  — DoS protection

  — IP spoofing prevention

  — Remote Authentication Dial-in User Service (RADIUS; see the "RADIUS Versus TACACS+" section) for network access management

  — Terminal Access Control Access System Plus (TACACS+; see the "RADIUS Versus TACACS+" section)

  — Logging

PAP Versus CHAP

Both PAP and CHAP are authentication schemes used by Point-to-Point Protocol (PPP) servers to validate the identity of remote clients, as defined in RFC 1334[3] (superseded by RFC 1994). PAP provides a simple method for the peer to establish its identity using a two-way handshake. This is done only upon initial link establishment. After the link establishment phase is complete, an ID/password pair is repeatedly sent by the peer to the authenticator until authentication is acknowledged or the connection is terminated. PAP is not a strong authentication method.

Passwords are sent over the circuit as clear text, and there is no protection from playback or repeated trial-and-error attacks. The peer is in control of the frequency and timing of the attempts.

CHAP is used to periodically verify the identity of the peer using a three-way handshake. This is done upon initial link establishment. After the link establishment phase is complete, the authenticator sends a "challenge" message to the peer. The peer responds with a value calculated using a "one-way hash" function. The authenticator checks the response against its own calculation of the expected hash value. If the values match, the authentication is acknowledged; otherwise, the connection should be terminated. CHAP provides protection against playback attack through the use of an incrementally changing identifier and a variable challenge value. The use of repeated challenges is intended to limit the time of exposure to any single attack. The authenticator is in control of the frequency and timing of the challenges.

RADIUS Versus TACACS+

Both RADIUS and TACACS+ are systems of distributed security that secure remote access into networks and network services against unauthorized access. Although the specification of RADIUS is defined in RFC 2865, TACACS+ is a Cisco proprietary enhancement to the original TACACS protocol. There are some other differences between them:

- RADIUS uses TCP, and TACACS+ uses UDP.

- RADIUS combines authentication and authorization in a user profile. The access-accept packets sent by the RADIUS server to the client contain authorization information. TACACS+ separates the two operations.

- RADIUS encrypts only the password in the access-request packet, from the client to the server. TACACS+ encrypts the entire body of the packet but leaves a standard TACACS+ header.

In this section, you have learned about the basic functions and security features of VoIP service devices (CPEs and call processing servers).

Summary

The network architecture of VoIP security consists of two groups of devices: service devices and security devices.

The security devices are primarily designed for providing security services like access control, intrusion detection, DoS protection, lawful interception, and so on. Examples of those devices are VoIP-aware firewall, NAT, SBC, and Lawful Interception server.

A VoIP-aware firewall has legacy firewall functions and additional capability to inspect and manipulate VoIP packets in the application layer for secure service, based on predefined policy. The capability includes dynamic port assignment, DoS protection, protocol message inspection, and bandwidth control. The policy consists of the range of IP addresses, port numbers, protocols, traffic directions, bandwidth consumption, and so on.

The benefit of NAT (NAPT) is reducing the usage of public IP addresses and providing access security. The access from external to internal hosts through NAT is almost impossible because the addresses of internal hosts are not publicly routable. The only way to make it work is that the internal host makes a mapping first on the NAT and the external host sends packets through the pinhole, which provides strict access security. However, this benefit has serious side effects on VoIP. NAT devices are application-unaware in that the translations are limited to IP, TCP, UDP, and ICMP.

Such NAT devices do not change the payload of the packets, as payloads tend to be application-specific. For this reason, there can be one-way or no-media issues with VoIP protocols such as SIP/SDP.

An SBC is a controlling device located on a border of two network sessions that are logical boundaries of a VoIP network. The role of an SBC is resolving border issues that include interoperability and security issues, such as Denial-of-Service, exposed topology of core network, traversing firewall or NAT, protocol conflict, lawful interception, ensuring quality of service, and so on.

LI, also known as wiretapping, is the lawfully authorized interception of communications and call-identifying information for a particular telecommunication subscriber, requested by a law enforcement agency. The LI servers perform multiple functions to provide LI service. The functions are broadly categorized as AF, DF, CF, SPAF, and LEAF. Each function could be performed by each logical server.

The service devices are primarily designed for providing VoIP services like call setup, media control, protocol conversion, voicemail access, user interaction, and so on. As a secondary purpose, most service devices provide limited security features. Examples of those devices are CPE (IP phone, softphone, ATA, IAD) and call processing servers (Softswitch, protocol proxy, B2BUA, IP PBX, rich media server, and media gateway).

There is no magic bullet; that is, a single device or architecture that can protect whole VoIP service network securely. The best practice is analyzing current vulnerability and applying a "consolidated" solution that includes all possible network devices.

End Notes

   1   RFC 2663, "IP Network Address Translator (NAT) Terminology and Considerations," P. Srisuresh, M. Holdrege, August 1999.

   2   RFC 3489, "STUN—Simple Traversal of UDP Through NAT," J. Rosenberg, J. Weinberger, C. Huitema, R. Mahy, March 2003.

   3   RFC 1334, "PPP Authentication Protocols," B. Lloyd, W. Simpson, October, 1992.

References

ATIS T1.678, Lawfully Authorized Electronic Surveillance (LAES) for Voice over Packet Technologies in Wireline Telecommunications Networks, Alliance for Telecommunications Industry Solutions, http://www.atis.org.

Cisco Unified Communications SRND, based on Cisco Unified Communications Manager Release 6.x, http://www.cisco.com/en/US/products/sw/voicesw/ps556/products_implementation_design_guide_book09186a008085eb0d.html.

RFC 1994, "PPP Challenge Handshake Authentication Protocol (CHAP)," W. Simpson, August 1996.

RFC 2865, "Remote Authentication Dial in User Service (RADIUS)," C. Rigney, S. Willens, A. Rubens, W. Simpson, June 2000.

RFC 3261, "SIP (Session Initiation Protocol)," J. Rosenberg, H. Schulzrinne, G. Camarillo, A. Johnston, J. Peterson, R. Sparks, M. Handley, and E. Schooler, June 2002.

RFC 4787, "Network Address Translation (NAT) Behavioral Requirements for Unicast UDP," F. Audet, C. Jennings, January 2007.

Security Considerations for VoIP Systems, NIST (National Institute of Standards and Technology), January 2005.

PART II

VoIP Security Best Practices

This chapter covers the simulation, analysis, and mitigation of the following threats:

- Denial of Service
- Malformed messages
- Sniffing/eavesdropping
- Spoofing/identity theft
- VoIP spam

CHAPTER 6

Analysis and Simulation of Current Threats

Several of the chapters in Part I introduced concepts and ideas behind current threats and protection methods at a high level. This chapter digs into the topic to find practical information that can be applied to real VoIP service environments.

In this chapter, you see the details of the threats and the methodology of protection. These are the threats that this chapter covers:

- Denial of Service (intentional and unintentional flooding)
- Malformed messages
- Sniffing/eavesdropping
- Spoofing/identity theft
- VoIP spam

Each section will approach the threat by

- Analyzing the detailed pattern, usage examples, and vulnerability of the threat
- Simulating the threat with a negative testing tool that is available on the web so that you can have a hands-on experience
- Providing the guidelines to mitigate the threat with practical methods

Because of the limited function of the tools and the restricted testing environments, each threat will be simulated simply as one of the most common patterns, which may be different from a specific pattern that you may expect or already know.

NOTE   The contents in this chapter are written more from the perspective of the enterprise or service provider that sees and manages VoIP networks from access to core network. The end users also can utilize the contents of this chapter to identify current threats and gain hands-on experience with them.

Denial of Service

A Denial-of-Service (DoS) attack is the most common threat in VoIP networks with so many different patterns, which are more than known patterns in a pure data network (for example, TCP SYN attack; see the following Note). The typical method of DoS is flooding; for example, an attacker floods valid or invalid heavy traffic to a targeted system, and as a result the performance drops significantly or the system breaks down.

NOTE   **TCP SYN attack**—The basic method of TCP connection between a client and a server is as follows:

Step 1   (Client) SYN -------------> (Server)

Step 2   (Client) <--------- SYN-ACK (Server)

Step 3   (Client) ACK -------------> (Server)

The client sends a SYN message to the server (Step 1), and the server acknowledges the SYN message by sending a SYN-ACK message (Step 2), and the client finishes establishing the connection by replying with an ACK message (Step 3). This flow applies to all TCP connections like Telnet, web, email, and so on.

An attacker (client) exploits this connection mechanism by flooding SYN messages with spoofed IP addresses, and then never responding to SYN-ACK from the server. That is, the server has sent acknowledgment (SYN-ACK) for the flooded SYN, but has not received ACK from the client (attacker), which leaves a lot of "half-open" connections on the server. The data structure of the half-open connections on the server system will eventually fill, and then the system will not be able to accept new legitimate connections until the table is emptied out.

There is generally a timeout for the pending connections so that the half-open connections will eventually expire and be dumped out. However, as long as the attacker keeps sending the flooded SYN with spoofed IPs, the timeout does not help.

There are many solutions in the market for data networks, but you cannot apply those in VoIP networks directly because there are many VoIP protocol-specific attacks, such as SIP INVITE message flooding. This section focuses on VoIP protocol layer attacks, rather than network layer.

Not only malicious and intentional attacks, but also unintentional attacks are possible, so-called self-attack, because of wrong configuration of devices, architectural service design issues, or unique circumstances.

The first example of DoS is intentional flooding, as described in the following section.

Intentional Flooding

Intentional flooding includes all malicious DoS flooding typically from external attackers.

The typical methods of flooding are as follows:

- **Valid or invalid registration flooding**—An attacker commonly uses this method because most registration servers accept the request from any endpoints in the Internet as an initial step of authentication. Regardless of whether the messages are valid or invalid, the large number of request messages in a short period of time (for example, 10,000 SIP REGISTER messages per second) impacts the performance of the server severely.

- **Valid or invalid call request flooding**—Most VoIP servers have a security feature that blocks flooded call requests from unregistered endpoints. So, an attacker registers first after spoofing a legitimate user (assuming the attacker stole the identity), and sends flooded call requests in a short period of time (for example, 10,000 SIP INVITE messages per second). It impacts the performance or functionality of the server regardless of whether the request message is valid or not.

- **Call control flooding after call setup**—An attacker may flood valid or invalid call control messages (for example, SIP INFO, NOTIFY, Re-INVITE) after call setup. Most proxy servers are vulnerable because they do not have a security feature to ignore and drop those messages.

- **Ping flooding**—Like Internet Control Message Protocol (ICMP) ping, VoIP protocols use ping messages in the application layer to check out the availability of server or keep the pinhole open in the local Network Address Translation (NAT) device, such as a SIP OPTIONS message. Although most IP network devices (for example, router or firewall) in the production network do not allow ICMP pings for security reasons, many VoIP servers should allow the application-layer ping for proper serviceability, which can be a critical security hole.

Simulation

Simulating a flooding attack can give you a better idea and understanding of the threat. A tool that generates malicious traffic is generally called a *negative testing tool*, which is used by testers who validate security features of a product. Of course, attackers use the tool in a malicious way.

There are many negative testing tools for generating flooded messages. One of the most popular tools is SIPSAK (SIP Swiss Army Knife), which is freeware; you can download it from http://www.sipsak.org/#download.

The contents of this section refer to the SIPSAK website.[1]

SIPSAK is a Session Initiation Protocol (SIP) stress and diagnostics utility. It sends SIP requests to the server within the sip-uri and examines received responses. It runs in one of the following modes:

- **default mode**—A SIP message is sent to destination in sip-uri and reply status is displayed. The request is either taken from a filename or generated as a new OPTIONS message.

- **traceroute mode (-T)**—This mode is useful for learning the request's path. It operates similarly to IP-layer utility traceroute.

- **message mode (-M)**—This mode sends a short message (similar to short message service [SMS] from mobile phones) to a given target. With the option **-B**, the content of the MESSAGE can be set. The options **-c** and **-O** might be useful in this mode.

- **usrloc mode (-U)**—Stress mode for SIP registrar. SIPSAK keeps registering to a SIP server at a high pace. Additionally, the registrar can be stressed with the **-I** or the **-M** option. If **-I** and **-M** are omitted, SIPSAK can be used to register any given contact (with the **-C** option) for an account at a registrar and to query the current bindings for an account at a registrar.

- **randtrash mode (-R)**—Parser torture mode. SIPSAK keeps sending randomly corrupted messages to torture a SIP server's parser.

- **flood mode (-F)**—Stress mode for SIP servers. SIPSAK keeps sending requests to a SIP server at a high pace.

Here is the full syntax for generating traffic with SIPSAK. You also can see it by typing the command in the command-line interface (CLI).

```
shoot  : sipsak [-f FILE] [-L] -s SIPURI
trace  : sipsak -T -s SIPURI
usrloc : sipsak -U [-IM] [-b NUMBER] [-e NUMBER] [-x NUMBER] [-z NUMBER] -s SIPURI
usrloc : sipsak -IM [-b NUMBER] [-e NUMBER] -s SIPURI
usrloc : sipsak -U [-C SIPURI] [-x NUMBER] -s SIPURI
message: sipsak -M [-B STRING] [-O STRING] [-c SIPURI] -s SIPURI
flood  : sipsak -F [-e NUMBER] -s SIPURI
random : sipsak -R [-t NUMBER] -s SIPURI

additional parameter in every mode:
   [-a PASSWORD] [-d] [-i] [-H HOSTNAME] [-l PORT] [-m NUMBER] [-n] [-N]
   [-r PORT] [-v] [-V] [-w]

  -h              displays this help message
  -V              prints version string only
  -f FILE         the file which contains the SIP message to send
                    use - for standard input
  -L              de-activate CR (\r) insertion in files
  -s SIPURI       the destination server uri in form
                    sip:[user@]servername[:port]
  -T              activates the traceroute mode
  -U              activates the usrloc mode
  -I              simulates a successful calls with itself
  -M              sends messages to itself
  -C SIPURI       use the given uri as Contact in REGISTER
  -b NUMBER       the starting number appendix to the user name (default: 0)
  -e NUMBER       the ending numer of the appendix to the user name
```

```
-o NUMBER      sleep number ms before sending next request
-x NUMBER      the expires header field value (default: 15)
-z NUMBER      activates randomly removing of user bindings
-F             activates the flood mode
-R             activates the random modues (dangerous)
-t NUMBER      the maximum number of trashed character in random mode
                  (default: request length)
-l PORT        the local port to use (default: any)
-r PORT        the remote port to use (default: 5060)
-p HOSTNAME    request target (outbound proxy)
-H HOSTNAME    overwrites the local hostname in all headers
-m NUMBER      the value for the max-forwards header field
-n             use FQDN instead of IPs in the Via-Line
-i             deactivate the insertion of a Via-Line
-a PASSWORD    password for authentication
                  (if omitted password="")
-u STRING      Authentication username
-d             ignore redirects
-v             each v produces more verbosity (max. 3)
-w             extract IP from the warning in reply
-g STRING      replacement for a special mark in the message
-G             activates replacement of variables
-N             returns exit codes Nagios compliant
-q STRING      search for a RegExp in replies and return error
                  on failure
-W NUMBER      return Nagios warning if retrans > number
-B STRING      send a message with string as body
-O STRING      Content-Disposition value
-P NUMBER      Number of processes to start
-A             print timing informations
-S             use same port for receiving and sending
-c SIPURI      use the given uri as From in MESSAGE
-D NUMBER      timeout multiplier for INVITE transactions
                  and reliable transports (default: 64)
-E STRING      specify transport to be used
```

The following shows the usage for this example:

To send an OPTIONS request to user@domain.com and display received replies:

```
Prompt> sipsak -vv -s sip:user@domain.com
```

To trace the SIP path to user@domain.com:

```
Prompt> sipsak -T -s sip:user@domain.com
```

To insert a forwarding contact for myself at work to me at home for one hour and authenticate with password if required:

```
Prompt> sipsak -U -C sip:me@home -x 3600 -a password -s sip:myself@company
```

To query the currently registered bindings for myself at work and authenticate with password if required:

```
Prompt> sipsak -I -C empty -a password -s sip:myself@work
```

To send the instant message "Lunch time!" to a colleague and show the result:

```
Prompt> sipsak -M -v -s sip:colleague@work -B "Lunch time!"
```

Now try to generate flooding traffic to a targeted SIP proxy server with SIPSAK. Here are the assumptions before the test:

- SIPSAK is installed on the Microsoft Windows system of your PC, which has IP connectivity with the proxy server.

- You already know the IP address (or fully qualified domain name [FQDN]) of the SIP proxy server.

- The phone number you test is a known number for a proxy server so that it will not reject the request message from SIPSAK.

- The network bandwidth between your PC and proxy server is enough to pass heavy traffic during a short period of time. It requires at least 1 Mbps.

WARNING This flooding test may cause serious damage to the performance or functionality of the SIP proxy server. It is highly recommended to use a lab system so that there is no real customer traffic. Do not try this on your production system or service provider's network.

Follow these steps to simulate flooding:

Step 1 Open a command window and go to the directory where SIPSAK is installed.

Step 2 Check out the options and usages with the **-h** parameter.

Step 3 This is a pretrial step. Send flooded SIP OPTIONS messages to the targeted SIP proxy server for 5 seconds as shown in Example 6-1 and stop sending (press **Ctrl-C**) as shown in Example 6-2. Make sure that there is no error message, and that those packets are going out to proxy server properly (you may use Ethereal trace to confirm).

Example 6-1 *Execution of SIP OPTIONS Message Flooding*

```
C:\sipsak>sipsak -vv -s sip:1111@192.168.10.10 -F
warning: redirects are not expected in flood. disabling
flooding message number 1
flooding message number 2
flooding message number 3
flooding message number 4
flooding message number 5
flooding message number 6
flooding message number 7
flooding message number 8
flooding message number 9
```

Example 6-1 *Execution of SIP OPTIONS Message Flooding (Continued)*

```
flooding message number 10
flooding message number 11
flooding message number 12
flooding message number 13
flooding message number 14
```

Example 6-2 *Stop Execution of Flooding*

```
flooding message number 15710
flooding message number 15711
flooding message number 15712
flooding message number 15713
flooding message number 15714
flooding message number 15715
flooding message number 15716
flooding message number 15717
flooding message number 15718
flooding message number 15719
flooding message number 15720
flooding message number 15721
flooding message number 15722

C:\sipsak>
```

NOTE   As you can see in Examples 6-1 and 6-2, SIPSAK generated about 15,000 SIP OPTIONS messages for 5 seconds; that is, about 3,000 messages per second. You can increase or decrease the number of messages per second by adding or deleting the **-v** parameter in the command line. Refer to the command syntax as explained previously.

Step 4   Log in to the SIP proxy server, turn on the system monitoring tool, and then check out the current usage of system resources, such as CPU and memory. Because this is before the flooding, you are supposed to see normal and low resource usage. Figure 6-1 is an example of a resource monitoring tool in the UNIX or Linux system using the **top** command.

Figure 6-1   *Resource Monitoring in UNIX/Linux*

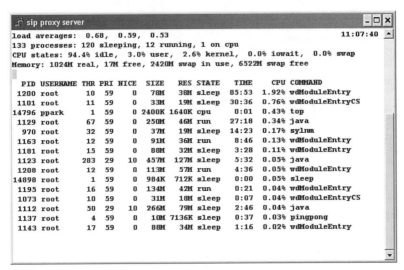

NOTE   If your proxy server is running on a Windows system, you can monitor the resources by
activating the Task Manager, as shown in Figure 6-2.

Figure 6-2   *Resource Monitoring in Windows*

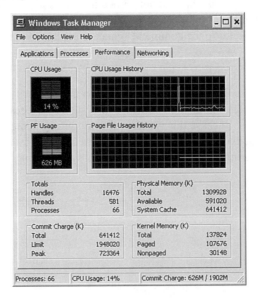

Step 5   While continuing to watch the monitoring screen, execute the flooding as instructed in Step 3. You may need to generate for more than 5 seconds to see consistent results on the server. Figure 6-3 shows an example.

Figure 6-3   *Resource Usage While Flooding*

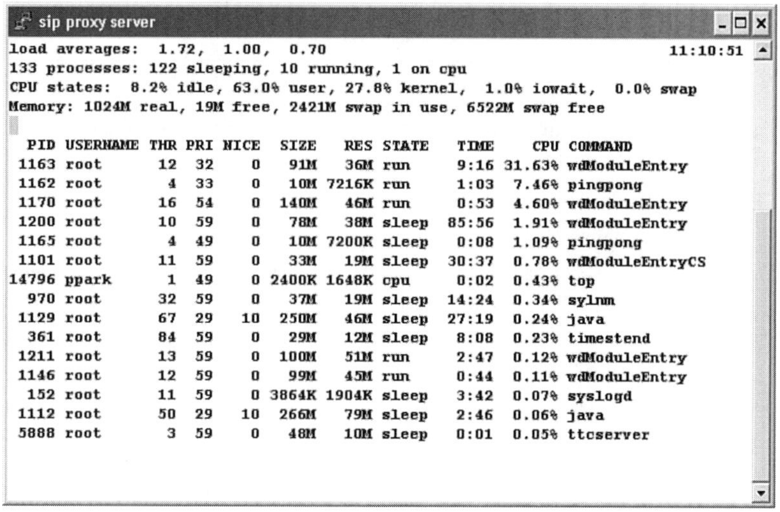

```
 sip proxy server                                                      - □ ×
load averages:   1.72,   1.00,   0.70                          11:10:51  ▲
133 processes: 122 sleeping, 10 running, 1 on cpu
CPU states:   8.2% idle, 63.0% user, 27.8% kernel,   1.0% iowait,   0.0% swap
Memory: 1024M real, 19M free, 2421M swap in use, 6522M swap free

   PID USERNAME THR PRI NICE   SIZE   RES STATE    TIME    CPU COMMAND
  1163 root      12  32    0   91M   36M run       9:16 31.63% wdModuleEntry
  1162 root       4  33    0   10M 7216K run       1:03  7.46% pingpong
  1170 root      16  54    0  140M   46M run       0:53  4.60% wdModuleEntry
  1200 root      10  59    0   78M   38M sleep    85:56  1.91% wdModuleEntry
  1165 root       4  49    0   10M 7200K sleep     0:08  1.09% pingpong
  1101 root      11  59    0   33M   19M sleep    30:37  0.78% wdModuleEntryCS
 14796 ppark      1  49    0 2400K 1648K cpu       0:02  0.43% top
   970 root      32  59    0   37M   19M sleep    14:24  0.34% sylnm
  1129 root      67  29   10  250M   46M sleep    27:19  0.24% java
   361 root      84  59    0   29M   12M sleep     8:08  0.23% timestend
  1211 root      13  59    0  100M   51M run       2:47  0.12% wdModuleEntry
  1146 root      12  59    0   99M   45M run       0:44  0.11% wdModuleEntry
   152 root      11  59    0 3864K 1904K sleep     3:42  0.07% syslogd
  1112 root      50  29   10  266M   79M sleep     2:46  0.06% java
  5888 root       3  59    0   48M   10M sleep     0:01  0.05% ttcserver
                                                                        ▼
```

NOTE   Depending on the capacity of the server machine, the resource usage could vary. You may adjust the verbosity option (**-v**) or time duration of flooding to see the degree of impairment on the server.

Step 6   You may make a regular call with an IP phone while the server is attacked by the flooding in Step 5 in order to experience the degradation (that is, late call setup time) or outage of the service.

Analysis

As you saw in Figure 6-3, 3,000 SIP OPTIONS messages per second consume more than 90 percent of CPU usage (8.2% idle), which is under very critical state. Especially if the high usage is sustained, the proxy server is not able to provide proper service for other call attempts; in the worst case, it could be down or rebooted.

Additionally, keep in mind that the proxy server being tested in this example is a well-known carrier-grade product, even though it is designed for a lab environment with a little lower hardware specification. Even a high-performance machine would suffer the same problems if the verbosity option is increased.

How is it possible for one PC to create a serious impairment on a carrier-grade machine that is designed for covering lots of customers, say, 50,000 endpoints? The reason is that the call request is very intensive within a short period of time.

Table 6-1 describes the difference between regular heavy traffic during busy hours and malicious flooding.

Table 6-1 *Comparison Between Regular Heavy Traffic and Malicious Flooding*

	Regular Heavy Traffic	**Flooding**
Call interval	Fairly intensive and various call intervals.	Extremely intensive and almost no call interval.
CPU usage	There could be high usage like a spike, but not sustained.	Sustained high usage.
Memory usage	It may have high usage, but it is refreshed quickly at the end of each call.	It constantly consumes high usage by sustaining each call transaction on purpose, which causes memory overflow.
Service impact	There could be minor call setup delay or call rejection according to Call Admission Control (CAC).	It causes major call setup delay or complete outage, especially when emergency calls (such as 911) are flooded.

What kind of VoIP messages (signals) can be a tool of flooding? One example is, as you already see, SIP OPTIONS. There are many more messages, and they can be categorized as shown in Table 6-2.

Table 6-2 *Flooding Messages*

	Function	**Example**	**Impact of Flooding**
Ping messages	Like an ICMP ping, to check out the availability of server, or keep the pinhole open within the local NAT device.	SIP OPTIONS H.323 Keepalive MGCP[1] RSIP[2] (keepalive)	It uses high CPU resources to reply to the endpoint. Some servers drop these messages for security purposes.
Registration messages	To request registration.	SIP REGISTER H.323 RRQ MGCP RSIP (restart)	It uses high CPU and memory resources to process the registration. It is one of the most vulnerable messages because most servers receive and process the authentication.

Table 6-2   *Flooding Messages (Continued)*

	Function	Example	Impact of Flooding
Call request messages	To initiate call setup.	SIP INVITE H.323 SETUP	It uses high CPU and memory. Even unauthorized call attempts (no registration before) can cause serious damage as long as the server generates error messages.
Dummy (invalid) messages	To receive error messages.	SIP NOTIFY without contents. Sudden H.323 CONNECT without session.	It uses high CPU usage to send back error messages.

1. MGCP = Media Gateway Control Protocol

2. RSIP = RestartInProgress

Mitigation

How can you mitigate those VoIP flooding attacks? There are several ways to mitigate, and they can be summarized as follows for your best practice:

- Do not allow ping messages, such as SIP OPTIONS, from endpoints. Also, do not allow the process to make response messages, so that the CPU of the server will not be engaged.

- Limit the number of registration requests within a certain period of time, such as only up to five times per second. The server must drop the exceeded packets without CPU engagement.

- Require credentials for registration and call requests so that unauthorized endpoints cannot occupy the resources of the server, such as registration cache or memory for call state information. Also, a server should limit the number of rejection messages to save CPU resources.

- Do not allow multiple call requests from single endpoints, except the multiple lines in a single endpoint.

- Maintain a "black list," put the misbehaving endpoint into the list, and drop all messages from it for a certain period of time, say, 60 seconds.

- Limit the total number of messages from the specific endpoint for a certain period of time, such as up to 30 messages for 30 seconds.

  The number can be calculated based on the normal behavior of the endpoint. Drop the exceeded packets or put the endpoint into the black list for demoting.

- Limit the total bandwidth for each endpoint and put it into the black list for a certain period of time when it exceeds the bandwidth. You may need to calculate the maximum bandwidth for normal phone usage, which varies depending on protocol and type of services.

- Use ACL (Access Control List) to block the source of unauthorized IP traffic.

NOTE   The legacy security tool of the network layer, such as a generic firewall blocking ICMP ping or TCP SYN attack, cannot mitigate these application (VoIP protocol) layer attacks.

The methods of mitigation described in this section are just guidelines for people who prepare secure VoIP networks, especially flooding protection. More specific or different methods of mitigation are possible, depending on the network architecture, type of service (ToS), type of protocol, type of endpoints, and so on.

Many VoIP servers like a Softswitch have some of the features described in this section, but they are very limited because the server manufacturers believe that a VoIP server itself is not a security device like a firewall. In reality, it is not a recommended method for the VoIP server to have all the security features, which use up significant resources as well. For example, maintaining a black list requires extra processing power and memory.

That is why an efficient method of mitigation is using external VoIP security devices like Session Border Controller (SBC), IP-to-IP gateway, or VoIP-aware firewall. Chapter 8, "Protection with Session Border Controller," and Chapter 9, "Protection with Enterprise Network Devices," show the details of the usage of those devices to mitigate the flooding.

Unintentional Flooding

It is possible to see unintentional flooding in a production service environment without any malicious external attacks. It is not common, but it happens because of wrong configuration of devices, wrong network design, unique circumstances or misbehaving devices, and so on.

It is generally easier to isolate and fix the problem of unintentional flooding compared to malicious flooding, because the legitimate devices are under the enterprise's or service provider's control. However, it is apt to damage the VoIP service quickly without being filtered by security devices.

This section analyzes the well-known cases and shows the methods of mitigation. Because of the lack of tools, actual simulation of each case is not included.

Analysis

Here are three well-known cases and their analysis: global power outage and backup, wrong configuration of devices, and misbehaving endpoints.

Global Power Outage and Backup

Here is a unique scenario as an example:

There was a global power outage and all IP phones (for example, 20,000 phones) within the same service network were down. After 5 minutes, the power is backed up and all 20,000 IP phones are booting up. What happens is that the SIP registrar server (or H.323 GK) will receive 20,000 REGISTER (or H.323 RRQ) messages at the same time. This causes high CPU usage and buffer overflow, which could make the server crash. (Refer to Figure 6-3 showing more than 90 percent CPU usage for 3,000 OPTIONS messages per second.)

To make the situation worse, the high CPU usage will not be just a spike but will be sustained because the failed or rejected phones keep sending the registration messages until they are successfully registered.

Because those phones are legitimate and distributed in a wide area, it is hard to control the flooding traffic proactively.

Wrong Configuration of Devices

The most common wrong configuration is setting endpoint devices (IP phone, integrated access device [IAD], media gateway, and so on) to send too many unnecessary messages, like these examples:

- Too short interval of ping messages (for example, SIP OPTIONS) to the server, such as every 10 seconds
- Too short interval of registration (for example, H.323 RRQ)

For better understanding, do some simple math for how many messages the SIP proxy server receives per second in the case of SIP OPTIONS from 20,000 endpoints every 10 seconds: 20000/10 = 2000. Two thousand messages per second are critical enough to affect current service because there are many other messages in service as well.

You may doubt who is going to set that short timer. Most VoIP engineers have common sense about a proper timer, but sometimes they mistakenly use the default setting of the phone, which has a very short timer.

The reason for the short timer in the default setting is that many phone manufacturers consider the worst case of NAT traversal: Some local NAT devices refresh the mapping table very quickly, like every 30 seconds, so the phone should send a dummy packet (for example, SIP OPTIONS; see the following Note) every less than 30 seconds in order to keep the pinhole open.

You may need to use the short timer if your service network is like that case, but it is not necessary in most cases.

NOTE   Using SIP messages, such as OPTIONS, is a common way of keeping the pinhole of NAT open, but the SIP Working Group does not recommend this method any more because of performance issues, as specified in draft-ietf-sip-outbound-13. Instead, the SIP Working Group selected the Session Traversal Utilities for NAT (STUN) mechanism, which is very robust, far less CPU-intensive, and allows the detection of a changed IP address. For more information, refer to the draft and RFC 3489 ("Simple Traversal of UDP Through NATs").

Not only endpoint devices, but also VoIP servers (registrar, gatekeeper, or call agent) may have wrong configuration that generates unnecessary heavy traffic like these examples:

- Too short interval of ping messages from a server (for example, MGCP AUEP, SIP OPTIONS)
- Too short registration timer, which makes endpoint devices send registration too frequently

You may need to set the server to have short intervals depending on service type or local environment, but it is not necessary in most cases.

Misbehaving Endpoints

There is a well-known flood problem with Address Resolution Protocol (ARP) broadcast that you might have seen before; for example, one PC has a network interface card (NIC) problem and floods lots of ARP packets sucking up all internal network bandwidth. It causes people to complain about the delay of downloading files, emails, or web contents. Sound familiar? Even in a VoIP network, you may see a similar situation because of device error.

A few years ago, when I was working for a Softswitch company, I found there was significant call setup delay in our corporate VoIP network along with high bandwidth consumption, even though not many users used the phones. Eventually, the problem was isolated: One MGCP phone that had a firmware or hardware error kept flooding RSIP messages until it was accepted by the Softswitch.

Like the experience I had, it gets worse if those problematic phones and servers are within the same corporate network because security devices like SBC are not apt to be involved for internal traffic.

Software (firmware) or hardware problems could create this kind of unexpected flooding, especially if multiple or anonymous types of endpoints are involved in the service network.

Mitigation

The method of mitigating unintentional (internal) flooding is somewhat easier than intentional (external) attack, in terms of manageability of the root cause. The basic steps of mitigation are as follows:

Step 1   Monitor traffic.

Monitor VoIP traffic regularly in the network to see whether unexpected heavy traffic happens, especially sustained heavy traffic. Or, monitor the resource usage (CPU, memory) of VoIP servers to see high sustained usage.

Step 2   Classify high resources and traffic.

When unexpected high traffic or resources are detected,

(a)   Check out the traffic direction: endpoint to server, server to endpoint, or both.

(b)   Check out how many nodes are involved: single or multiple endpoints or servers.

(c)   Check out what type of endpoint (for example, analog telephone adapter [ATA], IP phone, IAD) has the issue.

    (d) Check out whether those devices have the certified configuration.

    (e) Check out whether those endpoints are authorized or not: if unauthorized, it is most likely a malicious attack.

    (f) Check out whether the high usage is consistent or not: if consistent, it is most likely a configuration issue on either endpoints or servers.

    (g) Check out whether there was a unique environmental change like a global power outage or major network change, and so on.

Step 3 Isolate the root cause.

Sniff packets with tools (for example, Ethereal or tcpdump) and analyze the root cause:

    (a) What kind of message is flooded between endpoints and servers: ping, register, call request, and so on?

    (b) If a large number of endpoints request registration at the same time, it is because of a unique environmental change like a global power outage or major network change.

    (c) Analyze the message body and parameters, and isolate who initiated the frequent messages: either server or endpoint.

    (d) If there is no configuration issue on both endpoint and server, it is most likely a device error (firmware or hardware).

Step 4 Resolve issues.

    (a) Depending on the root cause, the method of resolution varies based on service policy, severity of issue, customer impact, other service impact, and so on.

    (a) Table 6-3 shows examples of resolving issues specified in the previous section.

Table 6-3   *Example of Resolution*

Case	Symptom	Resolution
Global outage and backup	Large number of phones register at the same time when power is up.	Let registration server or mediation device (for example, SBC) limit the number of concurrent registrations, and drop all exceeded requests without generating error messages.
Too frequent ping messages	Large number of endpoints send frequent ping messages (for example, SIP OPTION).	Increase the time interval to a reasonable number. If a short timer is necessary for certain endpoints using a local NAT device, segregate those endpoints and apply differently, rather than using one global configuration.
Too frequent registration messages	Large number of endpoints send frequent registration.	Increase the expiration timer on the server (for example, "expire" header in SIP OK for REGISTER message). If a short timer is necessary for a certain group of endpoints, segregate them from the others, rather than using one global configuration.
Device error (firmware or hardware)	Defective devices flood certain messages.	Isolate those devices, and replace or change the firmware or hardware.

Malformed Messages

Here is an experience that I had a few years ago:

Our demo Softswitch in the lab was down suddenly one day. I checked out network traffic, but there was no suspicious traffic like intrusion or DoS flooding or anything else suspicious. Internal logs in the Softswitch also did not show any critical error enough to crash the whole system. It was running back to normal after I rebooted, but the crash happened again a little while after. So, I sniffed all packets, analyzed, and found the root cause; the Softswitch was running on infinite loops after receiving a call from one IP phone that sent the wrong format of SIP header (the character ">" was missing in the contact header as in the following example):

```
Contact: <sip:192.168.11.11;transport=udp
```

The bug was fixed on both IP phone and Softswitch, and everything worked fine.

It may sound funny that one syntax error on the VoIP message caused the server crash, but this could happen in a real service environment, not only caused by a system bug but also by an external attacker generating massive malformed messages on purpose.

In fact, it is hard to prevent those attacks because there are so many possibilities of wrong syntax. That is, it is very difficult to code the fixes case by case. Fortunately, many testing tools have been released recently, and they help to verify the vulnerability before deploying a production system.

This section discusses those malformed messages from simulation to analysis and mitigation.

Simulation

There are many tools for testing malformed messages in the market. Some of them are free to use and already verified by many users, such as PROTOS created by the University of Oulu in Finland. For your simulation, download the PROTOS SIP version from the following link, or you can search "PROTOS" in the university website (www.ee.oulu.fi). The contents in this section refer to the website:[2]

http://www.ee.oulu.fi/research/ouspg/protos/testing/c07/sip/#download

Download the latest version of test-material as well. Because it is a JAR package, your PC should have the Java Virtual Machine to run it.

PROTOS manipulates only SIP INVITE message and generates 4,527 malformed INVITE messages for the whole test. One of the examples is shown in Example 6-3.

Example 6-3 *Malformed SIP Message*

```
Request-URI: aaaaaaaaa sip:1001@192.168.10.10 SIP/2.0
Message Header
   Via: SIP/2.0/UDP CAL-D600-5814.cc  ntd1.covad.com:5060;branch=z9hG4bK00002000005
   From::::::::: 2 <sip:user@CAL-D600-5814.cc-ntd1.covad.com>;tag=2
   To: Receiver <sip:1001@192.168.10.10>
   Call-ID: 5@CAL-D600-5814.cc-ntd1.covad.com
   CSeq: 1 INVITE
   Contact: 2 <sip:user@CAL-D600-5814.cc-ntd1.covad.com>
   Expires: 1200
   Max-Forwards: 70
```

Example 6-3 *Malformed SIP Message (Continued)*

```
    Content-Type: application/sdp
    Content-Length: 143

Message body
Session Description Protocol
    Session Description Protocol Version (v): = = = = = = 0
    Owner/Creator, Session Id (o): 2 2 2 IN IP4 CAL-D600-5814.cc-ntd1.covad.com
    Session Name (s): Session SDP
    Connection Information (c): IN IP4 192.168.10.10
    Time Description, active time (t): 0 0
    Media Description, name and address (m): audio 9876 RTP/AVP 0
    Media Attribute (a): rtpmap:0 PCMU/8000
```

You can find something wrong in the INVITE message. Three headers have the wrong format: one in Request-URI (aaaaaaaaa), another in From (;;;;;;;;;;), and the other in SDP version (======). Those error messages will be sent one at a time.

All the test cases (4,527) that PROTOS executes are grouped in Table 6-4.

Table 6-4   *Test Cases of PROTOS*

Name[1]	Exceptional Elements[2]	First Index #[3]	Test Cases[3]
valid	n/a	0	1
SIP-Method	overflow-general, overflow-space, overflow-null, fmtstring, utf-8, ansi-escape	1	193
SIP-Request-URI	sip-URI	194	61
SIP-Version	sip-version	255	75
SIP-Via-Host	ipv4-ascii	330	106
SIP-Via-Hostcolon	overflow-colon	436	16
SIP-Via-Hostport	integer-ascii	452	46
SIP-Via-Version	sip-version	498	75
SIP-Via-Tag	sip-tag	573	57
SIP-From-Displayname	overflow-general, overflow-space, overflow-null, fmtstring, utf-8, ansi-escape	630	193

continues

| SIP-From-Tag | sip-tag | 823 | 57 |

Table 6-4 *Test Cases of PROTOS (Continued)*

Name[1]	Exceptional Elements[2]	First Index #[3]	Test Cases[3]
SIP-From-Colon	overflow-colon	880	16
SIP-From-URI	sip-URI	896	61
SIP-Contact-Displayname	overflow-general, overflow-space, overflow-null, fmtstring, utf-8, ansi-escape	957	193
SIP-Contact-URI	sip-URI	1150	61
SIP-Contact-Left-Paranthesis	overflow-leftbracket	1211	16
SIP-Contact-Right-Paranthesis	overflow-rightbracket	1227	16
SIP-To	overflow-general, overflow-space, overflow-null, fmtstring, utf-8, ansi-escape	1243	193
SIP-To-Left-Paranthesis	overflow-leftbracket	1436	16
SIP-To-Right-Paranthesis	overflow-rightbracket	1452	16
SIP-Call-Id-Value	overflow-general, overflow-space, overflow-null, fmtstring, utf-8, ansi-escape	1468	193
SIP-Call-Id-At	overflow-at	1661	16
SIP-Call-Id-Ip	ipv4-ascii	1677	106
SIP-Expires	integer-ascii	1783	46
SIP-Max-Forwards	integer-ascii	1829	46
SIP-Cseq-Integer	integer-ascii	1875	46
SIP-Cseq-String	overflow-general, overflow-space, overflow-null, fmtstring, utf-8, ansi-escape	1921	193
SIP-Content-Type	overflow-general, overflow-space, overflow-null, fmtstring, utf-8, ansi-escape, content-type	2114	247
SIP-Content-Length	integer-ascii	2361	46

Table 6-4   *Test Cases of PROTOS (Continued)*

Name[1]	Exceptional Elements[2]	First Index #[3]	Test Cases[3]
SIP-Request-CRLF	crlf	2407	10
CRLF-Request	crlf	2417	10
SDP-Attribute-CRLF	crlf	2427	10
SDP-Proto-v-Identifier	overflow-general, overflow-space, overflow-null, fmtstring, utf-8, ansi-escape	2437	193
SDP-Proto-v-Equal	overflow-equal	2630	16
SDP-Proto-v-Integer	integer-ascii	2646	46
SDP-Origin-Username	overflow-general, overflow-space, overflow-null, fmtstring, utf-8, ansi-escape	2692	193
SDP-Origin-Sessionid	integer-ascii	2885	46
SDP-Origin-Networktype	overflow-general, overflow-space, overflow-null, fmtstring, utf-8, ansi-escape	2931	193
SDP-Origin-Ip	ipv4-ascii	3124	106
SDP-Session	overflow-general, overflow-space, overflow-null, fmtstring, utf-8, ansi-escape	3230	193
SDP-Connection-Networktype	overflow-general, overflow-space, overflow-null, utf-8, fmtstring	3423	188
SDP-Connection-Ip	ipv4-ascii	3611	106
SDP-Time-Start	integer-ascii	3717	46
SDP-Time-Stop	empty	3763	1
SDP-Media-Media	overflow-general, overflow-space, overflow-null, fmtstring, utf-8, ansi-escape	3764	193

continues

Table 6-4 *Test Cases of PROTOS (Continued)*

Name[1]	Exceptional Elements[2]	First Index #[3]	Test Cases[3]
SDP-Media-Port	integer-ascii	3957	46
SDP-Media-Transport	overflow-general, overflow-space, overflow-null, fmtstring, ansi-escape	4003	118
SDP-Media-Type	integer-ascii	4121	46
SDP-Attribute-Rtpmap	overflow-general, overflow-space, overflow-null, fmtstring, ansi-escape	4167	118
SDP-Attribute-Colon	overflow-colon	4285	16
SDP-Attribute-Payloadtype	integer-ascii	4301	46
SDP-Attribute-Encodingname	integer-ascii	4347	118
SDP-Attribute-Slash	overflow-slash	4465	16
SDP-Attribute-Clockrate	integer-ascii	4481	46

1. The "Name" column represents the tag-names of the test-groups. Tags reflect the header and field names in the protocol specification. Tags can be used to follow which parts of the Protocol Data Unit (PDU) are being tested.

2. The "Exceptional Elements" column describes which exceptional element categories are integrated in the test-group.

3. The "First Index #" and "Test Cases" columns describe the first test-case number for a test-group, and the number of cases from there on.

You can execute all of them sequentially, or individual cases indexed by the number. You can see the usage and syntax with a help option as in Example 6-4.

Example 6-4 *PROTOS Usage*

```
C:\PROTOS>java -jar c07-sip-r2.jar -help
Usage java -jar <jarfile>.jar [ [OPTIONS] | -touri <SIP-URI> ]

  -touri  <addr>        Recipient of the request
                        Example: <addr> : you@there.com
  -fromuri <addr>       Initiator of the request
                        Default: user@papark-wxp01.cisco.com
  -sendto <domain>      Send packets to <domain> instead of
                        domainname of -touri
  -callid <callid>      Call id to start test-case call ids from
                        Default: 0
  -dport <port>         Portnumber to send packets on host.
```

Example 6-4 *PROTOS Usage (Continued)*

```
                         Default: 5060
  -lport <port>          Local portnumber to send packets from
                         Default: 5060
  -delay <ms>            Time to wait before sending new test-case
                         Defaults to 100 ms (milliseconds)
  -replywait <ms>        Maximum time to wait for host to reply
                         Defaults to 100 ms (milliseconds)
  -file <file>           Send file <file> instead of test-case(s)
  -help                  Display this help
  -jarfile <file>        Get data from an alternate bugcat
                         JAR-file <file>
  -showreply             Show received packets
  -showsent              Show sent packets
  -teardown              Send CANCEL/ACK
  -single <index>        Inject a single test-case <index>
  -start <index>         Inject test-cases starting from <index>
  -stop <index>          Stop test-case injection to <index>
  -maxpdusize <int>      Maximum PDU size
                         Default to 65507 bytes
  -validcase             Send valid case (case #0) after each
                         test-case and wait for a response. May
                         be used to check if the target is still
                         responding. Default: off
```

The following steps show an example that runs all the test cases, along with a valid INVITE message to make sure the SIP proxy server runs properly right after each test case.

Here is an example of a command and its sequence of execution:

```
C:\PROTOS>java -jar c07-sip-r2.jar -touri 1001@192.168.10.10 -teardown -validcase
```

1 Sends the INVITE test-case to address 1001@192.168.10.10 default SIP port 5060 over UDP.

2 Sends CANCEL.

3 Sends ACK for the teardown.

4 Sends a valid INVITE.

5 Sends CANCEL for the valid INVITE.

6 Sends ACK for the valid INVITE teardown.

WARNING This test of malformed messages may cause serious damage to the functionality of a SIP proxy server. It is highly recommended to use a lab system on which there is no other traffic. Do not try this on your production system or service provider's network.

Example 6-5 is the initial output after executing the command in the example.

Example 6-5   *Test Output with PROTOS*

```
C:\PROTOS>java -jar c07-sip-r2.jar -touri 4084445555@192.168.10.10 -teardown -
  validcase
single-valued 'java.class.path', using it's value for jar file name
reading data from jar file: c07-sip-r2.jar
Sending Test-Case #0
     test-case #0, 563 bytes
        Received Returncode: 100
 Sending CANCEL
     test-case #0, 299 bytes
        Received Returncode: 487
 Sending ACK
     test-case #0, 293 bytes
Sending valid-cse
     test-case #0, 568 bytes
        Received Returncode: 100
 Sending CANCEL
     test-case #0, 304 bytes
        Received Returncode: 487
 Sending ACL
     test-case #0, 298 bytes
Sending Test-Case #1
     test-case #1, 562 bytes
        Received Returncode: 100
.......................................................
```

If you need to execute an individual test case, such as #3000 in Table 6-4, use the case number as in the following line:

```
C:\PROTOS>java -jar c07-sip-r2.jar -touri 1001@192.168.10.10 -teardown — single 3000
```

Analysis

After running the test-material package targeting your SIP proxy server, you may find certain errors on the server like memory overflow, high CPU usage, system crash or automatic reboot, and so on.

The result can be categorized into four different states:

- Failure (one of the symptoms in the following list)
    - The normal call request right after the test case is not processed.
    - The target server stops its service by being crashed or under freeze state.
    - The target server is rebooted automatically or requires manual reboot.
    - Any system errors like memory corruption, stack corruption, or buffer overflow.
    - High consumption of system resources like high memory or CPU usage.
- Inconclusive
    - The test case has not failed, but similar effects of failure are observed.
- Unknown
    - There is no way to have an accurate result because of previous server corruption or critical error while running the test-material.
- Pass
    - Successful result without any system error.

Table 6-5 shows an example of test results after running the test-material with multiple target servers.

Table 6-5   *Test Result of PROTOS[1]*

Test-group	Test-run #1	Test-run #2	Test-run #3	Test-run #4
Valid	–	–	–	–
SIP-Method	–	–	–	–
SIP-Request-URI	–	X	–	–
SIP-Version	–	–	–	–
SIP-Via-Host	–	–	X	–
SIP-Via-Hostcolon	–	–	X	–
SIP-Via-Hostport	–	X	X	–
SIP-Via-Version	–	–	X	–
SIP-Via-Tag	–	?	?	–
SIP-From-Displayname	X	X	X	–
SIP-From-Tag	X	X	–	–
SIP-From-Colon	X	X	–	–
SIP-From-URI	X	X	X	–

continues

Table 6-5 *Test Result of PROTOS[1] (Continued)*

Test-group	Test-run #1	Test-run #2	Test-run #3	Test-run #4
SIP-Contact-Displayname	X	–	–	–
SIP-Contact-URI	X	–	–	–
SIP-Contact-Left-Paranthesis	–	–	–	–
SIP-Contact-Right-Paranthesis	–	–	–	–
SIP-To	–	–	–	–
SIP-To-Left-Paranthesis	–	–	–	–
SIP-To-Right-Paranthesis	–	–	–	–
SIP-Call-Id-Value	X	X	?	–
SIP-Call-Id-At	X	X	–	–
SIP-Call-Id-Ip	X	X	–	–
SIP-Expires	X	–	–	–
SIP-Max-Forwards	X	X	?	–
SIP-Cseq-Integer	X	–	–	–
SIP-Cseq-String	–	X	X	–
SIP-Content-Type	–	–	–	–
SIP-Content-Length	–	X	–	–
SIP-Request-CRLF	–	–	–	–
CRLF-Request	–	–	–	–
SDP-Attribute-CRLF	–	–	–	–
SDP-Proto-v-Identifier	?	–	X	–
SDP-Proto-v-Equal	?	–	–	–
SDP-Proto-v-Integer	?	–	–	–
SDP-Origin-Username	–	X	–	–
SDP-Origin-Sessionid	X	–	–	–
SDP-Origin-Networktype	X	–	–	–
SDP-Origin-Ip	X	–	X	–
SDP-Session	X	–	–	–
SDP-Connection-Networktype	X	–	–	–

Table 6-5   *Test Result of PROTOS[1] (Continued)*

Test-group	Test-run #1	Test-run #2	Test-run #3	Test-run #4
SDP-Connection-Ip	X	–	–	–
SDP-Time-Start	X	–	–	–
SDP-Time-Stop	–	–	–	–
SDP-Media-Media	X	–	X	–
SDP-Media-Port	X	–	X	–
SDP-Media-Transport	X	–	X	–
SDP-Media-Type	X	–	–	–
SDP-Attribute-Rtpmap	X	–	–	–
SDP-Attribute-Colon	X	–	–	–
SDP-Attribute-Payloadtype	X	–	–	–
SDP-Attribute-Encodingname	X	–	–	–
SDP-Attribute-Slash	X	–	–	–
SDP-Attribute-Clockrate	X	–	–	–

1.   Meaning of symbols:

   X: Failure

   I: Inconclusive

   ?: Unknown

   –: Pass

As shown in Table 6-5, many SIP servers have vulnerability to malformed messages, which could be the method of DoS attack by external hackers.

There are two main reasons why even commercial products have this kind of security hole:

- Most VoIP solution providers focus on the general VoIP service itself like functionality, interoperability, features, and capacity. Many of them believe that additional security devices (for example, SBC) are required because VoIP server is not a security device.

- Technically, it is very difficult to implement a complete solution for every single malformed case. Even PROTOS with 4,527 test cases does not cover every possible case (limited to the SIP INVITE message as well).

Mitigation

There is no 100 percent complete solution for a malformed message attack, but you can mitigate the risk significantly with the methods like those in the following list. These guidelines are categorized by the different level of product life cycle.

- Development (protocol) level

  — Limit the buffer size on malformed message lines.

  — Prevent infinite loop caused by syntax errors (for example, unending clause in any message line).

  — Define a clear procedure of exception handling after the error is detected, like stopping the parsing process immediately and flushing the error.

- Test level

  — Use testing tools (for example, PROTOS) and verify whether the target server handles properly without abusing resources. If not, additional development is required.

  — Perform the qualification process for targeted endpoint devices to make sure they do not send any type of malformed message.

- Operational level

  — Whenever the VoIP server detects the error, it should send a trap to the administration server, so that a network administrator may handle the error immediately.

  — The VoIP server should demote the endpoint device sending the malformed message, like dropping all packets from the device for a certain period of time.

Sniffing/Eavesdropping

The biggest concern that most Internet telephony users have is that someone may hear their conversation somewhere in the middle of the network. It is technically possible but not as easy as they believe. The eavesdropper must have network access to the same local broadcasting domain or the media path to capture the packets, as well as special tools to decode voice conversation.

This section shows how the sniffing or eavesdropping works, and how to mitigate them.

Simulation

The call scenario of this simulation is simple: You (the caller) make a phone call to the callee while activating the sniffing tool on your local network. That is, you pretend to be the eavesdropper as well.

To make the test simple, it assumes the following conditions:

- You (caller) have an IP phone (or a softphone).
- You (caller) have a PC connected to the same hub that your IP phone uses.
- The PC has a sniffing tool that is able to capture all in and out packets of the phone.
- The callee can be anywhere, either an IP phone user or public switched telephone network (PSTN) user.
- SIP proxy server (or H.323 gatekeeper) is ready to accept and terminate the call.

Using the same hub is not necessary as long as you can capture all in and out packets of the phone; for example, if using a softphone, you can capture the packets in the same computer.

One of the most popular sniffing tools is Wireshark (formerly "Ethereal"), which is used in this test. It is freeware and you can download it from the following website:

http://www.wireshark.org/download.html

Download the latest installation file (.exe) for Windows users. For UNIX users, there are separate packages depending on the system.

When you install it, use default options if you are not sure. The main window will be similar to Figure 6-4 after activating the program.

Figure 6-4   *Main Window of Wireshark*

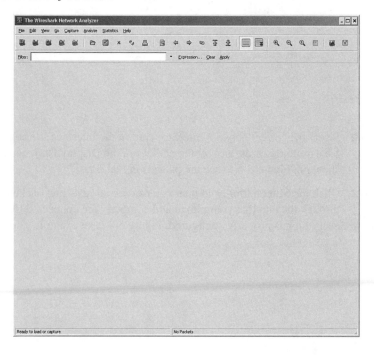

There are many options in this tool, but we will use only the essential ones to sniff VoIP packets. Follow these steps to make the tool ready.

Step 1 Click **Options** on the Capture menu in the main window (or press the shortcut key **Ctrl-K**). Then you can see the Capture Options window as shown in Figure 6-5.

Figure 6-5 *Capture Options Window of Wireshark*

Step 2 Select the correct network interface card in the Interface list box if you have multiple cards, and set the choices in the Display Options area as shown in Figure 6-6 to see the packets in real time.

Step 3 Click the **Start** button, and then you can see all real-time packets going through the hub that your phone and computer are connected to, if everything is properly configured. Figure 6-7 is an example.

Figure 6-6   *Setting the Options of Wireshark*

Figure 6-7   *Real-Time Packet Capture*

If you see some packets rolling down, you are ready to sniff VoIP packets.

Now, pick up the phone, make a phone call, talk a little bit, and hang up the phone. You can see many SIP and RTP packets rolling down on the Wireshark during the test. Stop the capture and save it as a file.

Analysis

Because the capture file has non-VoIP packets as well, you need to filter them out to see only VoIP packets.

To see the call setup messages as in Figure 6-8, type **sip** in the filter box and then click **Apply**.

Figure 6-8   *Filtered SIP Messages*

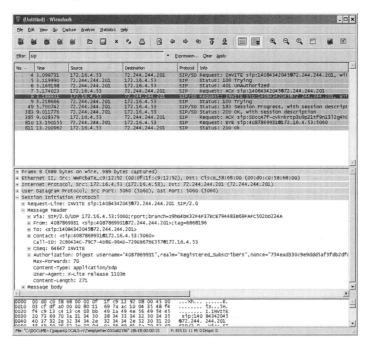

As shown in Figure 6-8, you can see some information about the targeted user and the call, such as:

- What phone number the user has
- What number the user dialed

- What ID and password were used (in this case, those are encrypted with Digest format)

- IP address and User Datagram Protocol (UDP) port of the user phone, proxy server, or media server

- The duration of the conversation

It is possible that an attacker may use this kind of information and spoof its identity or attack network nodes.

Now it is time to filter actual voice (RTP) packets and retrieve the voice with Wireshark. You can filter RTP packets as in Figure 6-9; type **rtp** in the filter box and then click **Apply**.

Figure 6-9 *Filtered RTP Packets*

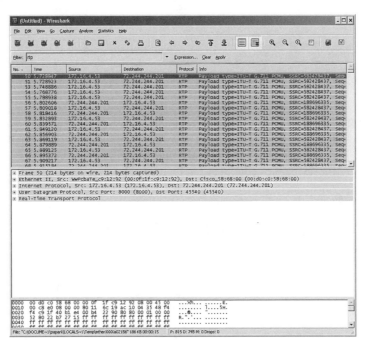

In order to hear the actual audio conversation, you need to take the following steps:

Step 1   Choose **Statistics > RTP > Stream Analysis**, and you can see the RTP Stream Analysis window as in Figure 6-10.

Figure 6-10 *RTP Stream Analysis*

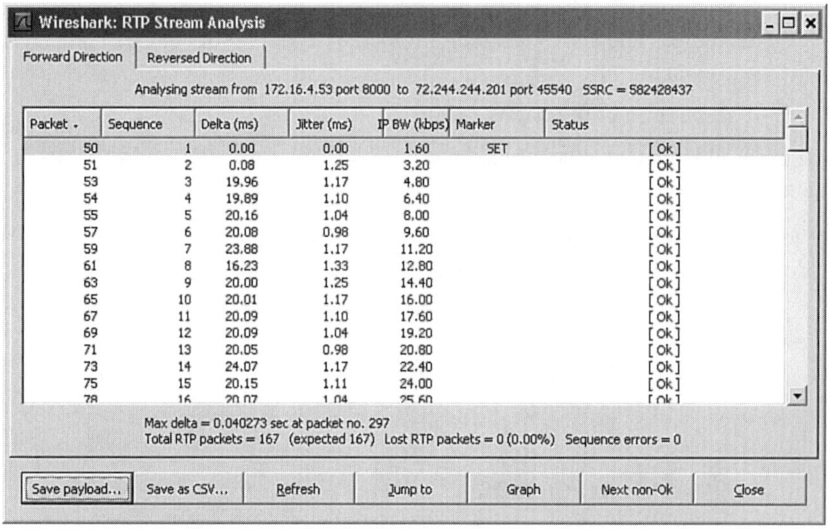

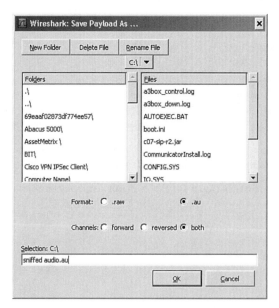

Step 2 Depending on the voice direction that you want to hear, you can choose it in the option. The default is, as shown in Figure 6-10, the caller to callee. Click the **Save payload** button, and you can see another window for saving the audio file as in Figure 6-11.

Figure 6-11 *Saving Audio*

Step 3   Select the audio type (.au) and filename (for example, voice.au) as
in Figure 6-11, and save it. Now, you can hear the original voice
conversation by playing the audio file (voice.au) with a media player. If
you want to hear the other direction of voice, you can select other options
in Step 2.

Therefore, it is possible for an eavesdropper to hear someone's conversation with this kind
of sniffing tool.

Mitigation

Someone may be surprised by this kind of sniffing and eavesdropping. It is realistically
possible, as you have seen, but not too difficult to prevent it.

There could be two solutions to mitigate at a high level: encrypting and non-broadcasting.
The non-broadcasting is the more common way these days because of its cost-effectiveness.
Table 6-6 shows the difference.

Table 6-6   *Two Solutions for Sniffing*

	Description	Pros	Cons
Non-broadcasting	It is a way of preventing broadcasted packets that an eavesdropper is able to sniff, especially within a Layer 2 broadcasting domain. The most common way of prevention is using a Layer 2 switch using unicast.	It is cost-effective and easy to implement.	This is only for a Layer 2 local network. If an eavesdropper sniffs on the backbone network or router, there is no way to prevent it.
Encrypting	It encrypts RTP packets with cryptographic methods like a Secure RTP.	Wherever packets are intercepted, it is almost impossible to retrieve original messages or voice without the key.	It comes with cost and performance degradation compared with nonencryption system, because each network node should have the capability and consumes extra processing power to encrypt and decrypt.

Spoofing/Identity Theft

Spoofing means that an attacker pretends to be an actual registered user and inserts fake messages in order to interrupt VoIP service or make toll calls. The following are examples of spoofing:

- Insert faked SIP REGISTER message to steal the registration
- Insert faked SIP BYE message to the current call session and tear it down
- Respond out-of-service messages (for example, 486 BUSY HERE) for the inbound calls after stealing the registration
- Make toll calls after stealing the user identity

In common cases, an attacker sniffs original registrations or call setup messages from legitimate users as exemplified in the previous section in order to spoof the user's identity.

Simulation

Many spoofing scenarios are possible, but the most common type of spoofing is that an attacker steals a user's identity (or session) first and generates a fake message to break the service, which will be simulated in this section.

There are two steps of preparation before generating the attack: prespoofing scan and identity theft. We will use a tool called SIPcrack to simulate both. You can download it from the following website. The content in this section refers to the website:[3]

http://www.remote-exploit.org/codes_sipcrack.html

This is running on a UNIX/Linux system. Download the tar.gz file and extract into a folder that you want. Switch to the folder and type the **make** command to build the files. If you do not have OpenSSL or some errors happen while building, try the **make no-openssl** command to build with integrated Message Digest 5 (MD5) function, which is slower than the OpenSSL implementation.

After that, you can see two modules in the package: the **SIPdump** command for scanning and the **SIPcrack** command for getting identity. Now, you are ready to do the simulation.

Prespoofing Scan

Prespoofing scan means collecting the user's session messages, such as registration or call setup messages, by means of any type of sniffing tools as shown in the previous section. The SIPdump has the function.

SIPdump sniffs SIP Digest authentications from all packets passing by and writes the password into the file that you specify.

You can see the usage with the help option:

```
Prompt> sipdump  - h
```

For example, if you want to sniff Ethernet 0 and write the password into the sniffed_passwords.dump file, use the following command:

```
Prompt> sipdump  - I eth0 sniffed_passwords.dump
```

If your phones and computer are using same broadcasting domain like using the same hub, you can see the hashed (or encrypted) passwords in the dump file after you make phone calls or reboot the phones. Now, you need another tool (SIPcrack) for decrypting them.

Identity Theft

The function of SIPcrack is that, when you select the hashed (or encrypted) password that you want to crack, SIPcrack reads a password dictionary file having millions of samples and hashes each word with MD5 and compares it with the target password until they are matched. So, you need an additional password dictionary file (see the following Note) to execute it.

NOTE To get the password dictionary, go to your favorite search engine and search for the phrase "password dictionary." Alternatively, you can create your own text-based dictionary with sample words just for this simulation.

For example, if you want to crack the sniffed_passwords.dump file with the dictionary file pass_dic.txt, the usage is as follows:

```
Prompt> sipcrack  - w pass_dic.txt sniffed_passwords.dump
```

Example 6-6 illustrates the output as an example.

Example 6-6 *Cracking Password*

```
SIPCrack 0.1  ( MaJoMu | www.remote-exploit.org )
-------------------------------------------------

* Reading and parsing dump file...
* Found Accounts:

Num   Server          Client          User   Algorithm   Hash / Password
1       192.168.19.81   192.168.19.120   500    PLAIN       12345
2       192.168.19.81   192.168.19.120   500    PLAIN       34after12
3       192.168.19.81   192.168.19.120   500   MD5          d3bc10e4f2c9c275fe7da2f20f17600f
4       192.168.19.81   192.168.19.120   500   MD5          e5827d8cda285252d5ce87ad8e3c64ca
5       192.168.19.81   192.168.19.120   500   MD5          6524e36531b0dd77efa87cede26b4af3
```

continues

Example 6-6   *Cracking Password (Continued)*

```
* Select which entry to crack (1 - 5): 3

* Generating static MD5 hash...1a24e68fa4904bd8ce0b7a2b37fffab2
* Starting bruteforce against user '500' (MD5 Hash:
  'd3bc10e4f2c9c275fe7da2f20f17600f')
* Loaded wordlist: 'pass_dic.txt'
* Tried 8462686 passwords in 13 seconds
* Found password: 'a1b2c3'
* Updating 'logins-sip.txt'...done
```

The analysis of this simulation is as follows.

Analysis

According to the simulation in Example 6-6, the password was cracked in 13 seconds even though it is hashed by MD5. You may have a question: Is it that easy to crack the password?

Technically, it is almost impossible to crack an encrypted password because the average time of cracking a password with a single PC is many years when using the method of inputting all possible words.

However, most passwords are created by humans (rather than computers) manually and there is a high possibility that they may use very similar ones that are simple and easy to remember. No one really wants to have more than 10 digits and random password to remember, except system administrators. For example, if someone has a name "John Kim," he is apt to have passwords like "jkim," "iamjohn," "johnkim," "john2kim," "john4me," and so on.

Therefore, if you are using a password dictionary containing millions of commonly used passwords, it does not take long to crack passwords that ordinary users created.

When the identity is exposed, an attacker can easily pretend and generate any type of spoofing messages as well as making toll calls. The attacks are categorized as in the following:

- Stealing registration
  - The user cannot make outbound calls or receive inbound calls: the phone goes into an out-of-service state.
  - The attacker receives all inbound calls and either rejects (for example, 486 BUSY HERE) or receives the call.
  - The attacker may send flooded registrations to the server in order to interrupt the service.

- Session interruption
  - The attacker sends Re-INVITE to either caller or callee, and this results in one-way or no audio.
  - The attacker sends BYE message to the current call session and tears it down.
- Toll call
  - The attacker sends INVITE with a stolen identity and makes toll calls.

Mitigation

The first and best way of mitigating this spoofing attack is preventing the prespoofing scan like a sniffing, because after the identity or call session information is exposed, there is a high possibility of being cracked or manipulated.

The prevention of sniffing is already described in Table 6-6 with two methods: designing non-broadcasting network and encrypting.

The other methods of mitigating are summarized as follows:

- Require authentication for call request message (for example, SIP INVITE) as well as registration: Some service providers do not require this for faster call setup.
- Do not use default ID and password when installing initially.
- Pre-provision a machine-generated random user ID and password into the phone, rather than giving users the option to set up their own ID and password.
- The proxy server should track the original IP address of caller and callee, and detect (or prevent) when other source of IP address sends any session message (for example, SIP BYE or Re-INVITE).

VoIP Spam

The general meaning of spam is unsolicited bulk email, which you may see every day. It wastes network bandwidth and system resources, as well as annoying email users.

The spam exists in VoIP space as well, so-called VoIP Spam, in the form of voice, instant message (IM), and presence Spam. This section looks into each type of VoIP Spam with the SIP protocol and provides several solutions for mitigation. The content in this section refers to RFC 5039.[4]

Voice Spam

Voice (or call) spam is defined as a bulk unsolicited set of session initiation attempts (that is, INVITE requests), attempting to establish a voice or video communications session. If the user answers, the spammer proceeds to relay a message over the real-time media. This is the classic telemarketer spam, applied to VoIP protocol (SIP). This is often called SPam over Ip Telephony, or SPIT.

The main reason that SPIT is getting popular is that it is cost-effective for spammers. As you know, the legacy PSTN-call spam already exists in the form of telemarketer calls. Although these calls are annoying, they do not arrive in the same kind of volume as email spam. The difference is cost; it costs more for the spammer to make a phone call than it does to send email. This cost manifests itself in terms of the cost for systems that can perform telemarketer calls, and in cost per call. However, the cost is dramatically dropped when switching to SPIT because of the following reasons:

- **Easy to write a spam application**—It is just a SIP User Agent that initiates, in parallel, a large number of calls. If a call connects, the spam application generates an ACK and proceeds to play out a recorded announcement, and then it terminates the call. This kind of application can be built entirely in software, using readily available off-the-shelf software components.

- **Low hardware cost**—It can run on a low-end PC and requires no special expertise to execute.

- **Low line cost**— A normal PSTN phone line allows only one call to be placed at a time. If additional lines are required, a user must purchase another line. Typically, a T1 or T3 would be required for a large-volume telemarketing service. However, SPIT uses a broadband Internet connection. For example, if a spammer uses a typical broadband Internet that provides 500 Kbps of upstream bandwidth, initiating a call requires just a single INVITE message that is about 1 KB, which allows about 62 call attempts per second.

- **No boundary for international calls**—Currently, there are few telemarketing calls across international borders, largely due to the large cost of making international calls. However, IP network provides no boundaries for them, and calls to any SIP URI are possible from anywhere in the world. This will allow for international spam at a significantly reduced cost.

- **Higher hitting rate**—Its content is much more likely to be examined by a user if a call attempt is successful, because a user has to listen to an initial announcement (spam) to judge whether it is a spam call or not.

- **Finite address space**—Unlike email addresses, phone numbers are a finite address space and one that is fairly densely packed. As a result, going sequentially through phone numbers is likely to produce a fairly high hit rate.

This low cost is enough to be attractive to spammers. For some cases, many spammers utilize computational and bandwidth resources provided by others, by infecting their machines with viruses that turn them into "zombies" that can be used to generate spam. This can reduce the cost of call spam to nearly zero.

IM Spam

Instant Message (IM) spam is similar to email spam. It is defined as a bulk unsolicited set of instant messages, whose content contains the message that the spammer is seeking to convey. IM spam is most naturally sent using the SIP MESSAGE request. However, any other request that causes content to automatically appear on the user's display will also suffice. That might include INVITE requests with large Subject headers (since the Subject is sometimes rendered to the user), or INVITE requests with text or HTML bodies. This is often called SPam over Instant Messaging, or SPIM.

SPIM is very much like email, but much more intrusive than email. In today's systems, IMs automatically pop up and present themselves to the user. Email, of course, must be deliberately selected and displayed. However, most popular IM systems employ white lists, which only allow IM to be delivered if the sender is on the white list. Thus, whether or not IM spam will be useful seems to depend a lot on the nature of the systems as the network is opened up. If they are ubiquitously deployed with white-list access, the value of IM spam is likely to be low.

It is important to point out that there are two different types of IM systems: page mode and session mode. Page mode IM systems work much like email, with each IM being sent as a separate message. In session mode IM, there is signaling in advance of communication to establish a session, and then IMs are exchanged, perhaps point-to-point, as part of the session. The modality impacts the types of spam techniques that can be applied. Techniques for email can be applied identically to page mode IM, but session mode IM is more like telephony, and many techniques (such as content filtering) are harder to apply.

Presence Spam

Presence spam (SPPP) is similar to IM spam. It is defined as a bulk unsolicited set of presence requests (that is, SIP SUBSCRIBE requests) in an attempt to get on the "buddy list" or "white list" of a user in order to send them IMs or initiate other forms of communications. This is occasionally called SPam over Presence Protocol, or SPPP.

The cost of SPPP is within a small constant factor of IM spam, so the same cost estimates can be used here. What would be the effect of such spam? Most presence systems provide some kind of consent framework. A watcher that has not been granted permission to see the user's presence will not gain access to their presence. However, the presence request is usually noted and conveyed to the user, allowing them to approve or deny the request.

In SIP, this is done using the watcherinfo event package. This package allows a user to learn the identity of the watcher, in order to make an authorization decision. This could provide a vehicle for conveying information to a user; for example, by generating SUBSCRIBE requests from identities such as sip:buy-this-product@spam.com, which brief messages can be conveyed to the user, even though the sender does not have permission to access presence. As such, presence spam can be viewed as a form of IM spam, where the amount of content to be conveyed is limited. The limit is equal to the amount of information generated by the watcher that gets conveyed to the user through the permission system.

Mitigation

There is no single magic bullet that prevents all voice, IM, and presence spam problems. However, the problems would be much less significant if solutions had been deployed globally before the problems became widespread.

RFC 5039 introduces dozens of solutions mostly coming from techniques for email spam. Here are some remarkable solutions from the RFC.

Content Filtering

In email space, the most common form of spam protection is content filtering: a spam filter analyzes the content of the email and looks for clues that the email is spam.

This is a useful technique for IM spam that is similar to email. IM spam filter can leverage the latest email filter.

However, this technique is not that effective for SPIT. There are two reasons. First, in the case where the user answers the call, the call is already established and the user is paying attention before the content is delivered. The call cannot be analyzed before the user hears it. Second, if the content is stored before the user accesses it (for example, with voicemail), the content will be in the form of recorded audio or video. Speech and video recognition technology is not likely to be good enough to analyze the content and determine whether or not it is spam. Indeed, if a system tried to perform speech recognition on a recording in order to perform such an analysis, it would be easy for the spammers to make calls with background noises, poor grammar, and varied accents, all of which will throw off recognition systems. Video recognition is even harder to do and remains primarily an area of research.

Turing Test

In email, Turing tests are mechanisms whereby the sender of the message is given some kind of puzzle or challenge, which only a human can answer. If the puzzle is answered correctly, the sender is placed on the user's white list. These puzzles frequently take the form of recognizing a word or sequence of numbers in an image with a lot of background noise. The tests need to be designed such that automata cannot easily perform the image recognition needed to extract the word or number sequence, but a human user usually can. Designing such tests is not easy because ongoing advances in image processing and artificial intelligence continually raise the bar.

Like many of the other email techniques, Turing tests are dependent on sender identity, which cannot easily be authenticated in email.

Turing tests can be used to prevent IM spam in much the same way they can be used to prevent email spam.

Turing tests can be applied to SPIT as well, although not directly, because SPIT does not usually involve the transfer of images and other content that can be used to verify that a human is on the other end. If most of the calls are voice, the technique needs to be adapted to voice.

This is not that difficult to do. The following sidebar shows how it could be done, for example.

User A calls User B and is not on User B's white or black list. User A is transferred to an Interactive Voice Response (IVR) system. The IVR system tells the user that they are going to hear a series of numbers (say 5 of them), and that they have to enter those numbers on the keypad. The IVR system reads out the numbers while background music is playing, making it difficult for an automated speech recognition system to be applied to the media. The user then enters the numbers on the keypad. If they are entered correctly, the user is added to the white list.

This kind of voice-based Turing test is extended to a variety of media, such as video and text.

In the case of voice, the Turing test would need to be made to run in the language of the caller. This is possible in SIP, using the Accept-Language header field, though this header is not widely used at the moment, and meant for languages of SIP message components, not the media streams.

The primary problem with the voice Turing test is the same one that email tests have: instead of having an automaton process the test, a spammer can pay cheap workers to take the tests.

As an alternative to paying cheap workers to take the tests, the tests can be taken by human users who are tricked into completing the tests to gain access to what they believe is a legitimate resource. This was done by a spambot that posted the tests on a pornography site, and required users to complete the tests in order to gain access to content.

Because of these limitations, Turing tests may never completely solve the problem.

Reputation System

A reputation system is also used in conjunction with white or black lists. Assume that User A is not on User B's white list, and A attempts to contact B. If a consent-based system is used,

B is prompted to consent to communications from A, and along with the consent, a reputation score might be displayed in order to help B decide whether or not they should accept communications from A.

Reputation is calculated based on user feedback. For example, a button on the user interface of the messaging client might empower users to inform the system that a particular user is abusive. Of course, the input of any single user has to be insufficient to ruin one's reputation, but consistent negative feedback would give the abusive user a negative reputation score.

Reputation systems have been successful in systems where centralization of resources (user identities, authentication, and so on) and monolithic control dominate. Examples of these include the large instant messaging providers that run IM systems that do not exchange messages with other administrative domains. That control, first of all, provides a relatively strong identity assertion for users (because all users trust a common provider, and the common provider is the arbiter of authentication and identity). Secondly, it provides a single place where reputation can be managed.

It would eliminate the need for centralization of the reputation system if there were a way to leverage the social network of your buddies and their buddies to constitute a social network of reputation. Your perception of a particular user's reputation might be dependent on your relationship to them in the social network. This web of trust would also have the very desirable property that circles of spammers adding one another to their own buddy lists would not affect your perception of their reputation unless their circle linked to your own social network.

If a user's machine is compromised and turned into a zombie, this allows spam to be sent and may impact the user's reputation in a negative way. When one's reputation decreases, it becomes extremely difficult to re-establish a positive reputation.

Address Obfuscation

Address obfuscation is a fundamental way of minimizing spam by preventing spammers from gathering email addresses through websites or other public sources of information. One way to minimize spam is to make your address difficult or impossible to gather. Spam bots typically look for text in pages of the form "user@domain" and assume that anything of that form is an email address. To hide from such spam bots, many websites place email addresses in an obfuscated form, usable to humans but difficult for an automaton to read as an email address. For example,

```
patrick at cisco dot com
p a t r i c k a t c i s c o d o t c o m
```

These techniques are equally applicable to prevention of VoIP spam, and are likely to be as equally effective or ineffective in its prevention.

It is worth mentioning that the source of addresses need not be a website—any publicly accessible service containing addresses will suffice. As a result, Telephone Number

Mapping (ENUM) has been cited as a potential gold mine for spammers. It would allow a spammer to collect SIP and other URIs by traversing the tree in e164.arpa and mining it for data. This problem is mitigated in part if only number prefixes, as opposed to actual numbers, appear in the Domain Name System (DNS). Even in that case, however, it provides a technique for a spammer to learn which phone numbers are reachable through cheaper direct SIP connectivity.

Limited-Use Address

The technique of using a limited-use address is that a user has a large number of email addresses at their disposal, each of which has constraints on its applicability. A limited-use address can be time-bound, so that it expires after a fixed period. Or, a different email address can be given to each correspondent. When spam arrives from that correspondent, the limited-use address they were given is terminated. In another variation, the same limited-use address is given to multiple users that share some property; for example, all work colleagues, all coworkers from different companies, all retailers, and so on. Should spam begin arriving on one of the addresses, it is invalidated, preventing communications from anyone else that received the limited use address.

This technique is equally applicable to SIP. One of the drawbacks of the approach is that it can make it hard for people to reach you; if an email address you hand out to a friend becomes spammed, changing it requires you to inform your friend of the new address. SIP can help solve this problem in part, by making use of presence. Instead of handing out your email address to your friends, you would hand out your presence URI. When a friend wants to send you an email, they subscribe to your presence, which can include an email address where you can be reached. This email address can be obfuscated and be of single use, different for each buddy who requests your presence. The addresses can also be constantly changed, as these changes are pushed directly to your buddies. In a sense, the buddy list represents an automatically updated address book, and would therefore eliminate the problem.

Another approach is to give a different address to each and every correspondent, so that it is never necessary to tell a "good" user that an address needs to be changed. This is an extreme form of limited-use address, which can be called a single-use address. However, the hard part remains a useful mechanism for distribution and management of those addresses.

Consent-Based Black/White List

This is a combination of consent-based solution and black/white list solution. That is, if User A is not on User B's white or black list, and User A attempts to communicate with User B, User A's attempt is initially rejected, and User A is told that consent is being requested. Next time User B connects, User B is informed that User A had attempted communications. User B can then authorize or reject User A.

These systems are used widely in presence and IM. Because most of today's popular IM systems only allow communications within a single administrative domain, sender identities can be authenticated. Email often uses similar consent-based systems for mailing lists. They use a form of authentication based on sending cookies to an email address to verify that a user can receive mail at that address.

This solution could mitigate call spams (SPIT), but it might just change the nature of the spam. Instead of being bothered with content, in the form of call spam or IM spam, users are bothered with consent requests. Those requests for communications do not convey much useful content to the user, but they can convey some. At the very least, they will convey the identity of the requester. The user part of the SIP URI allows for limited free-form text, and thus could be used to convey brief messages. For example, the SIP URI could be "sip:please-buy-my-product-at-this-website@spam.com". Fortunately, it is possible to apply traditional content-filtering systems to the header fields in the SIP messages, thus reducing these kinds of consent request attacks.

In order for the spammer to convey more extensive content to the user, the user must explicitly accept the request. This is unlike email spam, where, even though much spam is automatically deleted, some percentage of the content does get through, and is seen by users, without their explicit consent. Thus, if consent is required first, the value in sending spam is reduced, and perhaps it will cease for those spam cases where consent is not given to spammers.

Summary

This chapter analyzes, demonstrates, and provides guidelines for mitigation for current VoIP threats; Denial of Service, malformed messages, sniffing (eavesdropping), spoofing (identity theft), and VoIP spam.

The typical method of DoS is that an attacker floods valid or invalid VoIP messages to target VoIP servers in order to drop the performance or break down the system. To mitigate, limit the number of registration requests, require credentials for registration and call requests, maintain a dynamic "black list," limit the total number of messages for a certain period of time, limit the total bandwidth for each endpoint, use ACL to block the source of unauthorized IP traffic, and do not allow application-layer ping messages from endpoints. Unintentional flooding as well can occur because of wrong configuration of devices, architectural service design issues, or unique circumstances.

Malformed messages are another way of attacking VoIP servers by causing system errors. To mitigate, developers should limit the buffer size on malformed message lines, prevent infinite loops caused by syntax error, and define a clear procedure of exception handling after the error is detected. Testers should use sophisticated testing tools and verify whether the target server handles properly without abusing resources. Administrators should prepare a management system so that they can demote the malicious endpoints immediately after receiving the traps from VoIP servers.

The local broadcasting domain allows attackers to sniff (eavesdrop) someone's conversation or call information. To mitigate, encrypt signaling and media, and prevent packet broadcasting in the local domain.

The method of spoofing is that an attacker pretends to be a registered user after stealing the user's identity, and inserts fake messages in order to interrupt VoIP service or make toll calls. To mitigate, prevent prespoofing scan, require authentication for call request message, do not use default ID and password when installing initially, pre-provision machine-generated random user ID and password into the phone, and track the original IP address of caller and callee during the call session.

VoIP spam is unsolicited bulk voice (SPIT), IM (SPIM), and presence spam (SPPP). To mitigate, consolidate possible solutions like content filtering, Turing tests, reputation system, address confusing, limited-use address, and consent-based black/white list. The problems will be much less significant when selected solutions are deployed globally before the problems become widespread.

End Notes

1   SIPSAK, SIP Swiss Army Knife, http://www.sipsak.com.

2   PROTOS, Security Testing of Protocol Implementations, http://www.ee.oulu.fi/ research/ouspg/protos/index.html.

3   SIPcrack, SIP login dumper/cracker, http://www.remote-exploit.org/ codes_sipcrack.html.

4   RFC 5039, "SIP and Spam," J. Rosenberg, C. Jennings, http://www.ietf.org/rfc/ rfc5039.txt, January 2008.

References

CERT Advisory CA-1996-21 "TCP SYN Flooding and IP Spoofing Attacks," http:// www.cert.org/advisories/CA-1996-21.html.

draft-ietf-sip-outbound-13.txt, "Managing Client Initiated Connections in the Session Initiation Protocol (SIP)," C. Jennings, R. Mahy, March 2008.

RFC 3489, "STUN—Simple Traversal of User Datagram Protocol (UDP) Through Network Address Translators (NATs)," J. Rosenberg, J. Weinberger, C. Huitema, R. Mahy, March 2003.

RFC 3761, "The E.164 to Uniform Resource Identifiers (URI) Dynamic Delegation Discovery System (DDDS) Application (ENUM)," P. Faltstrom, M. Mealling, April 2004.

This chapter covers the methodology of protection with VoIP protocol (SIP) in the following sectors:

- Authentication
- Encryption
- Transport and network layer security
- Threat model and prevention
- Limitation

CHAPTER 7

Protection with VoIP Protocol

This chapter demonstrates how to make Voice over Internet Protocol (VoIP) service secure with VoIP protocols, Session Initiation Protocol (SIP), and other supplementary protocols. Other session protocols like H.323 also have similar specifications and recommendations for security, which are not described here to avoid redundancy. Chapter 3, "Security Profiles in VoIP Protocols," covers the security profiles of H.323.

This chapter focuses on the methodology of protection with SIP in the following categories:

- Authentication
- Encryption
- Transport and network layer security
- Threat model and prevention
- Limitation

In general, SIP itself is not secure enough to provide VoIP service through the public Internet, because when it was originally designed (RFC 2543), it did not consider many security issues; for example, it allowed user agents to send username and password with plain text format. Even though the next version (RFC 3261[1]) tried to add more security features, such as Digest authentication, it was still not enough to provide secure service.

However, these security features are essential to build up the whole security structure in conjunction with existing security models derived from other protocols, such as HTTP and Simple Management Transfer Protocol (SMTP). Indeed, RFC 3261 provides solid guidelines on how to use SIP with other security protocols, such as Secure/Multipurpose Internet Mail Extensions (S/MIME), Transport Layer Security (TLS), and IP Security (IPSec). The contents in this chapter refer to RFC 3261.[1]

Authentication

SIP provides challenge-based Digest authentication, which is defined in HTTP authentication (RFC 2617[2]). It challenges one direction between user agent client (UAC) and user agent server (UAS) including registrar, or between user agent (UA) and proxy server.

When UAS, proxy, or registrar receives a request, it may challenge the request to provide the assurance of the originator's identity. The originator can reply with its credential with encryption (for example, Message Digest Algorithm 5 [MD5]), or reject the challenge. When the credential is received, the server verifies and sends back respective response codes like 401 (Unauthorized) or 200 (OK).

The high-level mechanism is shown in Figure 7-1.

Figure 7-1 *Call Flow of Digest Authentication*

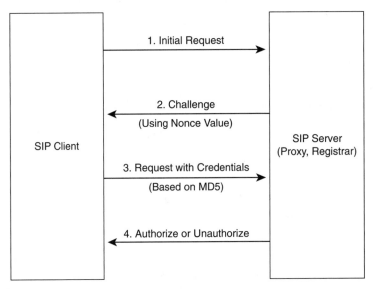

Because of the security issue, the previous method of Basic authentication (RFC 2543) is not acceptable anymore; it is supposed to be rejected or ignored.

The next section shows the details of the Digest mechanism and the usage among user agent and server.

User-to-Proxy Authentication

As mentioned, SIP uses Digest authentication derived from HTTP authentication based on RFC 2617. The typical authentication is between UA and the proxy server: Example 7-1 shows an example of one-way challenge from the proxy server.

Example 7-1   *SIP Registration with Digest Authentication*

```
Request-Line: REGISTER sip:10.10.10.40 SIP/2.0
    Message Header
        Via: SIP/2.0/UDP
        10.10.10.192;branch=z9hG4bKab46e4c000000011471e2cbf0000036800000000;rport
        From: "1000" <sip:papark@10.10.10.40>;tag=34eb553b475
        To: <sip:papark@10.10.10.40>
        Contact: <sip:papark@10.10.10.192>
        Call-ID: CE7F3F7B98CC4119A316B9830F2464EB0xab46e4c0
        CSeq: 1 REGISTER
        Max-Forwards: 70
        User-Agent: SJphone/1.65.377a (SJ Labs)
        Content-Length: 0
----------------------------------------------------------------
    Status-Line: SIP/2.0 407 Proxy Authentication Required
    Message Header
        Via: SIP/2.0/UDP
        10.10.10.192;branch=z9hG4bKab46e4c000000011471e2cbf0000036800000000;rport
            =5060
        Proxy-Authenticate: Digest
            nonce="1193156296:62de71f1d1e2f2f6fe4fa9b5ba5e2da2",algorithm=MD5,realm
            ="10.10.10.40",qop="auth,auth-int"
        To: <sip:papark@10.10.10.40>;tag=837dad48
        From: "1000"<sip:papark@10.10.10.40>;tag=34eb553b475
        Call-ID: CE7F3F7B98CC4119A316B9830F2464EB0xab46e4c0
        CSeq: 1 REGISTER
        Content-Length: 0
----------------------------------------------------------------
    Request-Line: REGISTER sip:10.10.10.40 SIP/2.0
    Message Header
        Via: SIP/2.0/UDP
        10.10.10.192;branch=z9hG4bKab46e4c000000016471e2cc000006d4d00000002;rport
        From: "1000" <sip:papark@10.10.10.40>;tag=34eb553b475
        To: <sip:papark@10.10.10.40>
        Contact: <sip:papark@10.10.10.192>
        Call-ID: CE7F3F7B98CC4119A316B9830F2464EB0xab46e4c0
        CSeq: 2 REGISTER
        Max-Forwards: 70
        User-Agent: SJphone/1.65.377a (SJ Labs)
        Content-Length: 0
        Proxy-Authorization: Digest
        username="papark",realm="10.10.10.40",nonce="1193156296:62de71f1d1e2f2f6f
            e4fa9b5ba5e2da2",uri="sip:10.10.10.40",response="39f8ec8f41b3bb72ca7af3
            58a8fe1e09",algorithm=MD5,cnonce="72b0553b4f2",qop=auth,nc=0000
----------------------------------------------------------------
    Status-Line: SIP/2.0 200 OK
    Message Header
        Via: SIP/2.0/UDP
        10.10.10.192;branch=z9hG4bKab46e4c000000016471e2cc000006d4d00000002;rport
            =5060
        Contact: <sip:papark@10.10.10.192;cid=0>;expires=3600
        To: <sip:papark@10.10.10.40>;tag=9b53b443
        From: "1000"<sip:papark@10.10.10.40>;tag=34eb553b475
        Call-ID: CE7F3F7B98CC4119A316B9830F2464EB0xab46e4c0
        CSeq: 2 REGISTER
        Content-Length: 0
```

Note that the comments ("Request-Line" and "Message Header") do not exist in actual SIP messages. In Example 7-1, there are four messages between UA and proxy server to accomplish the authentication. Each message corresponds to each step as follows:

Step 1   UA sends REGISTER without any credential.

— Most request messages can be challenged by a server; this example is REGISTER.

Step 2   Proxy server challenges with the response code 407 (Proxy Authentication Required) with "Proxy-authenticate" header (the shaded text), which has the information of method (Digest), nonce value, algorithm (MD5–refer to the following Note), realm, and qop.

— SIP authentication is meaningful for a specific realm, for example, protection domain.

— The realm string alone defines the protection domain and must be globally unique.

Note	MD5 is a cryptographic hash function with a 128-bit hash value, standing for Message Digest Algorithm 5. As defined in RFC 1321, the MD5 algorithm takes as input a message of arbitrary length and produces as output a 128-bit "fingerprint" or "message digest" of the input.
	It is conjectured that it is computationally infeasible to produce two messages having the same message digest, or to produce any message having a given prespecified target message digest. The MD5 algorithm is intended for digital signature applications, where a large file must be "compressed" in a secure manner before being encrypted with a private (secret) key under a public-key cryptosystem, such as Rivest, Shamir, and Adleman (RSA).
	The MD5 algorithm is designed to be quite fast on 32-bit machines. In addition, the MD5 algorithm does not require any large substitution tables; the algorithm can be coded quite compactly.

Step 3   UA creates its credentials based on the Proxy-authenticate header and adds to "Proxy-Authorization" header (the shaded text); password is encrypted (hashed) by MD5 with other values in the "response" parameter.

— Each protection domain has its own set of username and password.

— UA should contribute the contents of the realm parameter in the challenge to the user unless it already knows of the credential.

— If a server does not require particular authentication, it may accept username "anonymous" with no password (password of "").

— UACs representing many users, like public switched telephone network (PSTN) gateways, may have their own device-specific username and password, rather than accounts for particular users.

— Note that the user name is sent with clear text.

Step 4   The proxy server verifies the credentials by executing the same operation of MD5 that UA did after looking up the respective account information (username).

— The proxy server does not decrypt the credentials from UA, but encrypts with its own information and compares.

— It authorizes with 200 OK in this example, but it is possible to challenge again when the credentials are not matched.

— UA must not reattempt the request with the same credentials that have been rejected.

The authentication session lasts until the UA receives another authentication challenge from any server in the protection realm. UA should remember the username, password, nonce, nonce count, and opaque values associated with an authentication session to use to construct the authorization header in future requests within that protection realm.

Now that you are aware of user-to-proxy authentication, the next section takes a look at user-to-user authentication, which is somewhat different.

User-to-User Authentication

When a UAC sends a request to a UAS (including registrar), the UAS may authenticate the UAC before processing the request. Similar to the authentication between UAC and proxy server, the UAS challenges the UAC to provide credentials by rejecting the request with a status code 401 ("Unauthorized"), and the UAC sends the request again with its credentials based on the requested encryption (for example, MD5). The basic mechanism is shown in Figure 7-2.

Figure 7-2   *User-to-User Authentication*

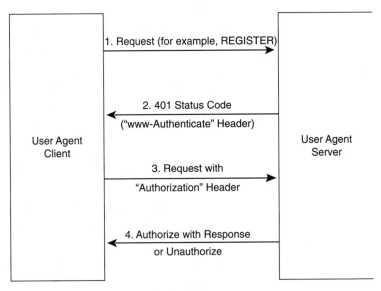

Note that the response codes (401) for the challenge and authentication headers are different from the case with proxy server. Example 7-2 shows an example with a SIP INVITE request.

Example 7-2   *SIP Messages for User-to-User Authentication*

```
Request-Line: INVITE sip:4084445555@192.168.10.197 SIP/2.0
    Message Header
        Via: SIP/2.0/UDP 10.10.10.155:5060;branch=z9hG4bK-a7140dfd
        From: "Patrick Park" <sip:8054445555@192.168.10.197>;
          tag=e4bc54109e8e72ebo0
        To: <sip:4084445555@192.168.10.197>
        Call-ID: 1c78e2b4-f2389497@10.10.10.155
        CSeq: 101 INVITE
        Max-Forwards: 70
        Contact: "Patrick Park" <sip:8054445555@10.10.10.155:5060>
        Expires: 240
        User-Agent: Linksys/SPA941-4.1.15
        Content-Length: 391
        Allow: ACK, BYE, CANCEL, INFO, INVITE, NOTIFY, OPTIONS, REFER, SUBSCRIBE
        Allow-Events: dialog
        Content-Type: application/sdp
- - - - - - - - - - - - - - - - - - - - - - - - - - - - - - - - - - - - - - - - - - - - - - - -
    Status-Line: SIP/2.0 401 UnAuthorized
    Message Header
        Via: SIP/2.0/UDP 10.10.10.155:5060;branch=z9hG4bK-a7140dfd
        From: "Patrick Park" <sip:8054445555@192.168.10.197>;tag=e4bc54109e8e72ebo0
        To: <sip:4084445555@192.168.10.197>;tag=1074824121846436
```

Example 7-2 *SIP Messages for User-to-User Authentication (Continued)*

```
        Call-ID: 1c78e2b4-f2389497@10.10.10.155
        CSeq: 101 INVITE
        WWW-Authenticate: Digest realm="Registered_
          Subscribers",domain="sip:cisco.com",nonce="6d21602c35c17795119785ad172e
          f8db",opaque="",stale=FALSE,algorithm=MD5
        Content-Length: 0
  ---------------------------------------------------------------------------------
    Request-Line: INVITE sip:4084445555@192.168.10.197 SIP/2.0
    Message Header
      Via: SIP/2.0/UDP 10.10.10.155:5060;branch=z9hG4bK-b1c67ebd
      From: "Patrick Park" <sip:8054445555@192.168.10.197>;tag=e4bc54109e8e72ebo0
      To: <sip:4084445555@192.168.10.197>
      Call-ID: 1c78e2b4-f2389497@10.10.10.155
      CSeq: 102 INVITE
      Max-Forwards: 70
      Authorization: Digest username="8054445555",realm="Registered_Subscribers",
        nonce="6d21602c35c17795119785ad172ef8db",uri="sip:4084445555@192.168.10.
        197",algorithm=MD5,response="7fca42e5293c3198f57400aa25927167",opaque=""
      Contact: "Patrick Park" <sip:8054445555@10.10.10.155:5060>
      Expires: 240
      User-Agent: Linksys/SPA941-4.1.15
      Content-Length: 391
      Allow: ACK, BYE, CANCEL, INFO, INVITE, NOTIFY, OPTIONS, REFER, SUBSCRIBE
      Allow-Events: dialog
      Content-Type: application/sdp
  ---------------------------------------------------------------------------------
    Status-Line: SIP/2.0 183 Session Progress
    Message Header
      Via: SIP/2.0/UDP 10.10.10.155:5060;branch=z9hG4bK-b1c67ebd
      From: "Patrick Park" <sip:8054445555@192.168.10.197>;tag=e4bc54109e8e72ebo0
      To: <sip:4084445555@192.168.10.197>;tag=2fa48d0c-1dd2-11b2-aa89-b0316
        2323164+2fa48d0c
      Call-ID: 1c78e2b4-f2389497@10.10.10.155
      CSeq: 102 INVITE
      Contact: <sip:SDtc4j0-cvknkrhu3u9p25092pf5c1232lkrtc3v9vin3qkgc
        cv1j72k4to7imn7i380jl6vmgvngvhh88jov84opovjm316s7@192.168.10.197:5060;
        transport=udp>
      Content-Type: application/sdp
      P-Asserted-Identity: "4084445555"<sip:4084445555@10.10.10.7>
      Content-Length: 186
```

Each message in Example 7-2 can be analyzed as a step to accomplish the authentication mechanism. Here is the detail of each message:

Step 1   UAC sends an INVITE request to UAS without any credentials.

Step 2   UAS challenges with a status code 401.

> — A "WWW-Authenticate" response header (the shaded text) must be included.

> — The field value consists of authentication scheme and parameters applicable to the realm.

Step 3   UAC sends INVITE again with its credentials.

— The "Authorization" header (the shaded text) includes the credentials containing the authentication information of the UA for the realm of the resource being requested, as well as parameters required in support of authentication and replay protection.

— UAC may require input from the user before proceeding.

— If no credentials for the realm can be located, UAC may attempt to request with "anonymous" username and no password (" ").

— If UAC resends the request with different credentials after being rejected, it must increment the CSeq header field value.

Step 4   UAS authorizes the request and processes it (in this example, UAS sends 183 Session Progress).

— UAS does not decrypt the password from UAC but encrypts its own information and compares.

— UAS can unauthorize it with 401 status code again if the credentials are wrong.

Now that you are aware of authentication mechanisms among UAs and proxy servers, the next section shows how the encryption mechanism works in SIP.

Encryption

End-to-end full encryption is the most common way to provide message confidentiality and integrity between communication endpoints. The SIP standard (RFC 3261) also recommends encryption for the purpose, but there is some limitation to providing the full encryption.

It is almost impossible, or we may say not practical, to encrypt all SIP requests and responses end-to-end because intermediaries like the proxy server have to look at the message fields to route properly. In particular, "Request-URI", "Route", and "Via" headers should be visible to the proxy server to route the call. Furthermore, the proxy server needs to modify some message field like "Via" header by adding its own IP address.

Therefore, you should have authentication mechanisms that proxy servers are trusted by SIP UAs before implementing this encryption. For this purpose, you should have low-layer security mechanisms like TLS or IPSec between UAs and proxy servers, which is discussed in the next section.

If there are limitations to end-to-end full encryption, what is the alternative? Two parts of a SIP transaction can be encrypted: message body and media. The message body encryption with S/MIME is recommended in RFC 3261. The media encryption is defined in RFC 3711.[3]

Next up is the detail of each method and usage example.

Message Encryption (S/MIME)

Because end-to-end full encryption is not practical, as mentioned previously, RFC 3261 recommends encrypting the message body, typically Session Description Protocol (SDP) information, by means of S/MIME (see the following Note). It allows SIP UAs to encrypt MIME bodies within SIP and secure the bodies end-to-end without affecting message headers.

The typical MIME types securing the contents are 'multipart/signed' and 'application/pkcs7-mime'.

- **multipart/signed**—The multipart/signed content type specifies how to support authentication and integrity services via digital signature. The multipart/signed content type contains exactly two body parts. The first body part is the body part over which the digital signature was created, including its MIME headers. The second body part contains the control information necessary to verify the digital signature. The first body part may contain any valid MIME content type, labeled accordingly. The second body part is labeled according to the value of the protocol parameter.

- **application/pkcs7-mime**—The application/pkcs7-mime type is used to carry cryptographic message syntax (CMS) objects of several types including envelopedData and signedData. For details, refer to RFC 2633 (S/MIME Version 3 Message Specification).

NOTE   S/MIME, as the name implies, is a combination of MIME format plus security specification. MIME was developed by the Internet Engineering Task Force (IETF) to define the format of email messages supporting characters beyond US-ASCII, non-text attachment, multi-purpose message bodies, and header information in non-ASCII characters. This MIME format is also adapted by other protocols like HTTP as a supplement (SIP is derived from HTTP). The security specification was originally defined in the de facto standard PKCS #7 by RSA Laboratories, showing how to encrypt messages with a public key. IETF adapted PKCS #7 and documented it in RFC 2315 (CMS, "Cryptographic Message Syntax").

However, there could be an issue if some network intermediaries rely on the message body (SDP) and modifying it. Typical proxy servers do not modify the SDP, but some servers like Back-to-Back User Agent (B2BUA) and Session Border Controllers (SBC) do modify the SDP. For information on SBC, refer to Chapter 5, "VoIP Network Elements," and Chapter 8, "Protection with Session Border Controller."

Now that you are aware of the general concept of S/MIME, the next topic is detailed usage of S/MIME with SIP.

S/MIME Certificates

The certificate for S/MIME is used to identify an end user, asserting that the holder is identified by an end-user address, which is a combination of the "userinfo", "@", and "domainname" portions of a SIP or SIPS Uniform Resource Indicator (URI; see the following Note), typically the user's address-of-record.

NOTE   A SIP or SIPS URI identifies a communications resource. Like all URIs, SIP and SIPS URIs may be placed in web pages, email messages, or printed literature. They contain sufficient information to initiate and maintain a communication session with the resource. Examples of communications resources include the following:

- A user of an online service

- An appearance on a multiline phone

- A mailbox on a messaging system

- A PSTN number at a gateway service

- A group (such as "sales" or "helpdesk") in an organization

A SIPS URI specifies that the resource be contacted securely. This means, in particular, that TLS is to be used between the UAC and the domain that owns the URI. From there, secure communications are used to reach the user, where the specific security mechanism depends on the policy of the domain. Any resource described by a SIP URI can be "upgraded" to a SIPS URI by just changing the scheme, if the goal is to communicate with that resource securely.

The certificate is associated with private/public keys that are used to sign or encrypt bodies of SIP messages. As a public-key–based cryptographic mechanism, bodies are signed with the private key of the sender (who may include their public key with the message as appropriate), but bodies are encrypted with the public key of the intended recipient. Obviously, senders must have foreknowledge of the public key of recipients in order to encrypt message bodies. Public keys can be stored within a UA on a virtual keyring.

Each user agent that supports S/MIME must contain a keyring specifically for end users' certificates. This keyring should map between address-of-record and corresponding certificates. Over time, users should use the same certificate when they populate the originating URI of signaling with the same address-of-record.

The certificate can be acquired from known public certificate authorities or well-known centralized directories that distribute end-user certificates. Note that there is no such way to obtain someone else's certificate. It is also possible for users to create self-signed certificates for particular service.

The next section shows how SIP distributes public keys through S/MIME.

S/MIME Key Exchange

SIP itself can also be used as a means to distribute public keys in the following steps:

Step 1   When a UAC sends a request containing S/MIME body that initiates a dialog, or sends a non-INVITE request outside the context of a dialog, the UAC should structure the body as an S/MIME "multipart/signed" CMS SignedData body. If the desired CMS service is EnvelopedData and the public key of the target user is known, the UAC should send the EnvelopedData message encapsulated within a SignedData message.

Step 2   When a UAS receives a request containing an S/MIME CMS body that includes a certificate, the UAS should first validate the certificate with any available root certificates for certificate authorities. If the certificate is successfully verified, the UAS should add it to a local keyring, indexed by the address-of-record of the requester. If the certificate cannot be verified because it is self-signed or signed by no known authority, the UAS must notify its users of the status of the certificate and request explicit permission before proceeding. If the certificate was successfully verified and the subject of the certificate corresponds to the From header field of the SIP request, or if the user (after notification) explicitly authorizes the use of the certificate, the UAS should add this certificate to a local keyring, indexed by the address-of-record of the holder of the certificate.

Step 3   When a UAS sends a response containing an S/MIME body that answers the first request in a dialog, or a response to a non-INVITE request outside the context of a dialog, the UAS should structure the body as an S/MIME 'multipart/signed' CMS SignedData body. If the desired CMS service is EnvelopedData, the UAS should send the EnvelopedData message encapsulated within a SignedData message.

Step 4   When a UAC receives a response containing an S/MIME CMS body that includes a certificate, the UAC should first validate the certificate, if possible, with any appropriate root certificate. The UAC should also determine the subject of the certificate and compare this value to the To field of the response. However, the two may very well be different, and this is not necessarily indicative of a security breach.

If the certificate cannot be verified because it is self-signed, or signed by no known authority, the UAC must notify its user of the status of the certificate (including the subject of the certificate, its signator, and any key fingerprint information) and request explicit permission before proceeding. If the certificate was successfully verified, and the subject of the certificate corresponds to the To header field in the response, or if the user (after notification) explicitly authorizes the use of the certificate, the UAC should add this certificate to a local keyring, indexed by the address-of-record of the holder of the certificate. If the UAC had not transmitted its own certificate to the UAS in any previous transaction, it should use a CMS SignedData body for its next request or response.

Note that this key exchange mechanism does not guarantee the secure exchange of keys when self-signed certificates, or certificates signed by an obscure authority, are used—it is vulnerable to well-known attacks. The last major section in this chapter, "Limitations," has more information.

The next section shows how to format the S/MIME bodies with examples.

Formatting S/MIME Bodies

Basically, SIP follows the format that the S/MIME specification defines when creating headers, except for a few variations. The key factors formatting S/MIME bodies can be listed based on RFC 3261:

- Content-Type header must be "multipart/signed" if CMS detached signature is used.

- Content-Disposition header should be used and its value of "handling" parameter is supposed to be "required".

- If a UAC has no certificate on its keyring, it cannot send an encrypted "application/pkcs7-mime".

- Senders of S/MIME bodies should use the "SMIMECapabilities" attribute to express their capabilities and preferences for further communications.

- S/MIME implementations must support at least SHA1 as a digital signature algorithm, and Triple Data Encryption Standard (3DES) as an encryption algorithm. All other signature and encryption algorithms may be used.

- Each S/MIME body should be signed with only one certificate.

- Examples 7-3 and 7-4 show examples of SIP messages with an S/MIME body. You can see more detailed examples of the S/MIME format in RFC 4134.

Example 7-3 *S/MIME Body with EnvelopedData*

```
INVITE sip:4084445555@192.168.10.197 SIP/2.0
      Via: SIP/2.0/UDP 10.10.10.155:5060;branch=z9hG4bK-a7140dfd
      From: "Patrick Park" <sip:8054445555@192.168.10.197>;tag=e4bc54109e8e72ebo0
      To: <sip:4084445555@192.168.10.197>
      Call-ID: 1c78e2b4-f2389497@10.10.10.155
      CSeq: 101 INVITE
      Max-Forwards: 70
      Contact: "Patrick Park" <sip:8054445555@10.10.10.155:5060>
```

Example 7-3 *S/MIME Body with EnvelopedData (Continued)*

```
                    Expires: 240
                    User-Agent: Linksys/SPA941-4.1.15
                    Content-Length: 391
                    Allow: ACK, BYE, CANCEL, INFO, INVITE, NOTIFY, OPTIONS, REFER, SUBSCRIBE
                    Allow-Events: dialog
                    Content-Type: application/pkcs7-mime; smime-type=enveloped-data;name=
                      smime.p7m
                    Content-Disposition: attachment; filename=smime.p7m; handling=required
                    23j+bv7dM3F9piuR10DcMkQiVm96nXvn89J8v3UOoi1TxP7AHCEdNXYjDw7Wz41UIddU5dh
                    DEeL3/nbCElzfy5FEbteQJllzzflvbAhUA4kemGkVmuBPG2o+4NyErYov3k80CgYAmONAUi
                    TKqOfs+bdlLWWpMdiM5BAI1XPLLGjDDHlBd3ZtZ4s2qBT1YwHuiNrhuB699ikIlp/R1z0oI
                    Xks+kPht6pzJIYo7dhTpzi5dowfNI4W4LzABfG1JiRGJNkS9+MiVSlNWteL5c+waYTYfEX/
                    Cve3RUP+YdMLRgUpgObo20QOBhAACgYBc47ladRSWC6163eM/qeysXty9txMRNKYWiSgRI9
                    k0hmd1dRMSPUNbb+VRv/qJ8qIbPiR9PQeNW2PIu0WloErjhdbOBoA/6CN+GvIkq1MauCcNH
                    u8Iv2YUgFxirGX6FYvxuzTU0pY39mFHssQyhPB+QUD9RqdjTjPypeL08oPluKOBgTB
```

Example 7-4 *S/MIME Body with Multiparty/Signed*

```
INVITE sip:4084445555@192.168.10.197 SIP/2.0
             Via: SIP/2.0/UDP 10.10.10.155:5060;branch=z9hG4bK-a7140dfd
             From: "Patrick Park" <sip:8054445555@192.168.10.197>;
               tag=e4bc54109e8e72ebo0
             To: <sip:4084445555@192.168.10.197>
             Call-ID: 1c78e2b4-f2389497@10.10.10.155
             CSeq: 101 INVITE
             Max-Forwards: 70
             Contact: "Patrick Park" <sip:8054445555@10.10.10.155:5060>
             Expires: 240
             User-Agent: Linksys/SPA941-4.1.15
             Content-Length: 391
             Allow: ACK, BYE, CANCEL, INFO, INVITE, NOTIFY, OPTIONS, REFER, SUBSCRIBE
             Allow-Events: dialog
             Content-Type: multipart/signed; micalg=SHA1; boundary="-------this is
             boundary indicator_31_Oct_2007----------"; protocol="application/
             pkcs7-signature"
         This is a multi-part message in MIME format.

         -------this is boundary indicator_31_Oct_2007----------

         This is some sample content.
         -------this is boundary indicator_31_Oct_2007----------
         Content-Type: application/pkcs7-signature; name=smime.p7s
         Content-Disposition: attachment; filename=smime.p7s

         d4z+p7Kxe3L23ExE0phaJKBEj2TSGZ3V1ExI9Q1tv5VG/+onyohs+JH09B41bY8i7RaWgSu
         OF1s4GgD/oI34a8iSrUxq4Jw0e7wi/ZhSAXGKsZfoVi/G7NNTSljf2YUeyxDKE8H5BQP1Gp
         2NOM/Kl4vTyg+W4o4GBMH8wDAYDVR0TAQH/BAIwADAOBgNVHQ8BAf8EBAMCBsAwHwYDVR0j
         BBgwFoAUcEQ+gi5vh95K03XjPSC8QyuT8R8wHQYDVR0OBBYEFL5sobPjwfftQ3CkzhMB4v3
         jl/7NMB8GA1UdEQQYMBaBFEFsaWNlRFNTQGV4YW1wbGUuY29tMAkGByqGSM44BAMDMAAwLQ
```

continues

Example 7-4 *S/MIME Body with Multiparty/Signed (Continued)*

```
IUVQykGR9CK4lxIjONg2q1PWdrv0UCFQCfYVNSVAtcst3a53Yd4hBSW0NevTFjMGECAQEwG
DASMRAwDgYDVQQDEwdDYXJsRFNTAgIAyDAHBgUrDgMCGjAJBgcqhkjOOAQDBC4wLAIUM/mG
f6gkgp9Z0XtRdGimJeB/BxUCFGFFJqwYRt1WYcIOQoGiaowqGzVI

--------this is boundary indicator_31_Oct_2007-------------
```

Now that you are aware of SIP message encryption with S/MIME, the next section takes a look at how media can be securely encrypted.

Media Encryption

Secure RTP (SRTP) is an extension of Real-time Transport Protocol (RTP), which provides security features, such as encryption and authentication.

The method of securing RTP packets was not defined when SIP (RFC 3261) was released. In 2004, researchers from Cisco and Ericsson proposed the specification and IETF listed it in RFC 3711.[3] It provides a framework for encryption and message authentication of RTP and Real-time Transport Control Protocol (RTCP) stream. Note that SRTP includes Secure RTCP (SRTCP) in this section.

SRTP has not been widely deployed yet for VoIP services because of some issues, such as performance, complexity of implementation, and interoperability. However, it is critical technology that you can use to provide the confidentiality and integrity of media streams.

It uses a common method of security mechanism in which communication parties exchange keys and encrypt/decrypt RTP packets.

The usage of SRTP is described in terms of key derivation and packet processing as follows, based on RFC 3711.[3] The method of simulating SRTP process is also introduced for your hands-on test.

NOTE   The following subsections give the high-level concept and idea of SRTP, rather than describing every detail. For more information, refer to RFC 3711.

Key Derivation

SRTP uses two types of keys to make RTP packets secure: master key and session key.

The master key is a random bit string provided by the key management protocol and it is used to derive session keys.

The session key is used in a cryptographic transform like encryption or message authentication.

The reasons for using two types of keys are as follows:

- **To reduce the load on the key management**—For each crypto context, six different keys (session keys) are needed: two encryption keys for SRTP/SRTCP, two encryption salts (see the following Note) for SRTP/SRTCP, and two authentication keys for SRTP/SRTCP. Apparently, managing six different keys is not that simple, but it is derived from a single master key in a cryptographically secure way. So, the key management protocol needs to exchange only one master key with a salt, and then local SRTP generates all session keys.

- **To prevent a decrypting attack**—It prevents an attacker from collecting a large amount of cipher text encrypted with same key because session keys are most likely to be changed frequently. Even in the worst case, that an attacker compromised the session key, the key is only valid for the specific context, not before or after context using different session keys.

NOTE   Like salting bland food, a salt key is used to salt a bland encryption system—in other words, to give more complexity to encryption/decryption. What is the benefit? It makes it almost impossible to decrypt ciphertext (for example, password) with a dictionary or brute-force attack.

For example, think about a regular authentication system like a Microsoft Windows login; a user creates a new password when requested and Windows hashes the password before storing it. You cannot guess the actual password with only the hashed characters, but you may easily crack it with a password-dictionary attack because a human uses very simple passwords compared to those generated by machine. Because of this vulnerability, the salt (machine-generated random values) is appended to the password before being hashed. Cracking this password is literally impossible without knowing the salt.

This salt key mechanism is applied to RTP packet encryption as well as generating session keys from master keys.

The key derivation can be depicted at a high level, as shown in Figure 7-3.

Figure 7-3 *Key Derivation*

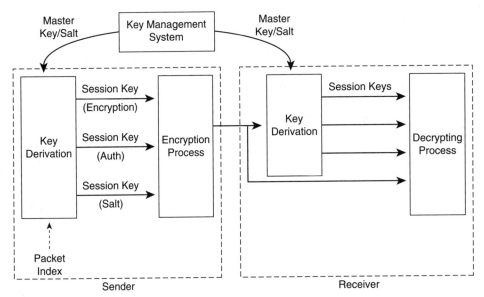

Note that RFC 3711 does not describe how to pass the master key and salt from the key management system to the sender or receiver. It could be implemented in many different ways (for example, containing the keys in the SDP during the call setup).

The next section shows how communication parties process SRTP packets.

SRTP Packet Processing

In this section, you follow the steps that show how a sender and receiver process SRTP packets. Assuming initialization of the cryptographic context has taken place via key management, the sender will take the following steps to construct SRTP packets:

Step 1 Determine cryptographic context that is a session identifier consisting of destination address, port number, and synchronization source (SSRC). Note that RTP uses only destination address and port number for the session.

Step 2 Determine the index of the SRTP packet using the rollover counter, the highest sequence number in the cryptographic context, and the sequence number in the RTP packet.

Step 3 Determine the master key and salt.

Step 4 Determine the session keys and session salts using master key, master salt, and packet index. (See Figure 7-3 for more information.)

Step 5   Encrypt the RTP payload (the default cipher is Advanced Encryption Standard [AES]).

Step 6   If the master key identifier (MKI) indicator is set to one, append the MKI to the packet.

Step 7   For message authentication, compute the authentication tag for the authenticated portion of the packet.

Step 8   If necessary, update the rollover counter using the packet index determined in Step 2.

These steps make the SRTP packets that the sender will send to the receiver.

The receiver will take the following steps to authenticate and decrypt the SRTP packets:

Step 1   Determine which cryptographic context to use.

Step 2   Get the index of the SRTP packet.

Step 3   Determine the master key and master salt (if the MKI indicator in the context is set to one, use the MKI in the SRTP packet; otherwise, use the index from the previous step).

Step 4   Determine the session keys and session salts by using the master key/salt, key derivation rate, and session key-lengths in the cryptographic context with the index, determined in Steps 2 and 3.

Step 5   For message authentication and replay protection, first check if the packet has been replayed by using the replay list (if the packet is replayed, the packet must be discarded).

Step 6   Decrypt the encrypted portion of the packet by using the decryption algorithm indicated in the cryptographic context, the session encryption key and salt found in Step 4.

Step 7   Update the rollover counter and highest sequence number in the cryptographic context.

Step 8   Remove the MKI and authentication tag fields from the packet.

Now that you are aware of the basic steps of constructing, authenticating, and decrypting SRTP packets, the next section gives you the opportunity to simulate the SRTP process with a test tool.

SRTP Test

You can simulate the SRTP process with a test tool, named libSRTP.[4] The libSRTP is an open-source implementation of the SRTP originally created by David McGrew of Cisco Systems, who is one of the authors of RFC 3711.

The libSRTP uses the default key derivation function that uses AES-128 in Counter Mode. It requires a 16-octet master key and a 14-octet master salt in order to generate session keys.

You can download the libSRTP in the following website (it is available under a Berkeley Software Distribution [BSD]-style license):

http://srtp.sourceforge.net/download.html

Download the latest version from the website and compile it to your target machine as follows:

```
> gunzip srtp-X.Y.Z.tgz
> tar xvf srtp-X.Y.Z.tar
> cd srtp
> autoconf
> ./configure
> make
```

You can see the basic usage with the **rtpw** command as follows:

```
[root@ test]# ./rtpw
error: neither sender [-s] nor receiver [-r] specified
usage: ./rtpw [-d <debug>]* [-k <key> [-a][-e]] [-s | -r] dest_ip dest_port
or      ./rtpw -l
where  -a use message authentication
       -e use encryption
       -k <key>  sets the srtp master key
       -s act as rtp sender
       -r act as rtp receiver
       -l list debug modules
       -d <debug> turn on debugging for module <debug>
```

Now, run the receiver first with a random 30-octet key/salt (you may use any generation tool) and then run the sender with same master key/salt. The libSRTP sender sends random words automatically, and you can see the same words displaying on the screen, as shown in Example 7-5.

Example 7-5 *SRTP Test with libSRTP*

```
[root@ test]# ./rtpw -k
  c1eec3717da76195bb878578790af71c4ee9f859e197a414a78d5abc7451 -a -e -s
  127.0.0.1 9999
security services: confidentiality message authentication
set master key/salt to c1eec3717da76195bb878578790af71c/
  4ee9f859e197a414a78d5abc7451
sending word: &c
sending word: 'd
sending word: 'em
sending word: 'll
sending word: 'm
sending word: 'mid
sending word: 'midst
sending word: 'mongst
sending word: 'prentice
sending word: 're
sending word: 's
sending word: 'sblood
```

Example 7-5 *SRTP Test with libSRTP (Continued)*

```
[root@ test]# ./rtpw -k
  c1eec3717da76195bb878578790af71c4ee9f859e197a414a78d5abc7451 -a -e -r
  127.0.0.1 9999
security services: confidentiality message authentication
set master key/salt to c1eec3717da76195bb878578790af71c/
  4ee9f859e197a414a78d5abc7451

        word: &c
        word: 'd
        word: 'em
        word: 'll
        word: 'm
        word: 'mid
        word: 'midst
        word: 'mongst
        word: 'prentice
        word: 're
        word: 's
        word: 'sblood
```

In Example 7-5, the first command is for a sender ("-s" parameter) and the second command is for a receiver ("-r" parameter). Both the sender and the receiver are in the same local machine (127.0.0.1) in this example. The receiver receives the same words sequentially in accordance of the sender's words.

You have learned about message encryption with S/MIME and media encryption with SRTP in this section. The next section shows how to secure VoIP service in the transport and network layers.

Transport and Network Layer Security

Ideally, the end-to-end full encryption of messages provides the best way to ensure confidentiality and integrity of messages. However, as mentioned previously, the full encryption is almost impossible within public service networks because of intermediary servers (for example, SIP Proxy) working on call routing. Those proxy servers need to see some message fields like "Request-URI", "Route", and "Via", as well as modifying them in most network architecture for proper call routing. Therefore, you need other security mechanisms in which proxy servers are trusted by UAs. For this purpose, you need a low-layer security mechanism that encrypts entire SIP requests and responses on the wire on a hop-by-hop basis, and allows UAs to verify the identity of proxy servers to whom they send requests.

In fact, the SIP standard (RFC 3261) recommends transport and network layer encryption as the low-layer security mechanism providing message integrity and confidentiality. Two existing security arts are recommended: TLS and IPSec.

Transport Layer Security

The main role of TLS is to provide transport-layer security over connection-oriented protocols (for example, TCP) as defined in RFC 4346.[5]

Typically, SIP uses TLS to provide hop-by-hop security in the service network and eventually give end-to-end security between UAs. For example, think about this common case, that a user agent A tries to make a call to a user agent B through A's proxy server and B's proxy server. Also, there is no trust between A and B, but A trusts A's proxy server and B trusts B's proxy server through TLS (or some other method, like IPSec). In this case, you can provide end-to-end security by exchanging certificates between A's and B's proxy server through TLS, which is shown in Figure 7-4.

Figure 7-4   *End-to-End Security Through TLS*

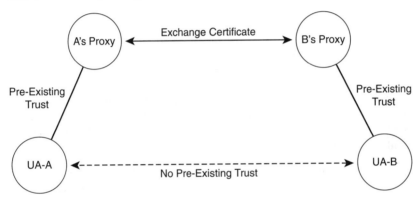

NOTE   The transport mechanisms are specified on a hop-by-hop basis in SIP, so a user agent that sends requests over TLS to a proxy server has no assurance that TLS will be used end-to-end.

TLS can be specified in SIP-URI or Via header signifying TLS over TCP, as shown in the following examples:

```
INVITE sip:4084445555@192.168.10.197; transport=tls
Via: SIP/2.0/TLS 10.10.10.155:5060;branch=z9hG4bK-a7140dfd
```

The Advanced Encryption Standard (AES) must be supported at a minimum when TLS is used in a SIP application. For the purpose of backward compatibility, all SIP servers (proxy, redirect, and registrar) should support triple DES (3DES).

SIP can also specify the usage of TLS when targeting a specific resource by means of SIPS URI format, which is the same as SIP URI except using "sips:" as follows:

```
Sips:patrick@company.com:5060;uri-parameters?headers
```

Using SIPS means that TLS is preferred to be used hop-by-hop until the terminating UAS has the target resource. However, in real service environments, some other security mechanism could be used partially rather than end-to-end TLS connection.

Now that you are aware of the basic usage of TLS with SIP, the next topic is network-layer security with IPSec.

IPSec (Tunneling)

IPSec is a suite of network-layer protocols that secure IP network communications by encrypting and authenticating data. It is generally used for virtual private network (VPN) connection.

Basically, the IPSec protocol (network-layer) is independent of the SIP protocol (application-layer) and there is no required integration between them. Unlike the integration with TLS, SIP does not provide any indication of IPSec in the messages. However, practically speaking, IPSec is very useful to provide security between SIP entities, especially between a UA and a proxy server. UAs that have a preshared keying relationship with their first-hop proxy server are good candidates to use IPSec.

Implementers should consider a separate security mechanism from SIP protocol because IPSec is usually deployed at the operating system level in a host, or on a security gateway (for example, a VPN server) that provides confidentiality and integrity for all traffic that it receives from a particular interface. (The detailed usage of IPSec is beyond the scope of this book. For more information on IPSec, go to Cisco.com.)

You have learned about transport and network layer security with SIP in this section. The next section shows threat models and prevention from a SIP perspective.

Threat Model and Prevention

Many different kinds of threats exist in the VoIP world, and most typical threats are introduced in Chapter 2, "VoIP Threat Taxonomy." In this section, you see the threat model and prevention from a SIP perspective; in other words, how the threat is implemented and prevented in SIP and supplementary protocols. RFC 3261 gives the guideline, which is summarized as follows.

Registration Hijacking

SIP registration allows a user agent to identify itself to a registrar as a device that a user is located. A registrar assesses the identity asserted in the From header field of a REGISTER message to determine whether this request can modify the contact addresses associated with the address-of-record in the To header field. In most cases, these two fields are same, which means the user agent registers its own. However, these two fields could be different in the case of third-party registration, which means the third party registers the user agent (address-of-record) on the user's behalf.

Here is a serious security hole in which the registration could be hijacked:

An attacker impersonates a user agent by modifying the From header and add the attacker's address to the To header when it sends a REGISTER message, which updates the address-of-record of the target user. Typically, the attacker unregisters first and registers its own and hijacks all the messages going to the target user.

This threat happens when the user agent server (registrar) is relying only on SIP headers to identify the user agent. The method of prevention is that the user agent server should authenticate the originator of requests based on cryptographic assurance; for example, by TLS.

The next threat is impersonating a server.

Impersonating a Server

Generally, a user agent sends a request to a server (proxy, registrar, or redirect server) in the target domain, which is specified in Request-URI. It is possible that an attacker impersonates the server, receives all requests, and manipulates them. Here is an example:

User agent A sends requests to its redirect server in the same domain (abc.com) when making a call. An attacker's redirect server in the different domain (xyz.com) impersonates A's redirect server by malicious means like attacking a Domain Name System (DNS) server. From now, A's requests go to the attacker's redirect server and the attacker redirects the call to any malicious proxy server that is totally under the attacker's control.

If a registrar server is impersonated as in this case, the situation is worse. The attacker responds SIP 301 (Moved permanently) with wrong contact information for a REGISTER request from the user agent, which makes the user agent register to the wrong registrar server all the time.

The method of prevention is providing the mechanism of cryptographic authentication from user agents to SIP servers; for example, by TLS.

The next threat is tearing down sessions.

Tearing Down Sessions

A SIP dialog between user agents is established based on From tag, To tag, and Call-ID while sending/receiving initial messages. After the establishment of the dialog, the user agent can either change the media session with re-INVITE or tear down the session with BYE. An attacker may use the characteristic to interrupt the session. Here is an example:

User agent A makes a call to user agent B. An attacker in the middle sniffs all SIP messages (for example, INVITE, OK, ACK) and memorizes the dialog based on the From tag, To tag, and Call-ID. Then, the attacker tears down the session by sending BYE to either A or B. Or, the attacker can eavesdrop the media by sending re-INVITE to either A or B and anchoring the media through the attacker's server.

The method of prevention is authenticating the sender of the BYE (or re-INVITE). The user agent needs to know that the BYE (or re-INVITE) came from the same party with whom the corresponding dialog was established. Another possible method of prevention is encrypting all headers so that an attacker may not see the session information, but this is generally not practical because many headers (for example, Via, From, To) are supposed to be visible to intermediaries like proxy. TLS also can be used to prevent the attack.

The next section shows the most common and critical threat: denial-of-service and amplification.

Denial-of-Service and Amplification

SIP is generally vulnerable to Denial-of-Service (DoS) attacks because servers (proxy, registrar, and redirect) are usually accessible from public networks in most VoIP service architecture. The common method of DoS attack is that an attacker sends an excessive number of SIP requests to a target server in order to make service resources (for example, bandwidth, CPU, and memory) unavailable. Typically, a Distributed Denial-of-Service (DDoS) is used, which allows one network user to cause multiple network hosts to flood a large number of SIP messages to a target server. The worst case is that those messages are malformed, which may cause a system crash. Here are a couple of examples:

An attacker floods a large number of REGISTER messages with randomly generated ID and password, let's say 1,000 messages per second (even a single PC can generate this much traffic), to a targeted registrar. Regardless of the identity (ID, password), the system resources (for example, CPU) in the Registrar would be exhausted as long as the Registrar replies with response messages (for example, 401 Unauthorized).

Another example is targeting a user agent client. An attacker creates an excessive number of requests with faked source IP address and a corresponding Via header field that identify a targeted host as the originator of the request and then send those to lots of SIP network elements that would reply with response messages to the target host. Especially if the attacker sends the request to the forking proxies with faked Route header, those response messages would be amplified.

The method of prevention with the SIP protocol is authenticating originators with possible ways that were already shown previously (for example, TLS, IPSec, S/MIME, and Digest authentication) so that the server may not process further requests. However, this is not enough at all to prevent so many different types of DoS attacks nowadays. Note that the SIP protocol is not originally designed for security. Therefore, you need to have a policy-based security device like SBC that is able to detect and prevent DoS attacks, as described in Chapter 8, "Protection with Session Border Controller."

Now that you are aware of the many different types of threats and protection methods with SIP, the next section takes a look at what limitations those methods have.

Limitations

The SIP protocol (RFC 3261) itself provides a few security features, and also introduces many guidelines with other protocols (for example, S/MIME, TLS, and IPSec) as described in the previous sections, which are very useful to build up secure VoIP service network. However, you also need to know what limitations exist.

Digest Authentication Limitations

Digest authentication is intended as a replacement of Basic authentication using clear text-based ID and password. There is nothing more than that. It uses password-based authentication just with hashing function (MD5), which is not as secure as any client-side private-key scheme. Also, there is no provision for the initial secure arrangement between user and server to establish the user's password.

The next limitations are on S/MIME, as follows.

S/MIME Limitations

The number one issue with S/MIME in SIP is the man-in-the-middle (MITM) attack because of its loose key management.

If self-signed certificates are used, which is allowed in SIP, an attacker in the way of the initial request can intercept, modify, and send the forged certificates to the other party. From now on, the attacker in the middle can monitor or manipulate all the messages between two parties.

Of course, this attack is only valid when the initial self-signed certificate is intercepted; otherwise, the UAs can detect any change of certificate. Therefore, how the keys are initially distributed from the key management system to UAs, or the keys are exchanged between UAs, is most critical.

The next limitations are on TLS, as follows.

TLS Limitations

The biggest limitation of TLS is that it cannot run over UDP. It requires a TCP (connection-oriented) connection that requires much more resources than UDPs, especially when a long-lived TCP connection is used. There is a relatively new protocol, Datagram Transport Layer Security (DTLS; see the following Note), that supports TLS-equivalent security over UDP, but DTLS is not commonly deployed yet.

In the same manner, it creates a scalability issue when a large number of user agents establish a long-lived TCP connection with a proxy or registrar server, which is very common in global VoIP networks. That is why TLS has not been widely deployed in large service networks even though it has significant security benefit.

TLS allows UAs to authenticate only the adjacent server, which means there is no guarantee of end-to-end TLS in a SIP transaction.

The next limitations are on SIPS URI as follows.

NOTE   DTLS (RFC 4347[6]) specifies the Datagram Transport Layer Security protocol, which provides communications privacy for datagram protocols. It allows client/server applications to communicate in a way that is designed to prevent eavesdropping, tampering, or message forgery. It is based on the TLS protocol and provides equivalent security guarantees. Datagram semantics of the underlying transport are preserved by the DTLS protocol.

SIPS URI Limitations

Using SIPS URI implies that TLS is used preferably hop-by-hop until the terminating UAs has the target resource. However, in reality, most VoIP service providers do not support end-to-end TLS connection because of complexity, especially when the call transports through different service networks that have different policies and capabilities. Some UAs in the request path may not support TLS, and even those UAs that do support TLS may be required to maintain a persistent TLS (TCP) connection that is not acceptable to other peers.

SIPS URI inherits the limitation of TLS, which runs over only TCP and creates a scalability issue as mentioned before.

You have learned about the limitations of SIP security features (Digest authentication, S/MIME, TLS, and SIPS URI) in this section.

Summary

This chapter demonstrates how to make VoIP service secure with SIP and other supplementary protocols (S/MIME, SRTP, TLS, and IPSec). It focuses especially on the methodology of protection in the area of authentication, encryption, and transport/network layer security in conjunction with threat models and limitation.

The SIP protocol itself is not secure enough to provide VoIP service through the public Internet because it was not originally designed for security, but its security features are essential to build up the whole security structure in conjunction with existing security models derived from other protocols, such as HTTP and SMTP.

SIP provides challenge-based Digest authentication between UAC and UAS, or between UA and proxy server. When a server receives a request, it may challenge the request to provide the assurance of the originator's identity. The originator can reply with its credential with encryption (for example, MD5), or reject the challenge. When the credential is received, the server verifies and sends back respective response codes.

End-to-end full encryption is the most common way to provide message confidentiality and integrity between communication endpoints. SIP also recommends encryption for the purpose, but there is a limitation; encrypting all SIP requests and responses end-to-end is not applicable because intermediaries like proxy server have to look at the message fields to route properly. Therefore, two parts of a SIP transaction are recommended to be encrypted: message body (with S/MIME) and media (with SRTP).

Another security mechanism is necessary so that proxy servers are trusted by UAs. For this purpose, you need a low-layer security mechanism that encrypts entire SIP requests and responses on the wire on a hop-by-hop basis, and allows UAs to verify the identity of proxy servers to whom they send requests. SIP recommends TLS and IPSec for the purpose.

SIP protocol-specific threat models exist, such as registration hijacking, impersonating a server, tearing down sessions, and DoS. These can be mitigated by authentication, encryption, or lower-layer security methods.

End Notes

1 RFC 3261, "SIP (Session Initiation Protocol)," J. Rosenberg, H. Schulzrinne, G. Camarillo, A. Johnston, J. Peterson, R. Sparks, M. Handley, E. Schooler, June 2002.

2 RFC 2617, "HTTP Authentication: Basic and Digest Access Authentication," J. Franks, P. Hallam-Baker, J. Hostetler, S. Lawrence, P. Leach, A. Luotonen, L. Stewart, June 1999.

3 RFC 3711, "Secure Real-time Transport Protocol (SRTP)," M. Baugher, D. McGrew, M. Naslund, E. Carrara, K. Norrman, March 2004.

4 "libSRTP, open-source implementation of SRTP," http://srtp.sourceforge.net/srtp.html.

5 RFC 4346, "Transport Layer Security (TLS) Protocol," T. Dierks, E. Rescorla, April 2006.

6 RFC 4347, "Datagram Transport Layer Security," E. Rescorla, N. Modadugu, April 2006.

References

RFC 2633, "S/MIME Version 3 Message Specification," B. Ramsdell, June 1999.

RFC 2315, "Cryptographic Message Syntax Version 1.5," B. Kaliski, March 1998.

This chapter covers the methodology of protection with a Session Border Controller (SBC). The main subjects are as follows:

- Network border issues
- Access and peer SBCs
- SBC functionality
- Service architecture design

CHAPTER 8

Protection with Session Border Controller

There is no single solution to secure a VoIP service network entirely. The best practice is to integrate all possible solutions according to service model, network architecture, protocol model, target customers, peering partners, and so on.

Chapter 7, "Protection with VoIP Protocol," demonstrated the methods of how to protect VoIP service with VoIP protocols. This chapter will demonstrate additional methods of protection with a major security device, Session Border Controller (SBC).

An SBC is, as the name implies, a controlling device located on a border of two network sessions. The session is a logical boundary of a VoIP network. For a better understanding, in this book it is also referenced as either *domain* or *realm*. Figure 8-1 shows an example of session borders among different VoIP networks.

The role of SBC is, simply speaking, resolving border issues. What are the border issues, then? They are interoperability and security issues taking place in the border, such as Denial-of-Service (DoS), call flooding, traversing media (one-way audio), coder-decoder (codec) conflict, and so on.

This chapter covers the details of border issues in a VoIP network, especially security issues, and the methodology of preventing them with an SBC.

NOTE   The content in this chapter is written from the perspective of VoIP service providers or enterprises, who generally design and deploy SBCs into their service network.

Figure 8-1 *Session Borders*

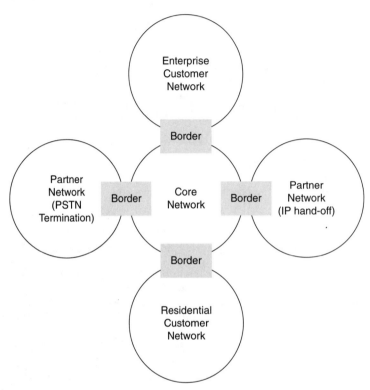

Border Issues

There are typically two network borders from a VoIP service provider's perspective. One is between the customer's access network and the service provider's network (core network). The other is between the core network and the other service provider's network (peer network).

The customer's access network is most likely that of the local Internet service provider (ISP) who provides Internet access service, which is generally different from the service provider's network (see the following Note).

NOTE   Many VoIP service providers, such as Vonage or Skype, do not provide the access network; however, some do provide it, especially for enterprise customers, to ensure quality of service and security. Some ISPs, such as Comcast or AT&T, also provide both the access and service network for their customers.

The peer network is typically a call-termination network like public switched telephone network (PSTN) termination. Figure 8-2 illustrates the VoIP service between the different networks at a high level.

Figure 8-2   *VoIP Service Borders*

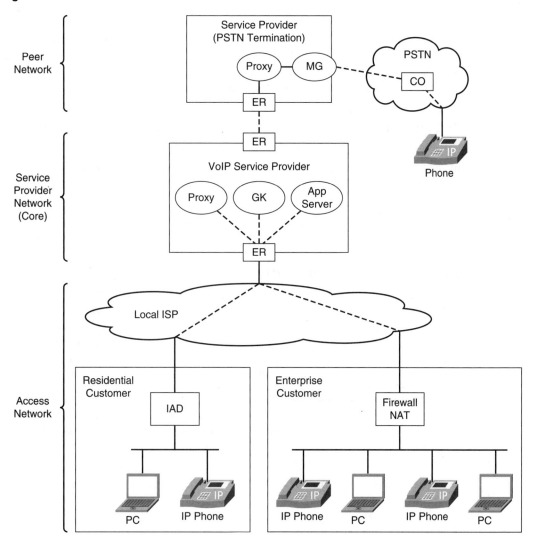

In an access network, most residential customers use an integrated access device (IAD; for example, digital subscriber line [DSL] or cable modem) that the local ISP provides in order to access the Internet. They can send and receive calls with IP phone or softphone through IP connectivity. IAD may have extra Foreign Exchange Station (FXS) port interfaces for regular PSTN phones. Enterprise customers, generally, maintain their internal network and use a local ISP to have Internet access through a firewall/Network Address Translation (NAT). They may use IP PBX, multiport IAD, IP phone, softphone, and so on for VoIP service.

In the core network, the service provider maintains all servers like Softswitch, proxy, gate-keeper, application server, and database in order to process call requests or registrations. Many servers have interfaces accepting call requests directly from clients in public (access) networks, and route the calls to either the service provider's own network or another service provider's network that is a peer network (for example, PSTN termination). Generally, a core network already has a fair degree of security level with a firewall.

In a peer network, the partner company also maintains some server groups and uses them to route the call to the corresponding destination. It is generally more secure than an access network, but there are still security issues facing it.

Some border issues among access, core, and peer networks are common, but mostly they have different types of issues because of their different policy, topology, management, and so on.

The next topic is the issues between access and core networks.

Between Access and Core Networks

Most issues in this border come from the nature of a "public" access network. Anybody in the world who has Internet access can access the servers (for example, Session Initiation Protocol [SIP] proxy or registrar) regardless of whether the user is legitimate or not. So, it is not difficult for attackers to jeopardize those servers with known hacking skills (some examples are presented in Chapter 6, "Analysis and Simulation of Current Threats"). The typical issues can be summarized as follows:

- **Denial-of-Service (intentional flooding)**—This is malicious traffic from a large number of infected devices around a public network (Distributed Denial-of-Service [DDoS]), or from an attacker's machine generating massive call requests. Most VoIP servers are vulnerable to this type of attack because it is very difficult to implement sophisticated access control.

- **Denial-of-Service (unintentional flooding)**—This is not malicious traffic, but the impact is almost the same as intentional flooding. For example, a large number of registration requests at the same time are issued after a global power outage followed by power backup.

- **Exposed topology of core network**—Most IP addresses and port numbers of VoIP servers are exposed for public service, which means that attackers may send probe messages to learn the characteristics of the servers and then generate many types of malicious calls, such as spoofed or malformed messages.

- **Traversing firewall or NAT**—Most enterprise customers use firewall or NAT for security purposes, but this may cause one-way or no-audio issues when traversing two different networks.

- **Regulatory mandate (lawful interception)**—There is a complicated governmental security issue when intercepting VoIP traffic in this border because of many different types of call routing through heterogeneous networks. The details of lawful interception are discussed in Part III, "Lawful Interception (CALEA)," in this book.

- **Ensuring quality of service**—This is a generic issue when VoIP traffic goes through a heterogeneous network (not directly related to border security).

These are typical border issues between access and core networks. The next section describes issues between core and peer networks.

Between Core and Peer Networks

Compared with access networks, similar issues can be found in this border because two different networks are facing each other, but there are some different types of issues as well. The typical issues can be summarized as follows:

- **Denial-of-Service**—It rarely happens that flooded malicious traffic comes from a peer network because of a decent level of security between network nodes, such as source/destination address (IP and port) filtering by an Access Control List (ACL). However, it is still possible to receive unexpected flooding from a peer network because of wrong configuration or detoured traffic, and so on.

- **Exposed topology of core network**—The topology of a VoIP service network could be visible to a peer network; for example, when the peer server receives a SIP message from the core proxy server, the peer knows where the call is being routed by means of the SIP "via" header. The exposed IP address and port number could be used for malicious purposes potentially.

- **Protocol conflict**—Each service provider has its own VoIP protocol and there are always interoperability issues between them, even if they use the same standard protocol, such as codec conflict. Most issues are not directly related to security, but some of them are related; for example, one requires Transport Layer Security (TLS) connection when sending SIP messages, but the other does not.

- **Ensuring quality of service**—This is a generic issue when VoIP traffic goes through a heterogeneous network (not directly related to border security).

In this section, you have learned about the border issues among access, core, and peer networks. In the next section, you learn the details about SBC.

Access and Peer SBCs

A VoIP service provider can deploy two logically separated SBCs (access and peer SBCs) in their service network, depending on where the SBC is located. The reason for the logical separation is that the function of each SBC is generally different because of different issues and policies.

- **Access SBC**—An access SBC is located on the border between the service provider's core network and access network in order to deal with border issues. Because the VoIP traffic comes from an unmanaged public network, an access SBC must have strict policies for a DoS attack, flooded call, malformed message, and spoofed call. Moreover, it must have the capability to apply the policy to individual users/devices; for example, only the misbehaving end device is supposed to be demoted (no call processing), without affecting other devices.

- **Peer SBC**—A peer SBC is located on the border between the service provider's core network and peer network in order to manage border issues. Because the traffic comes from a relatively safe network, typically through a VoIP trunk, it does not really require strict policy. It must have a capability of applying different policies to different peer networks.

Note that these two SBCs can be within one physical box, which is very common, even though each SBC uses a separate network interface VLAN and different configuration.

SBC Functionality

The primary function of an SBC is resolving the border issues that are listed in the section "Border Issues" of this chapter. This section covers the concept of the function of SBCs, the guidelines of functional design, and usage examples. Keep in mind that this content is explained at a high level; the actual implementation and utilization of the function can vary from company to company.

Network Topology Hiding

Network topology hiding is a key function of SBC, hiding the core network topology from either access or peer network. As mentioned previously, VoIP servers (for example, SIP proxy or registrar) are exposed to the external networks so that endpoints may access the servers to request calls or register, which means that the topology of the service network is partially visible and vulnerable. So, an SBC encapsulates the core network and provides a single logical interface for external networks. The external endpoints can see only the IP address and port of the SBC rather than actual VoIP servers, and the SBC routes the call to the corresponding server based on type of service, policy, protocol, and so on. Figure 8-3 illustrates the difference with and without SBC between access and core networks.

Figure 8-3   *Exposed and Hidden Topology of VoIP Network*

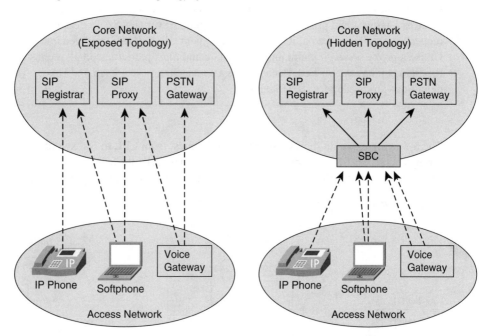

The external endpoints (Customer Premises Equipment [CPE]) cannot recognize the medi-ation device (SBC) that passes the same protocol messages as the VoIP servers except IP and port information. An SBC also typically has the capability to rewrite all headers in the message so that the endpoints cannot see any other node's information; for example, an SBC can rewrite a SIP Via header by removing history and adding only its own IP informa-tion. That is, a user cannot see where the actual server is and how the call is routed.

NOTE   Because an SBC is a single entity and its IP address/port is known to anything connecting to it, an SBC can become a point of attack, which is why an SBC has to have sophisticated security features, high capacity, robustness, and high availability.

Example of Topology Hiding

Now let us look at a detailed example of topology hiding with the SIP protocol. SBC typically plays a role of SIP Back-to-Back User Agent (B2BUA; see the following Note) in order to have full control of request and response messages, as well as providing transparent service.

The following example shows the simple call request from CPE to Softswitch (Proxy) through an access SBC that provides two separate network interfaces for each counterpart. Figure 8-4 illustrates the call flow with IP address change when going through SBC.

Figure 8-4   *Simple Call Flow Through SBC*

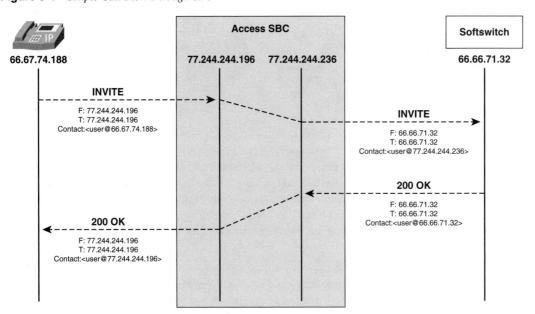

In Figure 8-4, the access SBC has two IP interfaces: 77.244.244.196 is the facing access network (CPE) and 77.244.244.236 is the facing core network (Softswitch).

CPE sends INVITE with its domain (IP), but the access SBC converts it with the other domain (IP) in the core network. 200 OK is also converted in the same way. The point is that CPE in the access network cannot see any core network information, even within headers and bodies in response messages. The actual messages in this dialog are listed in Example 8-1, which gives you the details of message conversion providing topology hiding. The important area is shaded.

Example 8-1 *Topology Hiding in SIP Message*

```
<From CPE to Access SBC>:
INVITE sip:4084342045@77.244.244.196 SIP/2.0
Via: SIP/2.0/UDP
66.67.74.188:5060;rport;branch=z9hG4bK92DD3413B67546F7B4255AF476556741
From: 4084003020 <sip:4084003020@77.244.244.196>;tag=498560566
To: <sip:4084342045@77.244.244.196>
Contact: <sip:4084003020@66.67.74.188:5060>
Call-ID: 2CACE82E-91B9-4AB3-85E8-A41306CEF2AB@66.67.74.188
CSeq: 8153 INVITE
Authorization: Digest
Max-Forwards: 70
Content-Type: application/sdp
Content-Length: 277

v=0
o=4084003020 26235624 26235644 IN IP4 66.67.74.188
c=IN IP4 66.67.74.188
t=0 0
m=audio 8000 RTP/AVP 0
a=rtpmap:0 pcmu/8000

<From Access SBC to Softswitch>:
INVITE sip:4084342045@66.66.71.32 SIP/2.0
Via: SIP/2.0/UDP 77.244.244.236:5060;branch=z9hG4bK009se930ageh1bste1s1.1
From: 4084003020 <sip:4084003020@66.66.71.32>;tag=498560566
To: <sip:4084342045@66.66.71.32>
Contact: <sip:4084003020-sipphoneo-f5mebkgfrd2v9-
mbqleqrmjm3jb@77.244.244.236:5060;transport=udp>
Call-ID: 2CACE82E-91B9-4AB3-85E8-A41306CEF2AB@66.67.74.188
CSeq: 8153 INVITE
Authorization: Digest
Max-Forwards: 69
Content-Type: application/sdp
Content-Length: 280

v=0
o=4084003020 26235624 26235644 IN IP4 77.244.244.236
c=IN IP4 77.244.244.236
t=0 0
m=audio 45572 RTP/AVP 0
a=rtpmap:0 pcmu/8000

<From Softswitch to Access SBC>:
SIP/2.0 200 OK
Record-Route: <sip:4084342045@cookie:5060;maddr=66.66.71.32>
Via: SIP/2.0/UDP 77.244.244.236:5060;branch=z9hG4bK009se930ageh1bste1s1.1
```

continues

Example 8-1 *Topology Hiding in SIP Message (Continued)*

```
CSeq: 8153 INVITE
Call-ID: 2CACE82E-91B9-4AB3-85E8-A41306CEF2AB@66.67.74.188
From: 4084003020 <sip:4084003020@66.66.71.32>;tag=498560566
To: <sip:4084342045@66.66.71.32>;tag=e0d01fb4-1dd1-11b2-ae1e-b03162323164+e0d01fb4
Contact: sip:4084342045@66.66.71.32:5075
Content-Type: application/sdp
Supported: timer
Allow: INVITE,BYE,ACK,CANCEL,PRACK,REFER,OPTIONS,REGISTER,NOTIFY
Content-Length: 217

v=0
o=- 2385770530 2385770531 IN IP4 66.66.71.32
s=SIP Call
c=IN IP4 66.66.71.16
t=0 0
m=audio 19546 RTP/AVP 0
a=rtpmap:0 PCMU/8000
```

<From Access SBC to CPE>:

```
SIP/2.0 200 OK
Via: SIP/2.0/UDP
66.67.74.188:5060;branch=z9hG4bK92DD3413B67546F7B4255AF476556741;rport=5060
From: 4084003020 <sip:4084003020@77.244.244.196>;tag=498560566
To: <sip:4084342045@77.244.244.196>;tag=e0d01fb4-1dd1-11b2-ae1e-
b03162323164+e0d01fb4
Call-ID: 2CACE82E-91B9-4AB3-85E8-A41306CEF2AB@66.67.74.188
CSeq: 8153 INVITE
Contact: <sip:SDavhu9-
    mnlsnius3k7o9nurau5sqd5v181vegv6gvjo7898040s840@77.244.244.196:5060;transport=udp>
Content-Type: application/sdp
Supported: timer
Allow: INVITE,BYE,ACK,CANCEL,PRACK,REFER,OPTIONS,REGISTER,NOTIFY
Content-Length: 226

v=0
o=- 2385770530 2385770531 IN IP4 77.244.244.196
s=SIP Call
c=IN IP4 77.244.244.196
t=0 0
m=audio 45572 RTP/AVP 0
a=rtpmap:0 PCMU/8000
```

Note that SBC converts the Session Description Protocol (SDP) ("c=" line) as well so that the media can be anchored (relayed) by SBC instead of end-to-end media, which is the most common service architecture to secure the media path and control the bandwidth. If any malicious endpoint floods media, SBC can detect it and demote the endpoint based on the policy.

DoS Protection

The major need for SBC came from the requirement of protecting VoIP servers from flooded traffic regardless of whether it is malicious or not. The DoS attack is typically formed of flooded traffic. You can see examples in Chapter 6, "Analysis and Simulation of Current Threats."

In reality, most VoIP servers (for example, Softswitch, proxy, and gatekeeper) are apt to support only a limited function of protecting flooded traffic, such as call admission control (CAC). Of course, that limited function cannot prevent the variety of DoS attacks. Why do those servers not support fully, then? The main reason is the capability issue on VoIP servers; supporting DoS prevention requires a large amount of system resources (CPU, memory, bandwidth, and so on), as well as sophisticated software and hardware architecture.

The method of implementing DoS protection functions in an SBC varies from company to company, but the general concept of function design and usage can be summarized as in the following section.

Policy-Driven Access Control

The primary method of preventing DoS is using access control that allows secure traffic, limits uncertain traffic, and denies insecure traffic. Let us categorize the different type of traffic with color names that come from the general term of "black or white list."

NOTE   "Black or white list" is not an officially used term but is used here just to give you a better understanding.

- **White traffic**—Secure signal or media from trusted endpoints. Generally, the VoIP service provider deploys these endpoints and maintains the static IP information. Some service providers manage even the access network as well and make sure all traffic within their network is secure; this is not a common service model, though.

  SBC should maintain White ACL and allow inbound and outbound traffic without restriction.

- **Black traffic**—Insecure signal or media from untrusted endpoints. These endpoints are either malicious or infected by attackers. Generally, this black traffic comes from an unmanaged access network in which the VoIP service provider cannot control the IP connectivity, which does not mean that all traffic from an unmanaged network is Black.

  SBC should maintain Black ACL and deny inbound and outbound traffic.

- **Gray traffic**—Undefined signal or media from unknown endpoints (the legitimacy of the endpoints is not yet known). Most initial traffic (for example, registration requests) from unmanaged access networks belongs to this category. After authentication or a certain type of validation, SBC decides whether it is white or black traffic.

  SBC should maintain Gray ACL and limit (not deny) inbound and outbound traffic with a certain threshold amount.

The reason for categorizing the traffic (or endpoints) is to apply different service policies, which are defined by an SBC administrator. For example, the administrator assigns 70 percent of bandwidth to endpoints in White ACL and 30 percent to Gray ACL, which means that any malicious or misbehaving endpoints in Gray ACL cannot use up all bandwidth (only up to 30 percent), and the service for White is not affected.

The ACL (White, Black, and Gray) can be dynamically changed according to the behavior of the endpoint. For example, Endpoint A was switched from Gray to White ACL after proper authorization, but all of sudden, Endpoint A sends flooded messages (whether malicious or not) hitting the maximum threshold, and the SBC puts Endpoint A into the Black ACL to deny the traffic for a certain amount of time.

In a real service environment, the method of judging that an endpoint belongs to the White, Black, or Gray list is not as simple as the preceding example. It is part of defining the overall policy for DoS, and the metrics of judging the type of endpoint (or traffic) can be exemplified as follows:

- Authentication and authorization (for example, an endpoint authorized is moved to White list)

- Messages per second (for example, an endpoint sending more than 15 messages per second is moved to the Black list for 1 minute)

- Call attempts per second (for example, an endpoint sending SIP INVITE more than 10 times per second is moved to the Black list for 5 minutes)

- Number of invalid or malformed messages (for example, an endpoint sending even a single malformed message is moved to the Black list for 60 minutes)

- Maximum bandwidth consumption per call (for example, an endpoint using more than 150 kbps with G.711 codec is moved to the Black list)

NOTE   The reason for time expiration in the Black list is that even normal endpoints may have malfunctions. The endpoints cannot have a service anymore even after recovery if there is no expiration time in the Black list.

Meanwhile, each ACL should include all information for the endpoint as follows:

- Source IP address
- Source port
- Transport protocol (Transmission Control Protocol [TCP] or User Datagram Protocol [UDP])
- Application Protocol (SIP, H.323, Media Gateway Control Protocol [MGCP], Skinny Call Control Protocol [SCCP])
- Destination IP address (SBC's)
- Destination port (SBC's)

Hardware Architecture

It is a much better idea to design SBC-specific hardware in order to apply the DoS policies effectively because software-only solutions have many limitations.

There are many possible architectures, and one of them is shown in Figure 8-5 from a high-level perspective.

Figure 8-5 *SBC Hardware Architecture for DoS Protection*

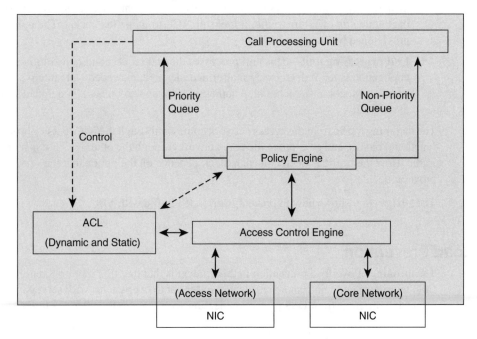

Here is the role of each functional block:

- **Network Interface Card (NIC)**—A physically separate NIC is required for each network, access (or peer) and core network. Each interface could be configured as a trunk supporting multiple access or peer networks. It is recommended to use different subnets and VLANs.

- **Access Control Engine (ACE)**—The ACE inspects the packet header and decides whether it drops the packet or passes it to the Policy Engine, by looking up ACL. This is a key module that blocks any malicious or flooded traffic in the network layer without going up to the call processing unit.

- **ACL**—ACL contains dynamic and static White, Black, and Gray lists with endpoint information (IP, port, protocol, and so on), and provides the lists to the Access Control Processor or Policy Engine on demand. Dynamic ACL is updated by the call processing unit, which decides the type of endpoints, and Static ACL is provisioned by an administrator.

- **Policy Engine**—The Policy Engine manages bandwidth and system resources based on the type of traffic. There are two different queues going to the call processing unit: Priority and Non-priority Queue. White traffic goes through Priority Queue being allocated much higher bandwidth (for example, 70 percent of total bandwidth), and Gray traffic goes through Non-priority Queue being allocated limited bandwidth. The main reason for the separation is, as mentioned, to prevent burst traffic from consuming the bandwidth of White traffic. It looks up ACL to judge the packet. The policy is provisioned by an administrator.

- **Call processing unit**—This unit processes the call request and registration in the application layer. It detects any malformed message, exceeded call attempts, invalid signal, protocol mismatch, failed authentication, and so on, and then updates ACL dynamically.

The incoming traffic from the access network comes in through the NIC, passes through the functional blocks, and goes out to the core network through the other NIC if it is legitimate traffic. How the traffic is treated in each block depends on the policy that the service provider decides.

The next section shows how to prevent overloaded traffic with SBC.

Overload Prevention

The meaning of overload prevention in this context is that the SBC monitors regular traffic from legitimate endpoints and controls it in order not to overwhelm VoIP servers, which is somewhat different from DoS protection dealing with malicious or flooded traffic.

The typical method of preventing the overload is that an SBC reduces redundant or unnecessary signals by controlling the frequency of messages (for example, periodical registration or keepalive), or distributes the load to multiple targets based on policy. The next section looks at the typical examples that an SBC can support.

Registration Timer Control

In the SIP protocol, a UAC sends a REGISTER message for registration request and then a registrar authorizes and replies 200 OK with an "expires" header indicating how often the UAC is supposed to reregister. For example, if the expires is 60 seconds, a UAC has to reregister in 60 seconds before the registration is expired in a registrar.

Now, take a look at the characteristics first according to the length of the timer.

If the expiration time is short:

- More bandwidth and resources are consumed because more signals go back and forth between a UAC and a registrar.
- There is better visibility and connectivity between them.

If the expiration time is long:

- There is a higher possibility of losing the connection when a UAC is behind a NAT device updating a mapping table frequently or a registrar is rebooted (registrar loses all registration entry).
- Less bandwidth and fewer resources are consumed.

So how can you decide the expiration time properly? It depends on the connection type of the endpoint, whether it is behind NAT or not. For example, if it is behind NAT (or it uses a dynamic IP address), a registrar should request more frequent registration to keep the pinhole of NAT open. If it uses a static IP address, the long interval of registration should be fine.

When VoIP service providers decide the default registration timer, they are most likely to choose the shortest one to prevent any service outage even though it requires more bandwidth, which could be a significant waste if major endpoints are not behind NAT, or do not have dynamic IP addresses.

One of SBC's functions can resolve this kind of issue by controlling the registration timer in the middle: short timer to endpoints and long timer to a registrar. The long timer could be much longer than a regular service timer for the endpoints having a static IP, because the SBC has a managed static IP address that the registrar always remembers (an administrator provisions).

Example 8-2 shows how an SBC manipulates the registration timer and controls the bandwidth and resources. Figure 8-6 shows the high-level call flow.

Figure 8-6 *Registration Timer Control by SBC*

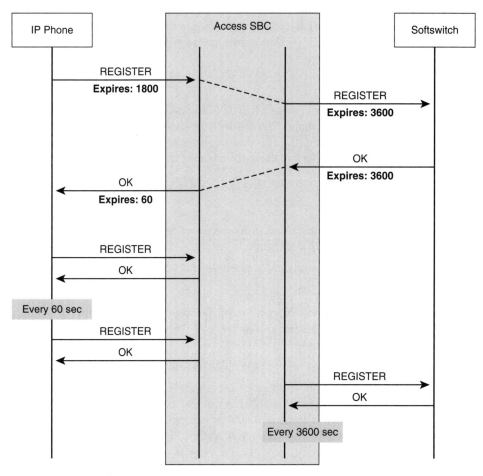

The actual SIP messages are listed in Example 8-2.

Example 8-2 *Registration Timer Control by SBC*

```
<IP phone to Access SBC>:
REGISTER sip:77.244.244.196 SIP/2.0
Via: SIP/2.0/UDP
66.67.74.188:5060;rport;branch=z9hG4bK5B8C2E16E35F4695A4CFD0B3F93519E0
From: 4084003020 <sip:4084003020@77.244.244.196>;tag=1006758284
To: 4084003020 <sip:4084003020@77.244.244.196>
Contact: "4084003020" <sip:4084003020@66.67.74.188:5060>
Call-ID: AF656D0A19AA45159D3F9A6E1EC078D5@77.244.244.196
CSeq: 7086 REGISTER
Expires: 1800
```

Example 8-2 *Registration Timer Control by SBC (Continued)*

```
Authorization: Digest username="4084003020",realm="Registered_Subscribers",
  nonce="02564c6a635153cac0d481f04b5c378d",response=
    "c8a7eab48ebc0d7d2434ed2845cbfb71",
  uri="sip:77.244.244.196",algorithm=MD5,opaque="acc9b8ee"
Max-Forwards: 70
User-Agent: X-Lite release 1103m
Content-Length: 0
```

<Access SBC to Softswitch>:
```
REGISTER sip:66.66.71.32 SIP/2.0
Via: SIP/2.0/UDP 77.244.244.236:5060;branch=z9hG4bK009se630boj17bstn2s1.1
From: 4084003020 <sip:4084003020@66.66.71.32>;tag=1006758284
To: 4084003020 <sip:4084003020@66.66.71.32>
Contact: "4084003020" <sip:4084003020-sipphoneo-f5meqrmjm3jb@77.244.244.236:5060;
  transport=udp>
Call-ID: AF656D0A19AA45159D3F9A6E1EC078D5@77.244.244.196
CSeq: 7086 REGISTER
Expires: 3600
Authorization: Digest username="4084003020",realm="Registered_Subscribers",
  nonce="02564c6a635153cac0d481f04b5c378d",response=
    "c8a7eab48ebc0d7d2434ed2845cbfb71",
  uri="sip:77.244.244.196",algorithm=MD5,opaque="acc9b8ee"
Max-Forwards: 69
User-Agent: X-Lite release 1103m
Content-Length: 0
```

<Softswitch to Access SBC>:
```
SIP/2.0 200 OK
Via: SIP/2.0/UDP 77.244.244.236:5060;branch=z9hG4bK009se630boj17bstn2s1.1
CSeq: 7086 REGISTER
Call-ID: AF656D0A19AA45159D3F9A6E1EC078D5@77.244.244.196
From: 4084003020 <sip:4084003020@66.66.71.32>;tag=1006758284
To: 4084003020 <sip:4084003020@66.66.71.32>;tag=1486403012856434
Contact: "4084003020" <sip:4084003020-sipphoneo-
mbqleqrmjm3jb@77.244.244.236:5060;transport=udp>
Date: Thu, 20 Jul 2006 23:39:58 GMT
Expires: 3600
Content-Length: 00
```

<Access SBC to IP phone>:
```
SIP/2.0 200 OK
Via: SIP/2.0/UDP
66.67.74.188:5060;branch=z9hG4bK5B8C2E16E35F4695A4CFD0B3F93519E0;rport=5060
From: 4084003020 <sip:4084003020@77.244.244.196>;tag=1006758284
To: 4084003020 <sip:4084003020@77.244.244.196>;tag=1486403012856434
Call-ID: AF656D0A19AA45159D3F9A6E1EC078D5@77.244.244.196
CSeq: 7086 REGISTER
Contact: <sip:4084003020@66.67.74.188:5060>;expires=60
Date: Thu, 20 Jul 2006 23:39:58 GMT
Expires: 60
Content-Length: 0
```

As shown in the preceding example, the access SBC manipulates the "Expires" header, and sets the timer to 60 seconds with the IP phone and 3600 seconds with the Softswitch, which saves a significant amount of bandwidth and resources on the Softswitch.

Ping Control

NOTE	In this context, the term "ping" is not ICMP Ping in the network layer, but ping messages in the application layer.

VoIP servers ping endpoints to check out the availability and keep the pinhole open if they use NATed IP addresses. The method of pinging is different depending on the protocol they use. For example, a Softswitch may send SIP OPTION or MGCP AUEP to an endpoint and validate the response.

The SIP OPTION itself is a very light message in terms of bandwidth and resource consumption. However, if the SIP server sends the OPTION to a large number of endpoints (say 50,000) very frequently, it becomes a significant issue.

SBC could be the solution by being located in the middle and controlling the number of pings to save bandwidth and resources. An administrator needs to configure an SBC to control the frequent OPTION messages to unmanaged endpoints so that SIP servers in the core network may not take care of the ping traffic.

Load Balancing

It happens intermittently that VoIP servers are overloaded during a certain period of time and users cannot make calls. There could be many reasons for this, but the typical one is a failure of load balancing among multiple identical servers.

Most service providers deploy multiple VoIP servers with the same functions to divide the traffic, after calculating expected traffic and capacity. However, this does not work well when the method of distributing traffic is not efficient; some service providers "statically" assign the server address (IP and port) to a CPE when initially deploying it. For example, a certain group of CPE (Group A) always connects to a dedicated server (Proxy A), Group B to Proxy B, Group C to Proxy C, and so on. The method of static assignment may work reasonably well if each group generates less traffic all the time than what the corresponding server can handle, but the reality does not quite work that way. Here are two main issues with the static load balancing:

- When a certain server is heavy loaded, others that have light traffic cannot share the overload. This happens commonly, especially in global VoIP service environments.

- The method of preventing overload (for example, deploying more servers to handle a small group of CPE) can be wasteful and not cost-effective.

To avoid these issues, some service providers deploy a redirect server in a core network to distribute the traffic, but it still has typical border issues (for example, flooding). Therefore, an SBC can be a good solution to resolve both overloading and border issues. Figure 8-7 shows before and after deploying an SBC in terms of load balancing.

Figure 8-7   *Load Balancing with SBC*

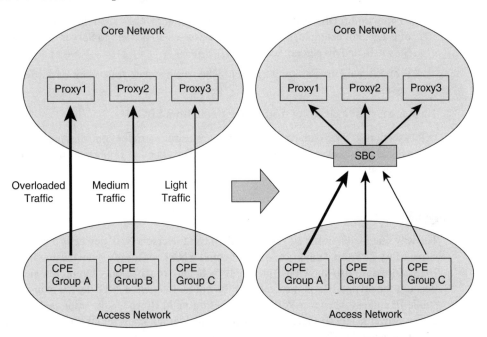

The method of distributing traffic from an SBC depends on the strategy that an administrator defines. Several methods are possible, and the following list describes some of them:

- **Round Robin**—Select each target server in turn and route a call request, which gives equal load to all servers.

  Round Robin is efficient when all servers have same capacity.

- **First Available**—There is a priority selecting each server, and the highest one is always selected first as long as it has not hit the threshold. If the highest is not available or overloaded, the second is selected. The configuration comes with the priority list.

  First Available is efficient when a primary server exists along with backups.

- **Random Select**—Each server is selected randomly, which distributes the load almost equally in the long run, like Round Robin.

  Random Select is efficient when all servers have same capacity.

- **Least Busy**—Select the target server having the least number of active sessions.

  Least Busy is efficient when distributing calls based on real-time resource consumption on the server. (Note that Round Robin or Random Select does not care about the number of active sessions.)

- **Proportional Distribution**—Select the target server based on the defined proportion of usage. For example, an administrator assigns 30 percent to Server A, 20 percent to Server B, and 50 percent to Server C.

  Proportional Distribution is efficient when each server or network has different capacity.

These are typical methods of distributing traffic from SBC.

In this section so far, you have learned about registration timer control, ping control, and load balancing to prevent overload. The next topic is another important function of SBC, NAT traversal.

NAT Traversal

The way that media traffic (voice and video) can traverse a NAT device is a very common issue. Most CPE these days are located behind a NAT (or firewall) device and have RFC 1918 addresses (also known as "private IP") that are routable only by internal network. Because the private IP is not routable in the public Internet, a NAT device maps it to its public IP address whenever VoIP traffic goes through. However, the thing is that a NAT device converts only IP addresses in Layer 3 and does not know about IPs in the application layer (for example, SIP messages), which can cause a one-way or no-audio problem, which you may have heard many times.

NOTE   There are also VoIP-aware NATs that convert IP addresses in the application layer as well, but these are not commonly deployed yet.

Example 8-3 shows an example with SIP INVITE message.

Example 8-3 *Private IP in SDP*

```
INVITE sip:4084445555@77.244.244.196 SIP/2.0
Via: SIP/2.0/UDP
192.168.10.10:5060;rport;branch=z9hG4bK92DD3413B67546F7B4255AF476556741
From: 4084003020 <sip:4084003020@77.244.244.196>;tag=498560566
To: <sip:4084445555@77.244.244.196>
Contact: <sip:4084003020@192.168.10.10:5060>
Call-ID: 2CACE82E-91B9-4AB3-85E8-A41306CEF2AB@192.168.10.10
CSeq: 8153 INVITE
Authorization: Digest
Max-Forwards: 70
Content-Type: application/sdp
Content-Length: 277

v=0
o=4084003020 26235624 26235644 IN IP4 192.168.10.10
c=IN IP4 192.168.10.10
t=0 0
m=audio 8000 RTP/AVP 0
a=rtpmap:0 pcmu/8000
```

The user agent sending the INVITE in Example 8-3 has a private IP 192.168.10.10 that is written in "Via", "Contact" header and SDP ("c" line). The private IP in the headers is not an issue when making a call setup with a proxy server dealing with a NATed public IP. However, the other user agent receiving the INVITE from the proxy looks at the SDP and sends media to the address in the "c" line having a private IP, which means the media will be dropped.

An SBC can be a solution to resolve this problem in the middle of the signaling path as a proxy server or B2BUA. There are two ways of resolving it in an SBC:

1 Replacing a private IP with the SBC's IP.

   This is the most common way of traversing a NAT device. An SBC anchors (relays) the media between user agents by replacing the IP ("c" line) and port ("m" line) with its own IP/port.

   It assumes that the endpoints behind a NAT device use symmetric Real-time Transport Protocol (RTP)/Real-time Transport Control Protocol (RTCP) (see the following Note).

   The downside is that it affects the performance of SBC anchoring all media.

2 Replacing a private IP with NATed IP.

Instead of anchoring the media, an SBC hands it off by replacing the private IP with the NATed IP so that the other user agent may send the media directly to the originator through the NAT device.

It assumes that a NAT device uses (maps) the same port number as an originator's, which is not a common feature. So, this method is not commonly used.

NOTE   Symmetric RTP/RTCP means that the IP address and port number used for outbound RTP/RTCP are reused for the inbound RTP/RTCP. An SBC learns the outbound IP/port pair of RTP/RTCP when receiving initial outbound media packets and passes inbound media to the same IP/port pair. Most CPE supports this feature.

Because anchoring media requires high bandwidth and processing power, it is not recommended for regular VoIP servers (for example, SIP B2BUA) to support this feature. A dedicated media server like an SBC is recommended.

The next topic is another important function of SBC, lawful interception, especially for government security purposes.

Lawful Interception

Lawful Interception (LI) or Communications Assistance for Law Enforcement Act (CALEA) is a VoIP service provider's duty to intercept call data (for example, call setup messages) or call contents (for example, voice), and forward them to a law enforcement agency according to a warrant. The detailed analysis of LI and its implementation with an SBC is described in Part III, "Lawful Interception (CALEA)," of this book.

The reason for utilizing an SBC for the interception is that it can see most of the signals and media going back and forth among CPE and VoIP servers as an access device. Figure 8-8 shows the functional architecture of LI and the location of SBC, which is based on the Telecommunications Industry Association (TIA) J-STD specification.

SBC should have the following functions as a part of Access Function (AF):

- Interface with Service Provider Administrative Function (SPAF) and receive the target information such as a phone number, start time, or end time.
- Intercept the target call information in accordance with the request from SPAF.
- Interface with Delivery Function (DF) and forward the call data and/or content.
- Provide the transparency of interception; in other words, the target user is not supposed to recognize any difference when being intercepted.

Figure 8-8 *Functional Architecture of LI and SBC Location*

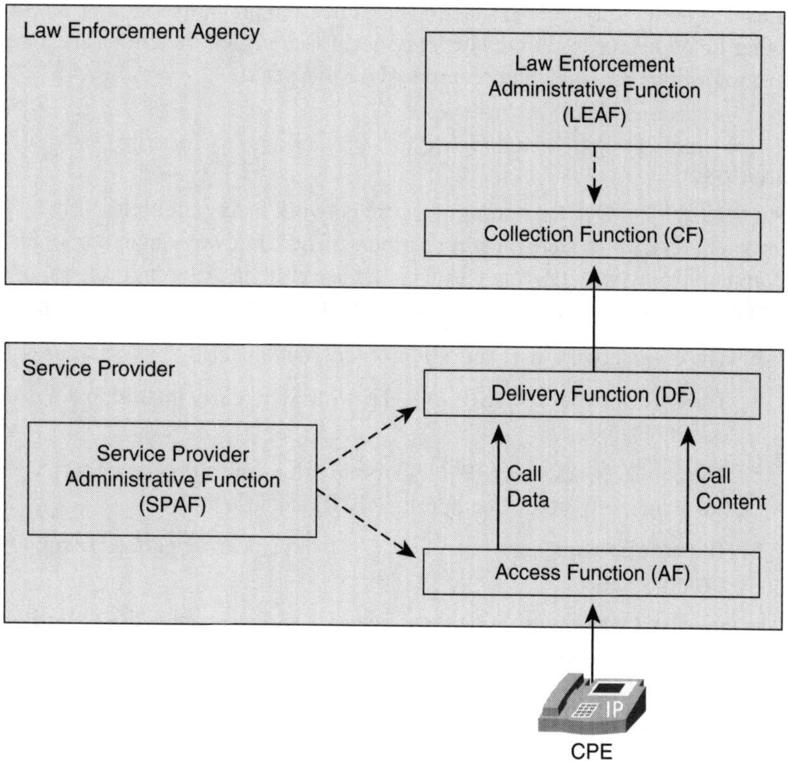

NOTE   All LI functions use an initial capital letter for each function's name followed by the letter "F," such as "DF" for "Delivery Function," because these names are defined by LI specifications and not as general terms.

For the details of LI, see Chapter 10, "Lawful Interception Fundamentals."

In this section so far, you have learned about the major functions of SBC, especially from the security perspective. The next section covers other important functions of SBC that you need to know.

Other Functions

Besides the security-related functions described in previous sections, an SBC has many other functions for resolving border issues. Other critical functions are introduced in this section, which are related to secure service in a sense.

Protocol Conversion

An SBC is located at the border of a core network facing multiple different domains, such as other service providers (peering partners). There is always an interoperability issue when communicating with peering partners that use either a different protocol or the same protocol but a different method of implementation. Here are some examples:

- The core network uses the SIP protocol, but a peering partner A uses H.323.

- The core network uses SIP INVITE with SDP (early media), but a peering partner B does not support.

- The core network uses SIP INFO for dual-tone multifrequency (DTMF) transmission, but a peering partner C supports only RFC 2833.

- The core network uses fax relay (T.38), but a peering partner D supports only fax pass-through.

The traditional way of resolving those issues is adding more codes to VoIP servers in order to support different protocols, which takes time and delays production service. An SBC can be the solution, converting protocols at the borderline without changing core VoIP servers (or making only minor changes). In fact, most current SBC products in the market support these features.

Figure 8-9 shows an example of converting protocols between SIP and H.323, which is a typical feature of SBC.

Converting protocols is not always as clear as the example in Figure 8-9 because each protocol may have complicated call flows that make it very hard to match one to one.

Transcoding

What codec will be used for the current call is decided after negotiating it during the call setup time. The method of negotiating is a little different depending on protocols, but the basic method is offer-and-answer; a call originator offers a list of codecs and a responder picks what it supports. Session Description Protocol (SDP) especially uses this offer-and-answer model as defined in RFC 3264.

For example, if the core network supports four codecs with priority (G.711u, G.711a, G.729, and iLBC) and a peering partner supports three codecs (G.729, iLBC, and G.723.1), G.729 will be picked as a final codec.

Figure 8-9 *Protocol Conversion*

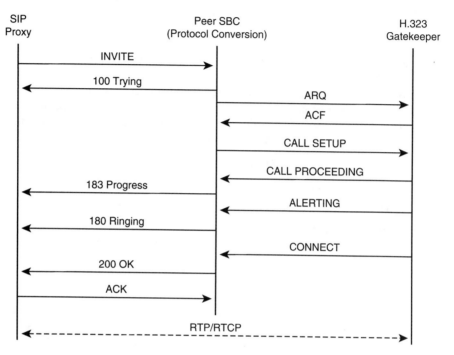

However, codec mismatching also may happen between different domains, which requires a mediation device transcoding them. An SBC is in the right location and can provide this feature.

Transcoding is required not only for the mismatching but also for bandwidth control. Suppose that, for example, a certain access network has limited bandwidth and cannot guarantee Quality of Service (QoS) when using a default codec, G.711 (64 Kbps). An SBC can resolve this issue by reordering a codec list and forcing it to use a low bit-rate codec like G.729 (8 Kbps).

Number Translation

Each peering partner may use a different format of phone number, which creates another interoperability issue. For example, the core network uses U.S. standard dialing format (for example, 14085556666 for domestic, 0118251864489 for international), but a peering partner A requires E.164 format (for example, +14085556666, +8251864489) and a peering partner B requires another format (for example, 4085556666, 8251864489). In the SIP protocol, these numbers are located in the Request-URI, From, To headers as in the following example. The other party not supporting this format will have a parsing error and return an error message.

```
INVITE sip:0118251864489@domain.com SIP/2.0
From: 14084003020 <sip:14084003020@domain.com>;tag=498560566
To: <sip: 0118251864489@domain.com>
```

It is possible that a VoIP server (for example, Softswitch) may apply different translation rules to each peering partner when routing the call. However, it will be more efficient for VoIP servers to use a unified format in the core network, and an SBC applies different rules to the peer interface, which gives the following benefits:

- Reduces complexity of handling multiple formats in core network.

- Saves processing resources in a core routing engine.

- Updating the translation rule does not affect the core routing engine.

- Makes it easier to apply different rules because an SBC generally has a separate interface (logically or physically) with each peering partner.

QoS Marking

One of the well-known techniques to provide QoS in VoIP networks is marking the type of service (ToS) byte in the IP headers to guarantee bandwidth for VoIP packets. The six most significant bits of the ToS byte, called the Differentiated Services Code Point (DSCP), can be used to differentiate the priority by marking them. This is a simple and efficient method of packet classification as long as the network nodes can recognize and differentiate them (for example, using a priority queue).

If an SBC at the border can mark the bits and send them to the access network, it is a big benefit especially for enterprise customers who have their own voice and data network. It is also beneficial for peer and core networks if their network nodes handle both real-time and non-real-time (for example, email) traffic at the same time.

Now that you are aware of the key functions of SBC, the next section looks at how to design secure service architecture with SBC.

Service Architecture Design

Designing VoIP service architecture with an SBC is a considerably broad topic in terms of implementing a variety of service requirements. Because it is not possible to cover every single case, this section focuses on the most common ones and provides the architecture guidelines at a high level. It will break down the topic into five different categories as follows:

- High availability

- Network connectivity
- Service analysis
- Virtualization
- Optimization

NOTE   Some SBC products may not have enough features or interfaces to implement all of the guidelines that this section covers.

High Availability

At the initial stage of VoIP service, people believed that VoIP service is much less stable than legacy PSTN service providing generally five 9s (99.999 percent availability), and hesitated to use it despite many advantages. It might be unfair to compare with the legacy system that has been stabilized for more than 100 years, but people are already used to it and expect that high level of availability. The techniques of providing high availability in VoIP have been developed fast, and some of them have demonstrated carrier-grade high availability recently.

SBC products providing carrier-grade high availability should have the following capability:

- Detect critical failure in the primary system and switchover to the backup (or secondary) system automatically
- Maintain current call sessions (for example, session timer, call state, and media state) in the backup system, as well as not losing them in the event of a primary system failure
- Preserve call detail records (CDR) even after the switchover
- Minimize the failover time (less than 60 ms)
- Should not drop new call requests while switching over
- Notify any failure of primary or backup system to a system administrator in real time (for example, using SNMP trap)
- Recover the primary system failure automatically (for example, auto reboot) after handing over its role to the backup system
- Should not affect network topology (for example, no change of IP address) while switching over

There are two different models for high availability: Active-Standby and Active-Active. Both have pros and cons, and can be chosen according to service model, policy, network capacity plan or Service Level Agreement (SLA), and so on.

The following sections give the details of each model.

Active-Standby

Active-Standby is a common model in which the primary system is active and the backup is standby; that is, only the primary handles all signals and media. The backup has to be fully synchronized with the primary in real time and maintain all call information in order to provide seamless backup service. Figure 8-10 illustrates simply the service model.

Figure 8-10   *Active-Standby Model*

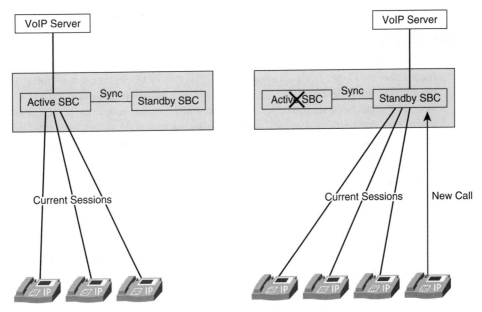

Note that the phones having active sessions or making new calls cannot recognize the failover, which is transparent.

Not only 1:1 (Active:Standby) mapping as shown in Figure 8-10, but also n:1 mapping is possible (multiple active nodes and single standby node), depending on the service model.

The Active-Standby model requires specific features and network connectivity between the pair of SBCs. Here are the characteristics:

- The pair of SBCs should use the same IP address and VLAN.

   This arrangement provides the transparency of IP connection from endpoints. It is recommended to use shared "virtual" IP address.

- The pair of SBCs should use the same Media Access Control (MAC) address.

  It is possible to provide transparency even with different MAC addresses, but using the same "virtual" MAC address can minimize the failover time.

- There should be a dedicated physical connection between the pair of SBCs.

  This is not only for checking out the heartbeat, but also synchronizing current call information.

- The pair of SBCs should have the same capacity (bandwidth and system resources).
- The pair of SBCs should have the same configuration.

The pros of this model are, as mentioned, being able to provide seamless and transparent service even after failover. However, the cons include wasting system resources; the standby system is just waiting without taking any call even when the active system is overloaded, that is, the standby is not involved in load-balancing. Also, real-time synchronization and heartbeat monitoring require additional resources.

Active-Active

Active-Active is another way of providing high availability by deploying multiple (typically, two) SBCs in parallel. The SBCs in the group are always active and have the same configuration with different network addresses, which means that endpoints are able to access any one of them. Whenever any failure happens on an SBC, the others take over the service. The endpoints decide the alternative based on their initial configuration. Figure 8-11 illustrates simply the service model.

The characteristics compared with the Active-Standby model are summarized as follows:

- It optimizes network and system resources because no standby node exists.
- The SBCs in the group do not have to have the same capacity.
- Current call sessions in the failed node will be dropped, and also new call attempts to this node will be rejected.
- The endpoints decide the alternative SBC when the current connection fails.
- There is no synchronization of call state between SBC nodes.

Despite the benefit of optimizing resources, the Active-Active model is not commonly used for large-scaled VoIP service because of the large number of call drops.

The next section shows how to design network connectivity to provide secure VoIP service.

Figure 8-11 *Active-Active Model*

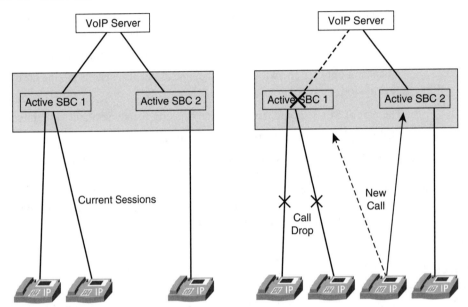

Network Connectivity

The question of

- A pair of SBCs is located at the border of the access and peer networks.
- The Active-Standby model is used for high availability.
- Each SBC has two physical network interfaces for VoIP service.
- Each SBC has the capability of setting up a VLAN on each interface.
- Each SBC has two additional interfaces; one for management and the other for synchronization (or heartbeat).
- Layer 2 switching and Layer 3 routing infrastructure are ready to use.

Figure 8-12 illustrates network Layer 2 and 3 connectivity (with high availability [HA]) with a pair of SBCs, focusing on high availability and efficient traffic control.

Figure 8-12 *Network Connectivity with HA*

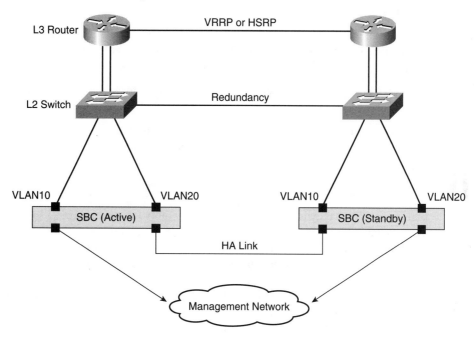

Here is the analysis of Figure 8-12:

1 Two Ethernet interfaces of each SBC are connected to its own Layer 2 Switch with separate IP subnet and VLAN; VLAN 10 for Outside network (access and peer) and VLAN 20 for Inside network (core).

2 The traffic segregation with different VLAN trunk makes it efficient to apply different policies such as bandwidth allocation, DoS threshold, access control, and so on.

3 An Active and Standby SBC share "virtual" IP and MAC address on the two Ethernet interfaces for high availability, which is similar to Virtual Router Redundancy Protocol (VRRP; see the following Note).

4 When a switchover happens due to network or system failure, the Standby SBC sends out Address Resolution Protocol (ARP) messages to the corresponding switch to obtain Layer 2 binding.

5 During the switchover, existing sessions are not interrupted because the MAC and IP addresses are still alive to the upstream router.

6 The pair of Layer 3 routers provides a fault-tolerant default gateway by means of a redundancy protocol, such as VRRP or Hot Standby Router Protocol (HSRP, Cisco proprietary).

7 There is an HA link between an Active and Standby for synchronizing state and detecting heartbeat.

8 There is another Ethernet port for management, which goes to a dedicated management network for monitoring, troubleshooting, maintaining, and so on.

NOTE   As defined in RFC 3768,[2] Virtual Router Redundancy Protocol (VRRP) specifies an election protocol that dynamically assigns responsibility for a virtual router to one of the VRRP routers on a LAN. The VRRP router controlling the IP address associated with a virtual router is called the Master, and forwards packets sent to these IP addresses. The election process provides dynamic failover in the forwarding responsibility should the Master become unavailable. This allows any of the virtual router IP addresses on the LAN to be used as the default first-hop router by end-hosts. The advantage gained from using VRRP is a higher-availability default path without requiring configuration of dynamic routing or router discovery protocols on every end-host.

Note that, in this design, there is no fixed active or standby node even though the name is assigned in the figure for simplicity. Whichever takes current calls is an Active SBC and the other is a Standby. It switches after a failover.

The next section provides

Service Policy Analysis

Before deploying an SBC, you need to analyze current VoIP service and decide what policies should be applied. The policy depends on the type of media (voice, video), protocol (SIP, H.323), QoS (low, high), endpoint (managed, unmanaged), peering partner (IP handoff, PSTN termination), and so on.

There can be many types of policies. Some of them are exemplified in Table 8-1 with their attributes.

Table 8-1   *Service Policy and Attribute*

Service Policy	Attributes
Media Policy	Media type (audio, video, IM, and data)
	Media bandwidth allocation per call (or per network)
	Codec assignment (G.711, G.729, and iLBC)
	Average rate limit
	Maximum rate limit
	Transport protocol (UDP, TCP)
	Media IP/port allocation
	Media anchoring for NAT Traversal
	Maximum flow time
	Media inactive timer (to drop hung calls)
	QoS marking (TOS/DiffServ)
	Maximum latency, jitter, and packet loss
Signal Policy	Signaling protocol (SIP, H.323, and MGCP)
	Transport protocol (UDP, TCP)
	Signal IP/port allocation
	Registration interval
	Ping method and timer
	Call session timer
	Minimum and maximum message length
	Maximum number of signals per second
	Invalid signal threshold
	Error handling (response code)
Routing Policy	Source and destination address
	Next hop (primary and secondary route path)
	Static or dynamic routing
	Time of effectiveness (start/end time, days of week, and holidays)
	Cost of route (least-cost routing)
	Codec preference for each route
	Maximum number of route recursion
	Transport method (UDP, TCP)
	Trunk group

continues

Table 8-1   *Service Policy and Attribute (Continued)*

Service Policy	Attributes
Access Control Policy	ACL
	Source and destination address
	Signaling protocol
	Transport protocol
	Restriction method (denying or limiting bandwidth)
	Denying or limiting period
	Trust threshold
	Trust level for each group of CPE
	Trust level for each peering partner

You can break down the policies in Table 8-1, and create a detailed policy group; for example, each VoIP protocol can have its own signal policy.

Other policies, such as authentication, call admission control, recovery, license, number translation, or protocol interworking, may be defined depending on the scope of service.

These polices are applied to each logical interface on an SBC with different values of attributes according to the target service plan. The logical interface is segregated by many factors, such as the following examples:

- Type of network (core vs. access/peer network)
- Type of access network (managed vs. unmanaged)
- Type of peering network (IP handoff vs. PSTN termination)
- VoIP protocol (SIP vs. H.323)
- Network bandwidth (T1 vs. T3)
- Type of media (voice vs. video)
- Target QoS (low vs. high quality)
- Type of core network element (Softswitch vs. media gateway)

Here are examples of applying policies to the logical interface:

Interface A:

    — Facing "unmanaged" access network with limited bandwidth

Policy A:

- Low trust level (the access network is relatively not secure)

- Limited number of signals per session (high possibility of misbehaving CPE or flooding attack)
- Short registration interval (keep NAT pinhole open)
- Short keepalive timer
- UDP transport protocol (reduces system resources)
- SIP signaling protocol
- Restricted size of SIP message (prevents malicious messages)
- Strict invalid signal threshold (prevents any malformed messages)
- Low bit-rate codec, G.729 (requires lower bandwidth)
- Anchoring media (for NAT traversal)
- QoS marking (for access network)

Interface B:

— Facing peer network for call termination (IP handoff)

Policy B:

- High trust level (relatively secure network)
- Limited number of signals per session
- Long registration interval
- Long keepalive timer
- UDP transport and SIP signaling protocol
- Restricted size of SIP message
- Strict invalid signal threshold
- High bit-rate codec, G.711
- No anchoring media
- No QoS marking (dedicated line is used)

The preceding example is just a simple guideline. The actual planning of service policy would be more complicated depending on the complexity of service.

The next section shows how to provide secure VoIP service by virtualizing SBC.

Virtualization

Virtualizing SBC is a technique of dividing a single SBC into multiple virtual (or logical) SBCs, named Virtual SBC (VSBC), in order to segregate traffic among the different services used in VoIP network. It provides simplicity of managing SBCs, and efficiency of applying different policies.

Each VSBC consists of two logical interfaces; one for the core network and the other for access (or peer) network. Figure 8-13 shows the example of virtualization with multiple VSBCs in an SBC. Note that this design approach may not be applicable to certain SBC products.

Figure 8-13 *Virtualization of SBC 1*

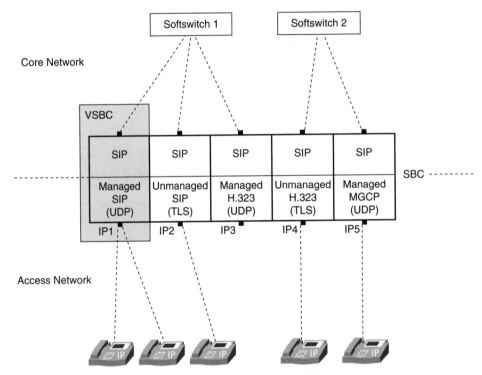

In Figure 8-13, there are five different VSBCs with two interfaces for access and core network, which looks as if there are five different SBCs. Each VSBC handles a different protocol, different type of CPE, and different security option. For example, whenever a CPE connects to IP1, the traffic (signal and media) goes to Softswitch1 through VSBC1, after being manipulated based on the policy.

It requires transcoding if a VSBC has two different protocol interfaces; for example, if a call goes to IP3 in Figure 8-13, it is transcoded between SIP and H.323.

This design is applied to the peering network as well, as shown in Figure 8-14.

The method of virtualization makes it much easier for you to design the service architecture, especially globalized VoIP service with multiprotocol, multivendors, and multiservers.

The next section shows how to optimize and secure traffic flow with SBC.

Figure 8-14   *Virtualization of SBC 2*

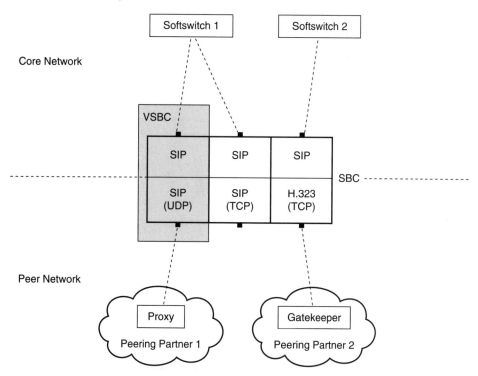

Optimization of Traffic Flow

An SBC controls the flow of VoIP traffic (signal and media) by anchoring or releasing it. How to design the traffic flow is a key to providing secure and cost-effective service. You can see some sample cases in this section so that you may understand the role of an SBC.

Deployment Location

First of all, think about the physical location of an SBC. Of course, the physical location might not be significant because it could be anywhere around the world as long as it has stable IP connectivity. However, generally, the physical distance is relative to the latency of traffic because packets pass by more network nodes (that is, more latency) if the distance is longer. The latency tends to come with packet loss or jitter as well.

Figure 8-15 illustrates an example of wrong deployment that does not consider the latency; a User A in Los Angeles makes a call to a local pizza store through an SBC located at a data center in New York.

Figure 8-15 *Wrong Deployment Location*

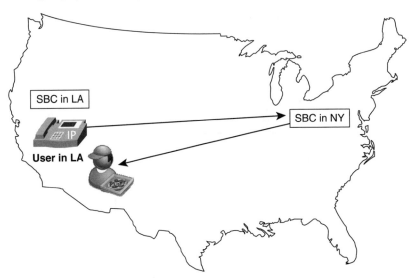

Therefore, either one of the following ways is recommended to minimize the latency:

- Configure CPE to connect the nearest SBC when provisioning them (static assignment).

- All CPE connect initially to a redirect server and receive the IP/port address of the corresponding SBC (it is possible to recognize the physical location of CPE based on its IP subnet).

Media Control

The signals always go through either access SBC or peer SBC providing topology hiding, but the media is either anchored (relayed) or released depending on the optimization of service architecture. It may waste network and system resources if an SBC always anchors media (unconditionally). Figure 8-16 is an example of unnecessary media anchoring; User A makes a call to User B in the same company through access SBC.

In Figure 8-16, because both parties are in the same company network, there is no issue of point-to-point media connection, actually, which gives better quality of service without any security issues. How does the SBC know that both are in the same network? It can be determined either from the same IP subnet or the same group of phone numbers.

Peer SBC also has the same mechanism of releasing media. For example, if a call session comes from and goes to the same peering network, peer SBC may release the media depending on the service agreement with the peering partner.

Figure 8-16   *Unnecessary Media Anchoring*

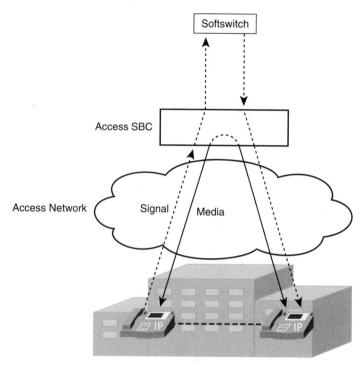

There can be four different models of media traversal with access and peer SBC:

- **Media anchoring in both access and peer SBC**—This is a typical service model that provides high-security architecture with topology hiding. Both access and peer network cannot see each other's network, not to mention the core network. Figure 8-17 illustrates the model with simple signal (SIP) and media traversal.

  Keep in mind that the access and peer SBCs are logical entities of an SBC, as mentioned before, so they can be within the same physical SBC or a separate SBC.

  Another benefit of this model is that it gives full control of signal and media so that an SBC can manipulate them, such as transcoding, QoS marking, DTMF interworking or RTCP control, and so on. Also, this model provides an easier interface for lawful interception (CALEA).

  However, the downside is that it consumes relatively high system resources (for example, CPU, memory) and network bandwidth, especially in a core network. It requires cautious routing policy and location design of both SBCs; otherwise, it may cause a serious latency issue.

Figure 8-17   *Media Traversal Through Access and Peer SBCs*

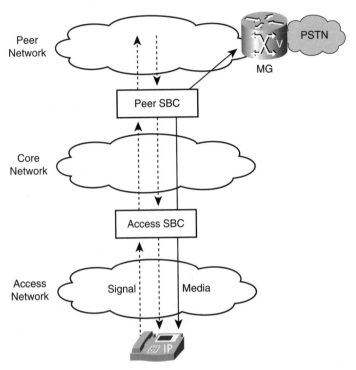

- **Media anchoring only in access SBC**—This model is generally used where the service provider has its own termination network (for example, managing time-division multiplexing [TDM] media gateways), or the peering partner does not require "strict routing." The strict routing means that inbound/outbound traffic (signal and media) has to come and go through a fixed IP address. In other words, the source and destination IP address between peer and core network is already fixed, that is, the service provider cannot terminate a call with a different source IP address. Some peering providers require this strict routing for security and performance purpose.

  Figure 8-18 illustrates the model. Stable and secure IP connectivity between core and peer network is necessary in this model.

Figure 8-18   *Media Traversal Only Through Access SBC*

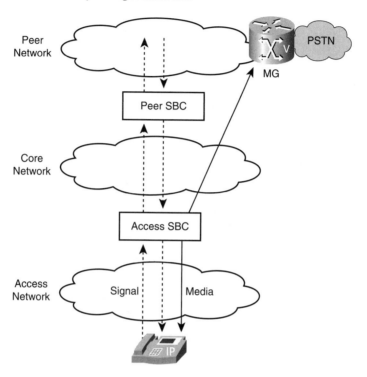

This model consumes fewer resources than the full anchoring model and provides the same security level to the access network that is most vulnerable. It is easier to design the routing architecture, especially to the peering network.

However, it exposes part of the core network topology to peering partner. It can be vulnerable to any malicious attack coming from the peering network, such as malformed messages or flooded DoS. So, it is necessary to confirm that the peering partner maintains a secure enough network.

- **Media anchoring only in peer SBC**—This model is not commonly used, but could be used where the service provider manages its own access network and controls CPE, assuming that all traffic from them is secure enough. Figure 8-19 shows media traversal only through peer SBC.

Figure 8-19 *Media Traversal Only Through Peer SBC*

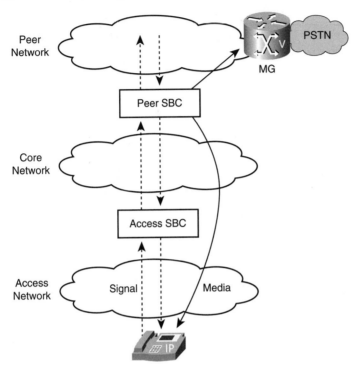

This model reduces the usage of resources and provides high security protection to the peering network.

However, it has a potential security issue because the topology of the core network is exposed to end users. It is very complicated to provide the feature of lawful interception (CALEA) in this model.

- **No media anchoring**—In this model, the media channel is opened end-to-end without going through an SBC. It is not commonly used, but could be used where the service provider manages both access and termination network, or carries only signals because of limited bandwidth or system resource.

  This model saves significant resources, but exposes a variety of security issues related to media and also restricts QoS control.

In this section, you have learned how to design secure VoIP service architecture with SBC, in terms of high availability, network connectivity, service policy analysis, virtualization, and optimization of

Summary

An SBC is a controlling device located in a logical boundary of a VoIP network in order to resolve border issues, such as DoS, call flooding, exposed network topology, traversing NAT/Firewall, codec conflict, lawful interception, QoS, and so on.

VoIP service providers can deploy two logically separated SBCs—access and peer SBC—in their service network depending on where the SBC is located.

The access SBC is located on the border between the service provider's core network and access network in order to deal with the border issues. Because the VoIP traffic comes from an unmanaged public network, the access SBC should have a strict policy for DoS attacks, flooded calls, malformed messages, and spoofed calls. Moreover, it should have the capability to apply the policy to individual users/devices without affecting other devices.

The peer SBC is located on the border between the service provider's core network and peer network in order to deal with border issues. Because the traffic comes from a relatively safe network, typically through a VoIP trunk, it does not require strict policy as much as access SBCs do. It should have the capability to apply different policies to different peer networks.

The primary function of SBC is network topology hiding; it encapsulates the core network and provides a single logical interface for external networks. The external endpoints can see only the IP address and port of SBC rather than actual VoIP servers, and the SBC routes the call to the corresponding server based on ToS, policy, protocol, and so on.

For DoS protection, SBC provides the function of policy-driven access control by categorizing VoIP traffic; white, black, and gray traffic (or endpoints). The method of judging the category is based on authentication, number of messages per second, number of call attempts per second, number of invalid (or malformed) messages, maximum bandwidth consumption per call, and so on.

The typical way to prevent overload with SBC is reducing redundant or unnecessary signals by controlling the frequency of messages, such as registration timer control or ping timer control. SBC also can distribute the load to multiple targets (for example, VoIP servers) based on the policy.

SBC also provides the function of NAT traversal by replacing a private IP of endpoint with either SBCs or NATed IP.

Lawful interception is another function of SBC that sees most of the signals and media going back and forth among endpoints and VoIP servers as an access device.

Other functions of SBC are protocol conversion, transcoding, number translation, QoS marking, and so on.

When designing VoIP service architecture with an SBC, you should consider high availability, network connectivity, service policy, virtualization, and deployment location for secure and optimized service.

End Notes

1 RFC 3261, "SIP (Session Initiation Protocol)," J. Rosenberg, H. Schulzrinne, G. Camarillo, A. Johnston, J. Peterson, R. Sparks, M. Handley, and E. Schooler, June 2002.

2 RFC 3768, "Virtual Router Redundancy Protocol (VRRP)," R. Hinden, ed., April 2004.

References

draft-ietf-sipping-sbc-funcs-05.txt, "Requirements from SIP Session Border Control Deployments," G. Camarillo, R. Penfield, A. Hawrylyshen, M. Bhatia, March 2008.

RFC 3264, "An Offer/Answer Model with the Session Description Protocol (SDP)," J. Rosenberg, H. Schulzrinne, June 2002.

RFC 5128, "State of Peer-to-Peer (P2P) Communication Across Network Address Translators," P. Srisuresh, B. Ford, D. Kegel, March 2008.

This chapter covers the methodology of protection with the following network devices in enterprise VoIP networks:

- Firewall
- Cisco Unified Communications Manager (Unified CM)
- Cisco Unified Communications Manager Express (Unified CME)
- Access device: IP phone
- Access device: Multilayer switch

CHAPTER 9

Protection with Enterprise Network Devices

Most network devices in an enterprise VoIP network have their own security features. Some devices (for example, a firewall) have strong capability with sophisticated features, and some devices (for example, an IP phone) have very limited capability.

As mentioned in previous chapters, there is no magic bullet—a single device or architecture that can protect the whole VoIP service network securely. The best practice is analyzing current vulnerability and applying a consolidated solution that includes all possible network devices and architectures.

This chapter demonstrates how to protect the enterprise VoIP network with the following devices. For practical information, products from Cisco Systems will be demonstrated, which are largely deployed around the world.

- Firewall
- Cisco Unified Communications Manager (Unified CM, formerly CallManager)
- Cisco Unified Communications Manager Express (Unified CME, formerly CallManager Express)
- Access device: IP phone
- Access device: Multilayer switch

Rather than specifying every security feature of those products, the chapter focuses on key features and their usage. The content refers to Cisco Unified Communications SRND.[1]

Firewall

There are two types of firewall in terms of capability of recognizing VoIP protocols: legacy and VoIP-aware firewalls. The legacy firewall handles packets only in the network and transport layers, and does not care what protocol is going through in the application layer. However, the VoIP-aware firewall has additional capability to inspect and manipulate VoIP packets in the application layer for secure service. This section describes the function and usage of the VoIP-aware firewall (shortening the name to just "firewall").

An Access Control List (ACL) is a primary method of a firewall to protect VoIP servers and media gateways from external devices that are not supposed to communicate with them. Using ACL for VoIP traffic is not simple because the media ports used by entities change dynamically based on the call setup. You may use a static configuration, such as a certain range being always opened or blocked, but it creates a potential vulnerability.

In general, an endpoint and a server are using the client/server model for signaling for call setup, and the media channel between endpoints is established directly; that is, end-to-end. If the call signaling did not go through the firewall, the media stream cannot pass through it because the firewall does not know which media ports need to be opened.

Because a firewall handles a large amount of traffic by nature, capabilities and performance need to be taken into account. Performance includes the amount of latency, which the firewall can increase if it is under high load or even under attack. The general rule in VoIP deployment is to keep the CPU usage less than 60 percent for normal usage. If the CPU usage goes up more than 60 percent, especially in sustained high usage, the quality of service (QoS) will degrade and phones will start to unregister. When this happens, the phones will attempt to reregister with a VoIP server, which increases the load on the firewall even more.

There are many ways to deploy firewalls for secure networks. This section focuses on Cisco ASA, PIX, and FWSM (see the following Note) in the Active-Standby mode in both routed and transparent scenarios. Figure 9-1 illustrates the Active-Standby mode for redundancy purposes.

Figure 9-1 *Active-Standby Mode of Firewall*

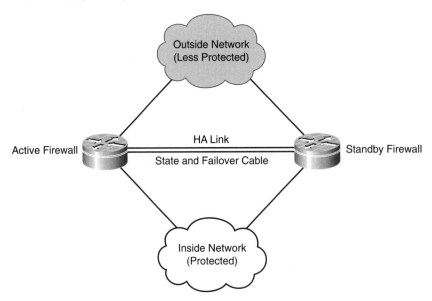

NOTE	Cisco ASA, PIX, and FWSM are defined as follows:
	Cisco ASA (Adaptive Security Appliance) is a new appliance of a firewall providing the capability of PIX firewall plus the flexibility to add other advanced security, such as IPS, Anti-X, and Virtual Private Network (VPN). It could take the place of three separate Cisco security devices: PIX Firewall, VPN 3000 Series, and IPS 4000 Series Sensor. Model numbers are in the 5500 Series.
	Cisco PIX (Private Internet Exchange) is a dedicated hardware firewall delivering application policy enforcement, multivector attack protection, and secure connectivity services. It runs a PIX operating system that is slightly different from the typical Cisco IOS. Model numbers are in the 500 Series.
	Cisco FWSM (Firewall Services Module) is a software module for Catalyst 6500 Series Switches and 7600 Series Routers, providing fast firewall data rates: 5-Gbps throughput, 100,000 connections per second (CPS) and 1M concurrent connections. Up to four FWSMs can be installed in a single chassis, providing scalability to 20 Gbps per chassis.

All of the Cisco firewalls can run in either multiple-context or single-context mode. In single-context mode, the firewall is a single firewall that controls all traffic flowing through it. In multiple-context mode, the firewalls can be turned into many virtual firewalls, which is the same concept as a Virtual Session Border Controller (VSBC; see Chapter 8). Each of these contexts or virtual firewalls has its own configurations and can be controlled by different groups or administrators. Each time a new context is added to a firewall, it will increase the load and memory requirements on the firewall.

Both the Cisco ASA and PIX firewalls operate in a different manner than the Cisco FWSM. Within an ASA and PIX, as long as there is no ACL on a more trusted interface, all traffic from that interface is trusted and allowed out to a less-trusted interface. When any ACL is applied to the more trusted interface on an ASA/PIX, all other traffic is denied and the firewall will then function very much like the FWSM.

ASA and PIX Firewalls

There are two types of operation mode in ASA and PIX: routed and transparent mode. Each mode targets different service with pros and cons.

Routed Mode

The ASA or PIX firewall in routed mode acts as a router between connected networks, and each interface requires an IP address on a different subnet. In single-context mode, the routed firewall supports Open Shortest Path First (OSPF) and Routing Information Protocol (RIP) in passive mode. Multiple-context mode supports static routes only. ASA version 8.x also supports Enhanced Interior Gateway Routing (EIGRP). Cisco recommends using the advanced routing capabilities of the upstream and downstream routers instead of relying on the security appliance for extensive routing needs.

The routed ASA or PIX supports QoS, Network Address Translation (NAT), and VPN termination to the ASA, which are not supported in the transparent mode. Figure 9-1 shows the logical placement of firewalls for both routed and transparent configurations in Active-Standby mode. With the routed configuration, each interface on the ASA or PIX would have an IP address.

Unlike with transparent mode, the device can be seen in the network and, because of that, it can be a point of attack.

Placing a routed ASA or PIX in a network changes the network routing because some of the routing can be done by the firewall. IP addresses must also be available for all the interfaces on the firewall, so changing the IP addresses of the routers in the network might also be required. If a routing protocol is to be allowed through the ASA or PIX firewall, an ACL will have to be put on the inside (or most trusted) interface to allow that traffic to pass to the outside (or less trusted) interface. That ACL must also define all other traffic that will be allowed out of the most trusted interface.

Transparent Mode

The ASA or PIX firewall can be configured to be a Layer 2 firewall (also known as "bump in the wire" or "stealth firewall"). In this configuration, the firewall does not have an IP address (other than for management proposes), and all of the transactions are done at Layer 2 of the network.

Even though the firewall acts as a bridge, Layer 3 traffic cannot pass through the security appliance unless you explicitly permit it with an extended access list. The only traffic allowed without an access list is Address Resolution Protocol (ARP) traffic.

This configuration has the advantage that an attacker cannot see the firewall because it is not doing any dynamic routing. Static routing is required to make the firewall work even in transparent mode. This configuration also makes it easier to place the firewall into an existing network because routing does not have to change for the firewall.

It also makes the firewall easier to manage and debug because it is not doing any routing within the firewall. Because the firewall is not processing routing requests, the performance of the firewall is usually somewhat higher with inspect commands and overall traffic than the same firewall model and software that is doing routing.

However, you are unable to use NAT on the firewall. If you are going to pass data for routing, you will also have to define the ACLs both inside and outside the firewall to allow traffic, unlike with the same firewall in routed mode. Cisco Discovery Protocol (CDP) traffic will not pass through the device even if it is defined. Each directly connected network must be on the same subnet. You cannot share interfaces between contexts; if you plan on running multiple-context mode, you will have to use additional interfaces. You must define all non-IP traffic, such as routing protocols, with an ACL to allow that traffic through the firewall. QoS is not supported in transparent mode. Multicast traffic can be allowed to go through the firewall with an extended ACL, but it is not a multicast device. Also, the firewall does not support VPN termination other than for the management interface.

If a routing protocol or RSVP is to be allowed through the ASA or PIX firewall, an ACL will have to be put on the inside (or most trusted) interface to allow that traffic to pass to the outside (or lesser trusted) interfaces. That ACL must also define all other traffic that will be allowed out of the most trusted interface.

TLS Proxy Feature

The Transport Layer Security (TLS) proxy feature adds the capability for an ASA firewall to perform inspection of encrypted Skinny Call Control Protocol (SCCP) signaling.

When an endpoint device is configured for encrypted signaling, an Application Layer Gateway (ALG; see Note) is unable to perform functions such as NAT fix-up because it is unable to inspect the signaling. The TLS proxy feature allows the ASA to participate in the TLS session over which the signaling is sent, and the ASA is then able to decode the signaling stream, perform any necessary fix-up, and then re-encrypt the signaling.

NOTE   Application Layer Gateways (or Application Level Gateways) are, as defined in RFC 2663,[2] application-specific translation agents that allow an application on a host in one address realm to connect to its counterpart running on a host in a different realm transparently. An ALG may interact with NAT to set up state, use NAT state information, modify application-specific payload, and perform whatever else is necessary to get the application running across disparate address realms.

ALGs may not always utilize NAT state information. They may glean application payload and simply notify NAT to add additional state information in some cases. ALGs are similar to proxies, in that both ALGs and proxies facilitate application-specific communication between clients and servers. Proxies use a special protocol to communicate with proxy clients and relay client data to servers and vice versa. Unlike proxies, ALGs do not use a special protocol to communicate with application clients and do not require changes to application clients.

When the ASA firewall is placed between an IP phone and the Unified CM to which it is registered, the TLS proxy is inserted into the TLS session. A phone with encrypted signaling uses TLS as a transport between itself and Unified CM. When the TLS proxy is involved, there are two TLS sessions for each phone registration, one between the phone and the ASA and the second between the ASA and Unified CM.

The ASA is the only firewall with an ALG that has a controlled method to allow a call with encrypted signaling to work, because it is able to inspect that signaling.

When a VPN design is not the desired solution for securing remote phones, the ASA can provide an alternative method of securing those devices.

The TLS proxy is added as a trusted entity to the Certificate Trust List (CTL) that is used by the phones. The CTL file is allowed to contain 16 entries, which include all servers that need to have a trust relationship with the phones. Therefore, the number of TLS proxies configured to work with a given cluster is limited by the number of free entries in the CTL.

Configuration Example

Example 9-1 is a configuration example listing the ports and inspect commands that are used to make the firewalls work with voice for ASA and PIX software Release 7.04. This is an example only, and you should review the ports list from all the applications that are used in your network before deploying any firewall. This configuration example shows only the voice sections.

Example 9-1 *Configuration Example of ASA and PIX*

```
!
object-group service remote-access tcp
description remote access
!Windows terminal
port-object range 3389 3389
!VNC
port-object range 5800 5800
!VNC
port-object range 5900 5900
port-object range 8080 8080
port-object eq ssh
!SSH
port-object eq ftp-data
!FTP data transport
port-object eq www
!HTTP Access
port-object eq ftp
!FTP
port-object eq https
!HTTPS Access
object-group service voice-protocols-tcp tcp
description TCP voice protocols
!CTI/QBE
port-object range 2428 2428
!SIP communication
port-object eq ctiqbe
!SCCP
port-object range 2000 2000
!Secure SCCP
```

Example 9-1   *Configuration Example of ASA and PIX (Continued)*

```
port-object range 2443 2443
object-group service voice-protocols-udp udp
!TFTP
port-object eq tftp
!MGCP Signaling
port-object range 2427 2427
!DNS
port-object eq domain
!RAS
port-object range 1719 1719
!SIP
!Object Group applied for remote-access
access-list OUTSIDE extended permit tcp any any object-group remote-access
!Object Group applied for voice-protocols-tcp
access-list OUTSIDE extended permit tcp any any object-group voice-protocols-tcp
!Object Group applied for voice-protocols-udp
access-list OUTSIDE extended permit udp any any object-group voice-protocols-udp
! Object Group applied for remote-access
access-list inside_access_in extended permit tcp any any object-group remote-access
! Object Group applied for voice-protocols-tcp
access-list inside_access_in extended permit tcp any any object-group voice-
    protocols-tcp
! Object Group applied for voice-protocols-udp
access-list inside_access_in extended permit udp any any object-group voice-
    protocols-udp
!Failover config
ip address 172.19.245.3 255.255.255.248 standby 172.19.245.4
failover
failover lan unit primary
failover lan interface failover GigabitEthernet0/3
failover polltime unit 1 holdtime 3
!Lowest and fastest setting for failover
failover polltime interface 3
failover link failover_state GigabitEthernet0/2
failover interface ip failover 192.168.1.1 255.255.255.0 standby 192.168.1.2
failover interface ip failover_state 192.168.0.1 255.255.255.0 standby 192.168.0.2
!
!Default inspection with inspects enabled
class-map inspection_default
match default-inspection-traffic
!
!
policy-map global_policy
class inspection_default
inspect h323 h225
inspect h323 ras
inspect skinny
inspect sip
inspect tftp
inspect mgcp
```

Now that you are aware of ASA and PIX firewalls, the next section looks at another type of firewall, FWSM.

FWSM Firewall

Cisco FWSM is a software module for Catalyst 6500 Series Switches and 7600 Series Routers, as mentioned before. Here are the usages of FWSM based on routed and transparent mode, as well as a configuration example.

Routed Mode

In routed mode, the FWSM is considered to be a router hop in the network. It performs NAT between connected networks and can use OSPF or passive RIP (in single-context mode). Routed mode supports up to 256 interfaces per context or in single mode, with a maximum of 1,000 interfaces divided between all contexts.

Unlike the transparent mode, the routed device is visible in the network and, because of that, it can be a point of attack. To place the device in a network, IP addressing and routing must be changed.

Transparent Mode

In transparent mode, the FWSM acts like a "bump in the wire," or a "stealth firewall," and is not a router hop. The FWSM connects the same network on its inside and outside interfaces, but each interface must be on a different VLAN. No dynamic routing protocols or NAT are required. However, like routed mode, transparent mode also requires ACLs to allow traffic to pass through. Transparent mode can also optionally use EtherType ACLs to allow non-IP traffic. Transparent mode supports only two interfaces, an inside interface and an outside interface.

You might use a transparent firewall to simplify your network configuration. Transparent mode is also useful if you want the firewall to be invisible to attackers. You can also use a transparent firewall for traffic that would otherwise be blocked in routed mode. For example, a transparent firewall can allow multicast streams using an EtherType ACL.

To avoid loops when you use failover in transparent mode, you must use switch software that supports Bridge Protocol Data Unit (BPDU) forwarding, and you must configure the FWSM to allow BPDUs.

Transparent mode does not support NAT, dynamic routing, or a unicast Reverse Path Forwarding (RPF) check.

NOTE   For information on BPDU and RPF, refer to Cisco.com.

Configuration Example

Example 9-2 is a configuration example listing the ports and inspect commands that are used to make the firewall work with voice for FWSM software Release 2.3.x. This is only an example, and you should review the ports list from all the applications that are used in your network before deploying any firewall. This configuration example shows only the voice sections.

Example 9-2   *Configuration Example of FWSM*

```
!
fixup protocol h323 H225 1720
!Enable fixup h3232 h225
fixup protocol h323 ras 1718-1719
!Enable fixup h323 RAS
fixup protocol mgcp 2427
!Enable fixup mgcp
fixup protocol skinny 2000
!Enable fixup
fixup protocol tftp 69
!Enable fixup
object-group service VoiceProtocols tcp
description Unified CM Voice protocols
port-object eq ctiqbe
port-object eq 2000
port-object eq 3224
port-object eq 2443
port-object eq 2428
port-object eq h323
!Defining the ports for TCP voice
object-group service VoiceProtocolsUDP udp
description UDP based Voice Protocols
port-object range 2427 2427
port-object range 1719 1719
port-object eq tftp
!Defining the ports for UDP voice
object-group service RemoteAccess tcp
description Remote Acces
port-object range 3389 3389
port-object range 5800 5809
port-object eq ssh
port-object range 5900 5900
port-object eq www
port-object eq https
!Defining remote access TCP ports
access-list inside_nat0_outbound extended permit ip any any
!
access-list phones_access_in extended permit tcp any any object-group RemoteAccess
   log
notifications interval 2
```

continues

Example 9-2 *Configuration Example of FWSM (Continued)*

```
access-list phones_access_in extended permit tcp any any object-group
  VoiceProtocols log
notifications interval 2
access-list phones_access_in extended permit udp any any object-group
  VoiceProtocolsUDP
log notifications interval 2
access-list phones_access_in extended deny ip any any log notifications interval 2
access-list outside_access_in extended permit tcp any any object-group
  VoiceProtocols log
notifications interval 2
access-list outside_access_in extended permit tcp any any object-group RemoteAccess
  log
notifications interval 2
access-list outside_access_in extended permit udp any any object-group
  VoiceProtocolsUDP
log notifications interval 2
!Access lists applying the object groups defined above for inside and outside
  interfaces
access-list outside_access_in extended deny ip any any log notifications interval 2
access-list inside_access_in extended deny ip any any
!Deny all other traffic
access-list phones_nat0_outbound extended permit ip any any
!
failover
failover lan unit primary
failover lan interface flan vlan 4050
failover polltime unit 1 holdtime 5
failover polltime interface 15
!Failover config - 15 seconds
failover interface-policy 50%
failover link flin vlan 4051
failover interface ip flan 1.1.1.1 255.255.255.252 standby 1.1.1.2
failover interface ip flin 1.1.1.5 255.255.255.252 standby 1.1.1.6
nat (inside) 0 access-list inside_nat0_outbound_V1
access-group outside_access_in in interface outside
access-group inside_access_in in interface inside
```

In this section so far, you have learned about ASA, PIX, and FWSM firewalls in terms of network architecture, usage, features, and configuration. The next section describes the limitations of using those firewalls.

Limitations

Not all IP telephony application servers or applications are supported through a firewall. Some applications that are not supported with firewalls or with an ALG in the firewall include Cisco Unity voicemail servers, Attendant Console, Cisco Unified Contact Center Enterprise, and Cisco Unified Contact Center Express. ACLs can be written for these applications to allow media and signaling traffic to flow through a firewall.

Versions of Cisco FWSM prior to version 3.0 do not support SCCP fragmentation. If an SCCP packet is fragmented from a phone, from Unified CM, or from a gateway to another IP telephony device, the fragmented packet will not be allowed through the FWSM. In cases where fragmentation occurs with an FWSM running version 2.x code, an ACL should be used without the ALG feature of the firewall for the signaling traffic. This configuration will allow the signaling traffic through the FWSM but will not do packet inspection as the signaling goes through the firewall.

If there are other applications that use the same port as SCCP (TCP 2000), those applications could be affected by the SCCP inspection. All traffic that is going to the SCCP TCP port will be inspected to see if it is SCCP traffic. If it is not SCCP traffic, it will be dropped.

To determine whether the applications running on your network are supported with the version of firewall in the network or if ACLs have to be written, refer to the appropriate application documentation available at Cisco.com.

Unified Communications Manager Express

The Unified CME (Cisco Unified Communications Manager Express, formerly CallManager Express) is a software module in Cisco IOS, providing telephony solutions to small to medium-size businesses. Typically, a Cisco router (for example, 2600 Series) has this module of CME and provides both data and voice service.

Like other Cisco IOS gateways, Unified CME supports the latest security features for small to medium-size enterprise VoIP networks to monitor and prevent malicious attacks or malfunctions of endpoints. The section focuses on the features and usage for your best practice. The contents refer to Cisco Unified CME Security.[3]

Access Control

Unified CME provides interfaces for system access locally and remotely. The system access control is the fundamental way of making VoIP service secure. The recommendation and command examples are listed as follows:

- Enable security and encrypt passwords

  Use **enable secret** to encrypt the enable password:

  ```
  enable secret <removed>
  no enable password
  ```

  The **enable secret** command takes precedence over the **enable password** command if both are configured.

  To increase security access, passwords can be encrypted to prevent any unauthorized users from viewing the passwords when packets are examined by protocol analyzers:

  ```
  Service password-encryption
  ```

- Create multiple privilege levels

  By default, Cisco IOS has two levels of access to commands: EXEC mode (level 1) and privileged EXEC mode (level 15), configuring up to 16 privilege levels (from 0, the most restricted level, to 15, the least restricted level) to protect the system from unauthorized access.

  ```
  Privilege mode level level
  Enable secret level level {0¦5} password string
  ```

- Restrict access to VTY

  Allow only certain users/locations to Telnet to the router via VTY by defining and applying an access list for permitting or denying remote Telnet sessions.

  ```
  line vty 0 4
  access-class 10 in
  access-list 10 permit 10.1.1.0 0.0.0.255
  ```

- Using AAA to secure access

  An authentication server can be used to validate user access to the system. The following commands allow an authentication, authorization, and accounting (AAA) server, Terminal Access Controller Access Control System Plus (TACACS+) server, to be used for authentication services.

  ```
  aaa new-model
  aaa authentication login default tacacs+ enable
  aaa authentication enable default tacacs+ enable
  ip tacacs source-interface Loopback0
  tacacs-server host 10.10.10.2
  tacacs-server host 10.10.10.10
  tacacs-server key xyz (defines the shared encryption key to be xyz)
  ```

- Command accounting/auditing on AAA

  The following commands use a TACACS+ server for command accounting and auditing purposes.

  ```
  aaa new-model
  aaa authentication login default tacacs+ enable
  (login uses TACACS+, if not available, use enable password)
  aaa authentication enable default tacacs+ enable
  aaa accounting command 1 start-stop tacacs+
  (runs accounting for commands at the specified privilege level 1)
  aaa accounting exec start-stop tacacs+
  ip tacacs source-interface Loopback0
  tacacs-server host 10.10.10.2
  tacacs-server host 10.10.10.10
  tacacs-server key xyz (defines the shared encryption key to be xyz)
  ```

  The sample command log shows the information contained in a TACACS+ command accounting record for privilege level 1.

  ```
  Wed Jun 25 03:46:47 1997 172.16.25.15 fgeorge tty3 5622329430/4327528 stop
  task_id=3 service=shell priv-lvl=1 cmd=show version <cr>
  Wed Jun 25 03:46:58 1997 172.16.25.15 fgeorge tty3 5622329430/4327528 stop
  task_id=4 service=shell priv-lvl=1 cmd=show interfaces Ethernet 0 <cr>
  Wed Jun 25 03:47:03 1997 172.16.25.15 fgeorge tty3 5622329430/4327528 stop
  task_id=5 service=shell priv-lvl=1 cmd=show ip route <cr>
  ```

- Configure local user authentication when AAA is not available

  Always require login even though the external AAA server is unreachable.

  ```
  username joe password 7 045802150C2E
  username jim password 7 0317B21895FE
  !
  line vty 0 4
  login local
  ```

- Configure Secure Shell (SSH) Access

  Use the following command to generate Rivest, Shamir, Adleman (RSA) key pairs for the router.

  ```
  router(config)#crypto key generate rsa
  ```

  By default, the VTY's transport is Telnet. The following command disabled Telnet and supports only SSH to the VTY lines.

  ```
  line vty 0 4
  transport input ssh
  ```

- ACLs for SNMP Access

  The community access string can be set up to permit access to the Simple Network Management Protocol (SNMP). The following example assigns the "changeme-rw" string to SNMP, allowing read-write access and specifies that IP access list 10 can use the community string:

  ```
  access-list 10 remark SNMP filter
  access-list 10 permit 10.1.1.0 0.0.0.255
  snmp-server community changeme-rw RW 10
  snmp-server community changeme-ro RO 10
  ```

  Because "read" and "write" are two common community strings for read and write access, respectively, change the community strings to different ones.

- Disable CDP Unless Needed

  Because CDP automatically discovers the neighboring network devices supporting CDP, disable CDP in an untrusted domain so that Unified CME routers will not show in the CDP table of other devices.

  ```
  no cdp run
  ```

  If CDP is needed, consider disabling CDP on a per-interface basis.

  ```
  Interface FastEthernet0/0
  no cdp enable
  ```

Phone Registration Control

The IP phones in the trusted domain should be able to register with a Unified CME. Assuming that the local segment is a trusted domain, use the **strict-match** option in the

ip source-address command, so that only locally attached IP phones will be able to register and get telephony services. The example of a command is:

Unified CME(config-telephony)# **ip source-address 1.1.1.1 port 2000 strict-match**

Use the following **access-list** if you want to block port 2000 access from the WAN side to prevent external SCCP phones from registering with Unified CME:

```
access-list 101 deny tcp any any eq 2000
```

NOTE   Unknown phones or phones that are not configured in Unified CME are allowed to register by default for ease of management, but they do not get dial tone until you configure them by associating the buttons with ephone-dns or configuring auto assign dns under telephony service.

Unified CME has the following syslog messages to generate and display all registration/ deregistration events:

```
%IPPHONE-6-REG_ALARM
%IPPHONE-6-REGISTER
%IPPHONE-6-REGISTER_NEW
%IPPHONE-6-UNREGISTER_ABNORMAL
%IPPHONE-6-REGISTER_NORMAL
```

The following message, for example, indicates that a phone has registered and is not part of the explicit router configuration; that is, ephone configuration has not been created:

```
%IPPHONE-6-REGISTER_NEW: ephone-3:SEP003094C38724 IP:1.4.170.6
   Socket:1 DeviceType:Phone has registered.
```

Unified CME also allows unconfigured IP phones to register in order to make provisioning of the Unified CME system more convenient. By default, IP phones designated as "new" are not assigned phone numbers and cannot make calls.

You can use the following configuration to enable syslogging to a router's buffer/console or a syslog server:

```
logging console ¦ buffer
logging 172.19.153.129 !!! 172.19.153.129 is the syslog server
```

The Cisco CallManager Express GUI provides call history table information so that a network administrator can monitor the call history information for unknown callers and use this information to disallow calling activities based on select calling patterns. The call history log should be configured to perform forensics and accounting and allow the administrator to track down fraudulent calling

```
dial-control-mib retain-timer 10080
dial-control-mib max-size 500
!
gw-accounting syslog
```

Secure GUI Management

Hypertext Transfer Protocol Security (HTTPS) (HTTP over Secure Socket Layer [SSL]) provides SSL version 3.0 support for the HTTP server and client within Cisco IOS Software. SSL provides server authentication, encryption, and message integrity to allow secure HTTP communications. SSL also provides HTTP client authentication.

This feature is supported only in Cisco IOS software images that support SSL.

Most IP phones do not serve as HTTPS clients. If HTTPS is enabled on the Unified CME router, IP phones will still attempt to connect to port 80. Because the SSL default port is 443, the phones will not be able to display local directory and system speed-dials.

The workaround for this is to enable both HTTP and HTTPS, as shown in the following example:

```
ip http server
ip http secure-server
ip http secure-port port_number (if https port is changed from default 443)
ip http authentication AAA ¦ TACACS ¦ local
```

Use the following command to generate an RSA usage key pair with a length of 1024 bits or greater:

```
crypto key generate rsa usage 1024
```

If you do not generate an RSA usage key pair manually, an RSA usage key pair with a length of 768 bits will be generated automatically when you connect to the HTTPS server for the first time. These automatically generated RSA keys are not saved to the startup configuration; therefore, they will be lost when the device is rebooted unless you save the configuration manually.

You should obtain an X.509 digital certificate with digital signature capabilities for the device from a certification authority (CA). If you do not obtain a digital certificate in advance, the device creates a self-signed digital certificate to authenticate itself.

If you change the device hostname after obtaining a device digital certificate, HTTPS connections to the device fail because the hostname does not match the hostname specified in the digital certificate. Obtain a new device digital certificate using the new hostname to fix this problem.

The **ip http secure-server** command will prevent clear-text passwords across the wires when a Unified CME administrator logs into the GUI. However, communication between the phone and the router will remain unsecured. A signed digital signature is required in the phone load and Cisco IOS for secure connection.

The following are the suggested best practices for using HTTP's interactive access to the Unified CME router:

- Use the **ip http access-class** command to restrict IP packets connecting to Cisco CallManager Express.

- Use the **ip http authentication** command with a central TACACS+ or Remote Authentication Dial-In User Service (RADIUS) server for authentication purposes. Configuring authentication for the HTTP and HTTPS servers adds additional security to communication between clients and the HTTP and HTTPS servers on the device.

- Do not use the same enable password as an HTTP/Unified CME login password, to prevent a regular user from gaining administrator rights.

Class of Restriction

The Class of Restriction (COR) is used to prevent toll fraud or restrict the permission of incoming/outgoing calls. There are two COR in the configuration: user and superuser along with various permissions allowed, such as local calling, long distance calling, 911 access, and 411 access. Example 9-3 shows how the "superuser" has access to everything and "user" has access to all resources with the exception of toll "1900," directory assistance "411," and international calling.

Example 9-3 *COR Example*

```
!
dial-peer cor custom
name 911
name 1800
name local-call
name ld-call
name 411
name int-call
name 1900
dial-peer cor list call911
member 911
!
dial-peer cor list call1800
member 1800
!
dial-peer cor list calllocal
member local-call
!
dial-peer cor list callint
member int-call
!
dial-peer cor list callld
member ld-call
!
dial-peer cor list call411
member 411
!
dial-peer cor list call1900
member 1900
dial-peer cor list user
member 911
```

Example 9-3 *COR Example (Continued)*

```
member 1800
member local-call
member ld-call
!
dial-peer cor list superuser
member 911
member 1800
member local-call
member ld-call
member 411
member int-call
member 1900
dial-peer voice 9 pots
corlist outgoing callld
destination-pattern 91..........
port 1/0
prefix 1
!
dial-peer voice 911 pots
corlist outgoing call911
destination-pattern 9911
port 1/0
prefix 911
!
dial-peer voice 11 pots
corlist outgoing callint
destination-pattern 9011T
port 2/0
prefix 011
!
dial-peer voice 732 pots
corlist outgoing calllocal
destination-pattern 9732.......
port 1/0
prefix 732
!
dial-peer voice 800 pots
corlist outgoing call1800
destination-pattern 91800.......
port 1/0
prefix 1800
!
dial-peer voice 802 pots
corlist outgoing call1800
destination-pattern 91877.......
port 1/0
prefix 1877
!
dial-peer voice 805 pots
corlist outgoing call1800
```

continues

Example 9-3   *COR Example (Continued)*

```
destination-pattern 91888.......
port 1/0
prefix 1888
!
dial-peer voice 411 pots
corlist outgoing call411
destination-pattern 9411
port 1/0
prefix 411
!
dial-peer voice 806 pots
corlist outgoing call1800
destination-pattern 91866.......
port 1/0
prefix 1866
ephone-dn 1
number 2000
cor incoming user
Ephone-dn 2
number 2001
cor incoming superuser
```

After-Hours Call Blocking

After-hours blocking can be added to restrict incoming calls after certain hours. After-hours blocking can also be used to restrict calls to numbers and area codes known as fraudulent calling patterns. The configuration example in Example 9-4 is used to restrict calls to certain area codes.

Example 9-4   *After-Hours Call Blocking*

```
telephony-service
after-hours block pattern 1 .1242
after-hours block pattern 2 .1264
after-hours block pattern 3 .1268
after-hours block pattern 4 .1246
after-hours block pattern 5 .1441
after-hours block pattern 6 .1284
after-hours block pattern 7 .1345
after-hours block pattern 8 .1767
after-hours block pattern 9 .1809
after-hours block pattern 10 .1473
after-hours block pattern 11 .1876
after-hours block pattern 12 .1664
after-hours block pattern 13 .1787
after-hours block pattern 14 .1869
after-hours block pattern 15 .1758
after-hours block pattern 16 .1900
after-hours block pattern 17 .1976
```

Example 9-4   *After-Hours Call Blocking (Continued)*

```
after-hours block pattern 18 .1868
after-hours block pattern 19 .1649
after-hours block pattern 20 .1340
after-hours block pattern 21 .1784
after-hours block pattern 22 .1684
after-hours block pattern 23 .1590
after-hours block pattern 24 .1456 zero
after-hours day Sun 00:00 23:59
after-hours day Mon 00:00 23:59
after-hours day Tue 00:00 23:59
after-hours day Wed 00:00 23:59
after-hours day Thu 00:00 23:59
after-hours day Fri 00:00 23:59
after-hours day Sat 00:00 23:59
```

In this section, you have learned how to make VoIP service secure with Unified CME in terms of access control, phone registration, GUI management, class of restriction, and after-hours call blocking. The next section covers security practices with Unified CM.

Unified Communications Manager

Unified CM (Cisco Unified Communications Manager, formerly CallManager) is an enterprise-class IP telephony call processing system providing voice, video, mobility, and presence service. It supports the latest security technology to establish and maintain authenticated communications along with encryption. This section covers the features and usages based on version 5.0 or above. The contents refer to Cisco CallManager Security Guide.[4]

NOTE   To avoid massive configuration snapshots, this section will approach the security applications at a high level, focusing on authentication, integrity, and encryption. If you need to see detailed configuration examples, refer to the administration guides at Cisco.com.

Security Features and Certificates

Unified CM uses a multilayered approach to call security, from the transport layer to the application layer.

The transport layer security includes TLS and IPsecurity (IPSec) for signaling authentication and encryption. Secure Real-time Transport Protocol (SRTP) adds media authentication and encryption to secure privacy and confidentiality for voice conversation and other media.

Media encryption keys derived by Unified CM get sent securely via encrypted signaling paths to IP phones through TLS (or TCP for some phone models) and to gateways over IPSec-protected links.

Table 9-1 shows the summary of security features that Unified CM can implement during a Session Initiation Protocol (SIP) or SCCP call.

Table 9-1 *Security Features on Unified CM*

Security Feature	Line Side	Trunk Side
Transport, Connection, Integrity	Secure TLS port	IPSec associations
		Security TLS port (SIP trunk only)
Device Authentication	TLS certificate exchange with CAPF	IPSec certificate exchange or preshared key
Digest Authentication	SIP phone users only	SIP trunk users or SIP trunk application users only
Signaling Authentication, Encryption	TLS mode: authenticated or encrypted	IPSec
		TLS mode
Media Encryption	SRTP	SRTP
Authorization	Presence SUBSCRIBE requests	Presence SUBSCRIBE requests
		Method list

Unified CM uses the following self-signed (own) certificate types:

- **HTTPS certificate (tomcat_cert)**—This self-signed root certificate gets generated during the Cisco CallManager installation for the HTTPS server.

- **Unified CM node certificate (ccmnode_cert)**—This self-signed root certificate automatically installs when you install Unified CM server. It provides server identification, including the server name and the Global Unique Identifier (GUID).

- **CAPF certificate (CAPF_cert)**—The system copies this root certificate to all servers in the cluster after you complete the Cisco CTL client configuration.

- **IPSec certificate (ipsec_cert)**—This self-signed root certificate gets generated during Unified CM installation for IPSec connections with MGCP and H.323 gateways.

- **SRST-enabled gateway certificate**—When you configure a secure SRST reference in Unified CM Administration, it retrieves the SRST-enabled gateway certificate from the gateway and stores it in the Unified CM database. After you reset the devices, the certificate gets added to the phone configuration file. Because the certificate is stored in the database, this certificate does not get integrated into the certificate management tool.

After root certificates are installed, certificates get added to the root trust stores to secure connections between users and hosts, integrate application devices, and so on. For security reasons, trusted certificate files typically get stored as an 8-digit number (such as f7a74b2c.0), which is a hashed value of the certificate name.

Unified CM imports the following certificate types to its trust store:

- **Cisco Unity server certificate**—Cisco Unity uses this self-signed root certificate to sign the Cisco Unity SCCP device certificates. The Cisco Unity Telephony Integration Manager manages this certificate.

- **Cisco Unity SCCP device certificates**—Cisco Unity SCCP devices use this signed certificate to establish a TLS connection with the Unified CM. Every Unity device (or port) gets issued a certificate that is rooted at the Unity root certificate. The Unity certificate name is a hash of the certificate's subject name, which is based on the Unity machine name.

- **SIP Proxy server certificate**—A SIP user agent that connects via a SIP trunk authenticates to Unified CM if the CM trust store contains the SIP user agent certificate and if the SIP user agent contains the CM certificate in its trust store.

Administrators have read-only access to certificates. Administrators can view the fingerprint of server certificates, regenerate self-signed certificates, and delete trust certificates at the Cisco IP Telephony Platform GUI.

Administrators can also regenerate and view self-signed certificates at the command-line interface (CLI).

Integrity and Authentication

Integrity and authentication protect against the following threats in a Unified CM domain:

- TFTP file manipulation (integrity)
- Modification of call processing signaling between the phone and Unified CM (integrity/authentication)
- Man-in-the-middle attack (integrity/authentication)
- Phone and server identity theft (authentication)
- Replay attack (authentication)

Authorization specifies what an authenticated user, service, or application can do. You can implement multiple authentication and authorization methods in a single session.

The following sections describe the methods of authentication, authorization, and integrity that Unified CM supports.

Image Authentication

This process prevents tampering with the binary image (that is a firmware load) prior to loading it on the phone. Tampering with the image causes the phone to fail the authentication process and reject the image. Image authentication occurs through signed binary files that are automatically installed when you install Unified CM. Likewise, firmware updates that you download from the web also provide signed binary images.

Device Authentication

The process of device authentication validates the identity of the device and ensures that the entity is who it claims to be. Device authentication occurs between Unified CM and supported IP Phones, SIP trunks, or JTAPI/TAPI/CTI applications (when supported).

An authenticated connection occurs between these entities only when each entity accepts the certificate of the other entity. This process of mutual certificate exchange is called mutual authentication. Device authentication relies on the creation of the Cisco CTL file for authenticating Unified CM server node, and the Certificate Authority Proxy Function for authenticating phones and JTAPI/TAPI/CTI applications.

File Authentication

The process of file authentication validates digitally signed files that the phone downloads; for example, the configuration, ring list, locale, and CTL files. The phone validates the signature to verify that file tampering did not occur after the file creation.

The TFTP server does not sign any files if you configure the cluster for non-secure mode. If you configure the cluster for secure mode, the TFTP server signs static files, such as ring list, localized, default.cnf.xml, and ring list WAV files, in .sgn format. The TFTP server signs files in *<device name>*.cnf.xml format every time the TFTP server verifies that a data change occurred for the file.

The TFTP server writes the signed files to disk if caching is disabled. If the TFTP server verifies that a saved file has changed, the TFTP server re-signs the file. The new file on the disk overwrites the saved file, which gets deleted. Before the phone can download the new file, the administrator must restart affected devices in Unified CM Administration.

After the phone receives the files from the TFTP server, the phone verifies the integrity of the files by validating the signature on the file. For the phone to establish an authenticated connection, ensure that the following criteria are met:

- The phone must have been provisioned with its own certificate.
- The CTL file must exist on the phone, and the Unified CM entry and certificate must exist in the CTL file.
- You configured the device for authentication or encryption.

Signaling Authentication

The process of signaling authentication, also known as signaling integrity, uses the TLS protocol to validate that no tampering has occurred to signaling packets during transmission. Signaling authentication relies on the creation of the CTL file.

Digest Authentication

The process of digest authentication for SIP trunks and phones allows Unified CM to challenge the identity of a SIP user agent (UA) when the UA sends a request to Unified CM. (A SIP user agent represents a device or application that originates a SIP message.)

Unified CM acts as a user agent server (UAS) for SIP calls originated by line-side phones or devices reached through the SIP trunk, as a User Agent Client (UAC) for SIP calls that it originates to the SIP trunk, or a back-to-back user agent (B2BUA) for line-to-line or trunk-to-trunk connections. In most environments, Unified CM acts primarily as a B2BUA connecting SCCP and SIP endpoints.

Unified CM can challenge SIP phones or SIP devices connecting through a SIP trunk (as a UAS) and can respond to challenges received on its SIP trunk interface (as a UAC). When digest authentication is enabled for a phone, Unified CM challenges all SIP phone requests except keepalive messages. Note that you can only effectively challenge on a SIP trunk if the UA belongs to your same realm and thus you know the valid username and password.

Unified CM defines a SIP call as having two or more separate call legs. For a standard two-party call between two SIP devices, two separate call legs exist: one leg between the originating SIP UA and Unified CM (the originating call leg) and the other leg between Unified CM and destination SIP UA (the terminating call leg). Each call leg represents a separate SIP dialog. Because digest authentication is a point-to-point process, digest authentication on each call leg stays independent of the other call legs. SRTP capabilities can change for each call leg, depending on the capabilities negotiated between the user agents.

Unified CM server uses a SIP 401 (Unauthorized) message to initiate a challenge, which includes the nonce and the realm in the header. (The nonce specifies a random number that gets used to calculate the Media Digest 5 [MD5] hash.) When a SIP user agent challenges the identity of Unified CM, Unified CM responds to SIP 401 and SIP 407 (Proxy Authentication Required) messages.

After you enable digest authentication for a SIP phone or trunk and configure digest credentials, Unified CM calculates a credentials checksum that includes a hash of the username, password, and realm. Unified CM encrypts the values and stores the username and the checksum in the database. Each digest user can have one set of digest credentials per realm.

When Unified CM challenges a user agent, Unified CM indicates the realm and nonce value for which the user agent must present its credentials. After receiving a response, Unified CM validates the checksum for the username that is stored in the database against the credentials received in the response header from the UA. If the credentials match, digest authentication succeeded, and Unified CM processes the SIP request.

When responding to a challenge from a user agent that is connected through the SIP trunk, Unified CM responds with the Unified CM username and password that are configured for the realm, which is specified in the challenge message header. When Unified CM gets challenged, the Unified CM looks up the username and encrypted password based on the realm that the challenge message specifies. Unified CM decrypts the password, calculates the digest, and presents it in the response message.

Administrators configure SIP digest credentials for a phone user or application user. For applications, you specify digest credentials in the Applications User Configuration window in Unified CM Administration. For SIP phones, you specify the digest authentication credentials, which are then applied to a phone, in the End User window in Unified CM Administration.

To associate the credentials with the phone after you configure the user, you choose a Digest User, an end user, in the Phone Configuration window. After you reset the phone, the credentials exist in the phone configuration file that the TFTP server offers to the phone.

If you enable digest authentication for an end user but do not configure the digest credentials, the phone will fail registration. If the cluster mode is nonsecure and you enable digest authentication and configure digest credentials, the digest credentials get sent to the phone and Unified CM still initiates challenges.

Administrators configure the SIP realm for challenges to the phone and for challenges that are received through the SIP trunk. The SIP Realm GUI provides the trunk-side credentials for UAC mode. You configure the SIP realm for phones with the service parameter SIP Station Realm. You must configure a SIP realm and username and password in Unified CM Administration for each SIP trunk user agent that can challenge Unified CM.

Administrators configure the minutes that the nonce value stays valid for the external device before that value gets rejected and a new number gets generated by Unified CM.

Authorization

Unified CM uses the authorization process to restrict certain categories of messages from SIP phones, from SIP trunks, and from SIP application requests on SIP trunks.

For SIP INVITE messages and in-dialog messages, and for SIP phones, Unified CM provides authorization through calling search spaces and partitions.

For SIP SUBSCRIBE requests from phones, Unified CM provides authorization for user access to presence groups.

For SIP trunks, Unified CM provides authorization of presence subscriptions and certain non-INVITE SIP messages; for example, out-of-dial REFER message, unsolicited notification, and any SIP request with the replaces header. You specify authorization in the SIP Trunk Security Profile window when you check the related check boxes in the window.

Authorization occurs for the SIP trunk first (as configured in the SIP Trunk Security Profile) and then for the SIP application user agent on the SIP trunk (as configured in the Application User Configuration), when application-level authorization is configured. For the trunk, Unified CM downloads the trunk ACL information and caches it. The ACL information gets applied to the incoming SIP request. If the ACL does not allow the SIP request, the call fails with a 403 Forbidden message.

If the ACL allows the SIP request, Unified CM checks whether digest authentication is enabled in the SIP Trunk Security Profile. If digest authentication is not enabled and application-level authorization is not enabled, Unified CM processes the request. If digest authentication is enabled, Unified CM verifies that the authentication header exists in the incoming request and then uses digest authentication to identify the source application. If the header does not exist, Unified CM challenges the device with a 401 message.

To enable SIP application authorization on the SIP trunk, you must check the **Enable Application Level Authorization** check box in the SIP Trunk Security Profile window. Before an application-level ACL gets applied, Unified CM authenticates the SIP trunk user agent through digest authentication. Therefore, you must enable digest authentication in the SIP Trunk Security Profile for application-level authorization to occur.

Encryption

Unified CM supports three types of encryption: signaling, media, and configuration file encryption.

Signaling Encryption

Signaling encryption ensures that all SIP and SCCP signaling messages that are sent between the device and the Unified CM server are encrypted.

Signaling encryption ensures that the information that pertains to the parties, dual-tone multifrequency (DTMF) digits that are entered by the parties, call status, media encryption keys, and so on, are protected against unintended or unauthorized access.

Cisco does not support NAT with Unified CM if you configure the cluster for secure mode; NAT does not work with signaling encryption because the encrypted signaling does not work in conjunction with the NAT ALG.

Firewall ALGs also break with encrypted signaling. As a workaround, you can enable User Datagram Protocol (UDP) ALG in the firewall to allow media stream firewall traversal. Enabling the UDP ALG allows the media source on the trusted side of the firewall to open a bidirectional media flow through the firewall by sending the media packet through the firewall.

SIP trunks support signaling encryption but do not support media encryption.

Media Encryption

Media encryption, which uses SRTP, ensures that only the intended recipient can interpret the media streams between supported devices. Support includes audio streams only. Media encryption includes creating a media master key pair for the call, delivering the keys to the endpoints, and securing the delivery of the keys while the keys are in transport.

If the devices support SRTP, the system uses an SRTP connection. If at least one device does not support SRTP, the system uses an RTP connection. SRTP-to-RTP fallback may occur for a variety of reasons: transfers from a secure device to a non-secure device, conferencing, transcoding, music on hold, and so on.

For most security-supported devices, authentication and signaling encryption serve as the minimum requirements for media encryption; that is, if the devices do not support signaling encryption and authentication, media encryption cannot occur. Cisco IOS gateways and trunks support media encryption without authentication. For Cisco IOS gateways and trunks, you must configure IPSec when you enable the SRTP capability (media encryption).

Secure SIP trunks can support secure calls over TLS; be aware, though, that the trunk supports signaling encryption but does not support media encryption (SRTP). Because the trunk does not support media encryption, the shield icon may display on the phones during the call, that is, if all devices in the call support authentication or signaling encryption.

The following example demonstrates media encryption for SCCP and MGCP calls:

1 Device A and Device B, which support media encryption and authentication, register with Unified CM.

2 When Device A places a call to Device B, Unified CM generates two sets of media session master values from the key manager function.

3 Both devices receive the two sets: one set for the media stream, Device A–Device B, and the other set for the media stream, Device B–Device A.

4 Using the first set of master values, Device A derives the keys that encrypt and authenticate the media stream, Device A–Device B.

5 Using the second set of master values, Device A derives the keys that authenticate and decrypt the media stream, Device B–Device A.

6 Device B uses these sets in the inverse operational sequence.

7 After the devices receive the keys, the devices perform the required key derivation, and the SRTP packet can be sent and received by both Device A and B.

Configuration File Encryption

Unified CM pushes digest credentials and other secured data to the phone as part of the configuration file download for phones that support encrypted configuration files. Only the device configuration file is encrypted for download. Unified CM encodes and stores encryption keys in the database.

To enable encrypted configuration files, set the TFTP Encrypted Configuration enterprise parameter to True. The TFTP server encrypts and decrypts configuration files by using symmetric key and public key encryption.

When the TFTP Encrypted Configuration enterprise parameter is set to False, Unified CM displays a warning message that digest credentials will be sent in the clear when digest authentication gets enabled in the SIP phone or trunk security profile.

Configuration Guideline

The following list gives the recommended steps to implement integrity, authentication, and encryption when configuring Unified CM based on version 5.

Note that you may have a different interface or options depending on the version and specific features you are implementing.

Step 1 On each server in the cluster, activate the Cisco CTL Provider service in Unified CM Serviceability. If you activated this service prior to a Unified CM upgrade, you do not need to activate the service again. The service automatically activates after the upgrade.

Step 2 On the first node, activate the Cisco Certificate Authority Proxy service in Unified CM Serviceability to install, upgrade, troubleshoot, or delete locally significant certificates.

Step 3 If you do not want to use the default port settings, configure ports for the TLS connection. If you configured these settings prior to a Unified CM upgrade, the settings migrate automatically during the upgrade.

Step 4 Obtain at least two security tokens and the passwords, hostnames/IP addresses, and port numbers for the servers that you will configure for the Cisco CTL client.

Step 5   Install the Cisco CTL client. You cannot use the Cisco CTL client that was available with Unified CM 4.0. To update the Cisco CTL file after an upgrade to Unified CM 5.0(1), you must install the plug-in that is available in Unified CM Administration 5.0(1).

Step 6   Configure the Cisco CTL client. If you created the Cisco CTL file prior to a Unified CM upgrade, the Cisco CTL file migrates automatically during the upgrade.

Step 7   Configure the phone security profiles. Perform the following tasks when you configure the profiles.

Step 8   Configure the device security mode (for SCCP and SIP phones).

Step 9   Configure CAPF settings (for some SCCP and SIP phones). Additional CAPF settings display in the Phone Configuration window.

Step 10   If you plan to use digest authentication for SIP phones, check the **Enable Digest Authentication** check box.

Step 11   Apply the phone security profiles to the phones.

Step 12   Configure CAPF to issue certificates to the phones.

Step 13   Verify that the locally significant certificates are installed on supported Cisco IP Phones.

Step 14   Configure digest authentication for SIP phones.

Step 15   Configure encryption for phone configuration files.

Step 16   Perform phone-hardening tasks.

Step 17   Configure voicemail ports for security.

Step 18   Configure security settings for SRST references.

Step 19   Configure IPSec.

Step 20   Configure the SIP trunk security profile.

   — If you plan to use digest authentication, check the **Enable Digest Authentication** check box in the profile.

   — For trunk-level authorization, check the authorization check boxes for the allowed SIP requests.

   — If you want application-level authorization to occur after trunk-level authorization, check the **Enable Application Level Authorization** check box. You cannot check application-level authorization unless digest authentication is checked.

Step 21 Apply the SIP trunk security profile to the trunk.

Step 22 Configure digest authentication for the trunk.

Step 23 If you checked the **Enable Application Level Authorization** check box
in the SIP trunk security profile, configure the allowed SIP requests by
checking the authorization check boxes in the Application User
Configuration window.

Step 24 Reset all phones in the cluster.

Step 25 Reboot all servers in the cluster.

In this section, you have learned how to make VoIP service secure with Unified CM, in
terms of authentication, authorization, and encryption. The next section covers the same
topic with access devices.

Access Devices

The access devices in this context are IP phones (for example, Cisco 7960s) and multilayer
switches (for example, Cisco Catalyst 6500s) that provide security features and interfaces
at the user's network. These features can be enabled or disabled on a phone-by-phone or
service-by-service basis to increase the security of an IP telephony deployment.

Figure 9-2 illustrates the typical layout of an access network.

Figure 9-2 *Access Devices*

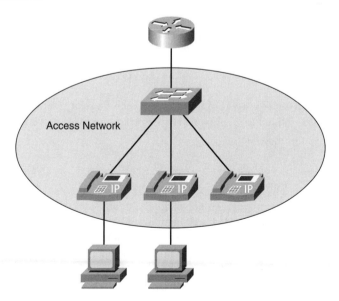

To make a secure access network, the section recommends the following method of using IP phone, VLAN, switch port, and ACL with configuration examples.

IP Phone

IP phones (Cisco Unified IP Phones) have built-in features to increase the security on the network even though the number of features is relatively small compared to other network devices. The best practices of usage can be summarized as follows:

- Disable unused PC ports to prevent a device from plugging into the back of the phone and getting network access through the phone itself. A phone in a common area such as a lobby would typically have its port disabled.

- Enable Gratuitous ARP (ARP announcement) to prevent man-in-the-middle attacks to the phone.

- Isolate the voice VLAN not to allow any devices from the PC port to access the voice VLAN.

- Restrict access to the built-in web server so that an attacker cannot get any information from the interface.

- Disable access to the network settings page on the phone so that an attacker cannot obtain network information like IP addresses of TFTP, default gateway (GW), or Unified CM.

- Integrate authentication and encryption with Unified CM and CME (refer to previous sections).

- Keep in mind that enabling video capabilities, as it is designed, could possibly allow communication to the phone from the PC connected to that phone.

Switch

Switch (Cisco Catalyst Switch) also provides many security features to protect IP telephony network. The following section present the methodology of preventing typical treats in the access network with the switch.

Mitigate MAC CAM Flooding

A classic attack on a switched network is a Media Access Control (MAC) content-addressable memory (CAM) flooding attack. This type of attack floods the switch with so many MAC addresses that the switch does not know which port an end station or device is attached to. When the switch does not know which port a device is attached to, it broadcasts the traffic destined for that device to the entire VLAN. In this way, the attacker is able to see all traffic that is coming to all the users in a VLAN, and the network becomes saturated with the traffic.

An attacker may use any flooding tool (for example, "macof") to generate MAC flooding from random source to random destination MAC address, which can fill up the CAM quickly and disrupt the functionality of the switch.

To prevent malicious MAC flooding, limit the number of MAC addresses allowed to access individual ports based on the connectivity requirements for those ports. For example, with a switch port with only a workstation attached to it, you would want to limit the number of learned MAC addresses to one. In the case of a port with an IP phone and a workstation behind it, you would want to set the number of learned MAC addresses to two.

Prevent Port Access

This is a form of device-level security authorization to prevent port access from non-legitimate devices. Only devices designated by their MAC addresses on the port will have the access.

This requirement is used to authorize access to the network by using the single credential of the device's MAC address. By using port security (in its nondynamic form), a network administrator would be required to associate MAC addresses statically for every port. However, with dynamic port security, network administrators can merely specify the number of MAC addresses they would like the switch to learn and, assuming the correct devices are the first devices to connect to the port, allow only those devices access to that port for some period of time.

The period of time can be determined by either a fixed timer or an inactivity timer (nonpersistent access), or it can be permanently assigned. The feature to permanently assign a MAC address on a Cisco 6000 switch is called "autoconfigure," and on the Cisco 4500, 2550, 2750, or 2950 switches, the feature is called "sticky." In both cases, the MAC address learned will remain on the port even in the event of a reload or reboot of the switch. Persistent assignment of MAC addresses via autoconfigure or sticky can be cleared only by a command.

The most common default behavior seen across the Cisco Catalyst switching platforms currently is the nonpersistent behavior; the only behavior prior to Cisco CatOS Release 7.6(1) was persistent. No provision is made for device mobility by static port security or persistent dynamic port security. Although it is not the primary requirement, MAC flooding attacks are implicitly prevented by port security configurations that aim to limit access to certain MAC addresses.

From a security perspective, there are better mechanisms for both authenticating and authorizing port access based on user-id and/or password credentials rather than using MAC address authorization. MAC addresses alone can easily be spoofed or falsified by most operating systems.

Prevent Network Extensions

Prevent rogue network extensions via hub or wireless access points (APs). Because it limits the number of MAC addresses to a port, port security can also be used as a mechanism to inhibit user extension to the IT-created network. For example, if a user plugs a wireless AP into a user-facing port or data port on a phone with port security defined for a single MAC address, the wireless AP itself would occupy that MAC address and not allow any devices behind it to access the network.

Example 9-5 illustrates the Cisco IOS commands to configure an access port with dynamic port security, running a phone with a device plugged into the data port on the phone.

Example 9-5 *Restrict Access Port*

```
switchport access vlan 10
switchport mode access
switchport voice vlan 20
switchport port-security
switchport port-security maximum 2
switchport port-security violation restrict
! This command is the recommended configuration. The default is to disable the port.
    If you restrict the port, it will learn up to the maximum number of MAC
        addresses and then stop learning any new MAC addresses. If you have the port
        on the default setting of disable and the maximum number of MAC addresses is
        exceeded, the port will error-disable and turn off power to the phone.
        The default timer for the port to re-enable is 5 minutes. Depending on
        your security policy, it might be preferable to restrict the port and
        not shut down the phone by disabling the port.
switchport port-security aging time 2
!This command sets the amount of time that the MAC address will remain on the
    port without any traffic from that MAC address. Because of CDP communication
    between some switches and the phone, the recommended minimum time is 2 minutes.
switchport port-security aging type inactivity
!This command defines the type of aging that will be used on the port to time-out
    the learned MAC address.
```

Prevent Fraudulent DHCP Server

DHCP Snooping prevents a non-approved DHCP or fraudulent DHCP server from handing out IP addresses on a network. It does this by blocking all replies to a DHCP request, except those replies from the authorized DHCP server.

Because most phone deployments use DHCP to provide IP addresses to the phones, you should use the DHCP Snooping feature in the switch to secure DHCP messaging. Without this protection, a fraudulent DHCP server can attempt to respond to the DHCP broadcast messages from a client to give out incorrect IP addresses, or it can attempt to confuse the client that is requesting an address.

When enabled, DHCP Snooping treats all ports in a VLAN as untrusted by default. An untrusted port is a user-facing port that should never make any reserved DHCP responses.

If an untrusted DHCP-snooping port makes a DHCP server response, its response will be dropped. However, legitimately attached DHCP servers or uplinks to legitimate servers must be configured as trusted.

Mitigate DHCP DoS Attacks

DHCP address starvation attacks create a DHCP Denial-of-Service (DoS) attack by starving the DHCP server of an IP address for legitimate clients. One such tool, Gobbler, makes DHCP requests from different random source MAC addresses. You can prevent it from starving a DHCP address space by using port security to limit the number of MAC addresses.

However, a more sophisticated DHCP starvation tool can make the DHCP requests from a single-source MAC address and vary the DHCP payload information. With DHCP Snooping enabled, untrusted ports will make a comparison of the source MAC address to the DHCP payload information and fail the request if they do not match.

Example 9-6 illustrates the Cisco IOS commands to configure an access port with DHCP Snooping, running a phone with a device plugged into the data port on the phone.

Example 9-6 *Prevent DHCP DoS Attack*

```
!!!!!!!! Global commands
ip dhcp snooping vlan 10, 20
! This command specifies which VLANs have DHCP Snooping enabled.
no ip dhcp snooping information option
! This command should be used so that Option 82 information is not required
  to lease a DHCP address. The Option 82 information must be supported by
  the DHCP server, but most enterprise servers do not support this feature. Option
  82 is supported in Cisco IOS DHCP servers.
ip dhcp snooping
! This command enables DHCP Snooping at the global level on the Switche.

!!!!!!!!! Interface commands
no ip dhcp snooping trust (Default)
! This command sets the interface to not trust any information coming into the port
  from a DHCP server.
ip dhcp snooping limit rate 10 (pps)
! This command sets the default rate limit that is configured on the interface when
  DHCP Snooping is initially configured. This value can be changed depending on your
  security policy.
ip dhcp snooping trust
! You must use this command on the port through which DHCP information will be sent
  from a DHCP server. If you do not trust the port from which the DHCP information
  is coming, then none of the devices will ever receive a DHCP address. At least
  one port (access port or trunk port) with the DHCP server on it must be configured
  to allow this information to get to the clients. This command can also be used to
  trust any device connected to a port that has a static IP address and that will
  not use DHCP to get an IP address. Note that the uplink port to the DHCP server,
  or the trunk port to the DHCP server, will also have to be trusted.
```

Limit ARP Responses

Another function of DHCP Snooping is to record the DHCP binding information for untrusted ports that successfully get IP addresses from the DHCP servers. The binding information is recorded in a table on the switch. The DHCP binding table contains the IP address, MAC address, lease length, port, and VLAN information for each binding entry. The binding information from DHCP Snooping remains in effect for the length of the DHCP binding period set by the DHCP server (that is, the DHCP lease time). The DHCP binding information is used to create dynamic entries for Dynamic ARP Inspection (DAI) to limit ARP responses for only those addresses that are DHCP-bound. The DHCP binding information is also used by the IP source guard to limit sourcing of IP packets to only those addresses that are DHCP-bound. Essentially, this causes the switch to enforce the device to use the IP address and MAC address that were indicated in the DHCP request and response. Example 9-7 shows the binding information from DHCP Snooping.

Example 9-7 *Binding Information*

```
!!!!! Displaying binding information for Cisco IOS:
show ip dhcp snooping binding
MacAddress IpAddress Lease(sec) Type VLAN Interface
---------- --------- ---------- ------------- ---- ---------

00:03:47:B5:9F:AD 10.120.4.10 193185 dhcp-snooping 10 FastEthernet3/18

!!!!! Displaying binding information for Cisco CatOS:
ngcs-6500-1> (enable) show dhcp-snooping bindings
MacAddress IpAddress Lease(sec) VLAN Port
----------------- --------------- ---------- ---- -----

00-10-a4-92-bf-dd 10.10.10.21 41303 10 2/5
```

VLAN ACL

You can use VLAN ACLs to control VoIP traffic that flows in the access network. Cisco multilayer switches have the capability of controlling Layers 2 to 4 within a VLAN ACL. Depending on the types of switches in a network, VLAN ACLs can be used to block traffic into and out of a particular VLAN. They can also be used to block intra-VLAN traffic to control what happens inside the VLAN between devices.

If you plan to deploy a VLAN ACL, you should verify which ports are needed to allow the phones to function with each application used in your VoIP network. Normally any VLAN ACL would be applied to the VLAN that the phones use. This would allow control at the access port, as close as possible to the devices that are plugged into that access port.

Example 9-8 represents a VLAN ACL that allows only the traffic for a Cisco 7960 IP Phone to boot and function in a VLAN. The example uses the following IP address ranges:

- Phones are in the range 10.0.20.
- Servers are in the range 10.0.10.

- Gateways are in the range 10.0.30.

- Default gateways are 10.0.10.2 and 10.0.10.3.

- DNS server IP address is 10.0.40.3.

Example 9-8   *VLAN ACL*

```
20 permit udp host 10.0.10.2 eq 1985 any
30 permit udp host 10.0.10.3 eq 1985 any
!permit HSRP from the routers
40 permit udp any any eq bootpc
50 permit udp any any eq bootps
!permit DHCP activity
60 permit udp 10.0.10.0 0.0.0.255 range 49152 65535 10.0.20.0 0.0.0.255 eq tftp
70 permit udp 10.0.20.0 0.0.0.255 range 1024 5000 10.0.10.0 0.0.0.255 range 49152
   65535
80 permit udp 10.0.10.0 0.0.0.255 range 49152 65535 10.0.20.0 0.0.0.255 range 1024
   5000
!permit the tftp traffic from the tftp server and phone
90 permit udp 10.0.10.0 0.0.0.255 range 49152 65535 host 10.0.40.3 eq domain
100 permit udp host 172.19.244.2 eq domain 10.0.10.0 0.0.0.255 range 49152 65535
!permit DNS to and from the phone. Only UDP is used here.
110 permit tcp 10.0.10.0 0.0.0.255 range 49152 65535 10.0.20.0 0.0.0.255 eq 2000
120 permit tcp 10.0.20.0 0.0.0.255 eq 2000 10.0.10.0 0.0.0.255 range 49152 65535
!permit signaling to and from the SCCP phone.
130 permit udp 10.0.10.0 0.0.0.255 range 16384 32767 10.0.10.0 0.0.0.255 range 16384
   32767
140 permit udp 10.0.0.0 0.0.255.255 range 16384 32767 10.0.10.0 0.0.0.255 range
   16384
32767
150 permit udp 10.0.10.0 0.0.0.255 range 16384 32767 10.0.0.0 0.0.255.255 range
   16384
43767
!permit all phones to send udp to each other
160 permit tcp 10.0.10.0 0.0.0.255 range 49152 65535 10.0.20.0 0.0.0.255 eq www
170 permit tcp 10.0.20.0 0.0.0.255 eq www 10.0.10.0 0.0.0.255 range 49152 65535
180 permit tcp 10.0.20.0 0.0.0.255 range 49152 65535 10.0.10.0 0.0.0.255 eq www
190 permit tcp 10.0.10.0 0.0.0.255 eq www 10.0.20.0 0.0.0.255 range 49152 65535
!permit web access to and from the phone
200 permit Intelligent Contact ManagementP any any
!allow all icmp - phone to phone, gateway to phone, and NMS to phone
220 permit udp 10.0.30.0 0.0.0.255 rang 16384 327676 10.0.10.0 0.0.0.255 rang 16384
   32767
!permit udp to the gateways in the network for pstn access
```

Note that the ports do change when either the application is updated or the OS is updated. This note applies to all the IP telephony devices in the network, including phones. To obtain the latest list of ports used by a product, refer to the appropriate documentation for the version of the product that is running on your network.

As this example of an ACL illustrates, the more well-defined the IP addresses are in a network, the easier it is to write and deploy an ACL.

The next section shows a detailed example with a specific scenario.

Deployment Example

Example 9.9 illustrates one possible way to configure a phone and a network for use in an area with low physical security, such as a lobby area. None of the features in this example are required for a lobby phone, but if your security policy states more security is needed, you could use the features listed in this example.

Because you would not want anyone to gain access to the network from the PC port on the phone, you should disable the PC port on the back of the phone to limit network access. You should also disable the settings page on the phone so that potential attackers cannot see the IP addresses of the network to which the lobby phone is connected. The disadvantage of not being able to change the settings on the phone usually will not matter for a lobby phone.

Because there is very little chance that a lobby phone will be moved, you could use a static IP address for that phone. A static IP address would prevent an attacker from unplugging the phone and then plugging into that phone port to get a new IP address. Also, if the phone is unplugged, the port state will change and the phone will no longer be registered with Unified CM. You can track this event in just the lobby phone ports to see if someone is trying to attach to the network.

Using static port security for the phone and not allowing the MAC address to be learned would mean that an attacker would have to change his MAC address to that of the phone, if he were able to discover that address. Dynamic port security could be used with an unlimited timer to learn the MAC address, so that it would not have to be added. Then the switchport would not have to be changed to clear that MAC address unless the phone is changed. The MAC address is listed in a label on the bottom of the phone. If listing the MAC address is considered a security issue, the label can be removed and replaced with a "Lobby Phone" label to identify the device.

A single VLAN could be used, and CDP could be disabled on the port so that attackers would not be able to see any information from the Ethernet port about that port or switch to which it is attached. In this case, the phone would not have a CDP entry in the switch for E911 emergency calls, and each lobby phone would need either a label or an information message to local security when an emergency number is dialed.

A static entry in the DHCP Snooping binding table could be made because there would be no DHCP on the port. When the static entry is in the DHCP Snooping binding table, Dynamic ARP Inspection could be enabled on the VLAN to keep the attacker from getting other information about one of the Layer 2 neighbors on the network.

With a static entry in the DHCP Snooping binding table, IP Source Guard could be used. If an attacker got the MAC address and the IP address and then started sending packets, only packets with the correct IP address could be sent.

A VLAN ACL could be written to allow only the ports and IP addresses that are needed for the phones to operate. Example 9-9 contains a very small ACL that can be applied to a port at Layer 2 or at the first Layer 3 device to help control access into the network. This example is based on a Cisco 7960 IP Phone being used in a lobby area, without music on hold to the phone or HTTP access from the phone. It uses the following IP address ranges:

- The lobby phone has an IP address of 10.0.40.5.
- The Unified CM cluster uses the address range of 10.0.20.*
- The DNS server has an IP address of 10.0.30.2.
- The HSRP routers have IP addresses 10.0.10.2 and 10.0.10.3.
- Other phones in the network use IP addresses in the range 10.0.*.*

Example 9-9   *ACL Example for Lobby Phone*

```
10 permit icmp any any
! Allow all icmp - phone to phone, gateway to phone and NMS to phone
20 permit udp host 10.0.10.2 eq 1985 any
!Allow HSRP information in, do not allow out
30 permit udp host 10.0.10.3 eq 1985 any
! Allow in from HSRP neighbor
40 permit udp host 10.0.40.5 range 49152 65535 10.0.20.0 0.0.0.255 eq tftp
! Using ip host from ephemeral port range from phone to the TFPT server port 69 (start of
   tftp)
50 permit udp 10.0.20.0 0.0.0.255 range 1024 5000 host 10.0.40.5 range 49152 65535
!Using IP subnet from TFTP server with ephemeral port range to ip host and ephemeral
   port range for phone
60 permit udp host 10.0.40.5 range 49152 65535 10.0.20.0 0.0.0.255 range 1024 5000
! Using host from phone to TFTP server with ephemeral port range to ip range and
   ephemeral port range for TFTP (continue the TFTP conversation)
70 permit udp host 10.0.40.5 range 49152 65535 host 10.0.30.2 eq domain
! Using IP host and ephemeral port range from phone to DNS server host
80 permit udp host 10.0.30.2 eq domain host 10.0.40.5 range 49152 65535
! Using IP from DNS server to phone host ip and ephemeral port range
90 permit tcp 10.0.40.5 range 49152 65535 10.0.20.0 0.0.0.255 eq 2000
! Using IP host and ephemeral port range from phone to Unified CM cluster for SCCP
100 permit tcp 10.0.20.0 0.0.0.255 eq 2000 host 10.0.40.5 range 49152 65535
! Using IP range and SCCP port to phone IP host and ephemeral port range
110 permit udp 10.0.0.0 0.0.255.255 range 16384 32767 host 10.0.40.5 range 16384 32767
! Using IP range and ephemeral port range from all phones or gateways outside a vlan
   to the IP host to phone
120 permit udp host 10.0.40.5 range 16384 32767 10.0.0.0 0.0.255.255 range 16384 43767
! Using IP host and ephemeral port range from vlan to all other phones or gateways
130 permit udp host 172.19.244.3 range 1024 5000 host 10.0.40.5 eq snmp
!From IP host of NMS server and ephemeral port range (Different for Windows vs Sun) to IP
   host of phones and SNMP port (161)
140 permit udp host 10.0.40.5 eq snmp host 172.19.244.3 range 1024 5000
! From IP host of phone with SNMP port (161) to IP host of NMS server and ephemeral port
   range
```

In this section, you learned how to make VoIP service secure with IP phones and switches. Many methods and configuration examples were demonstrated to prevent unauthorized access, MAC CAM flooding, unauthorized network extensions, fraudulent DHCP server, DoS attack, and so on.

Summary

This chapter demonstrates how to protect the enterprise VoIP network with five different types of Cisco network devices; VoIP-aware firewall, Unified CME, Unified CM, IP phone, and multilayer switch.

The VoIP-aware firewalls (Cisco ASA, PIX, and FWSM) use an ACL as a primary method of protecting VoIP servers and media gateways from external devices that are not supposed to communicate with them. The ACL for the VoIP traffic should be dynamically updated because the ports used by entities are dynamically changed based on the call setup. The Cisco firewalls are running in the Active-Standby mode for high availability, and routed or transparent mode for operation. Each mode targets different service with pros and cons.

Unified CME supports the latest security features for small or medium-size enterprise VoIP networks to monitor and prevent malicious attacks or malfunctions of endpoints. To make a network secure, you should utilize the features of system access control, phone registration control, secure GUI management, class of restriction, and call blocking according to the policy and service requirements.

Unified CM supports the latest security technology to establish and maintain authenticated communications along with encryption as an enterprise-class IP telephony call processing system providing voice, video, mobility, and presence service. To make a network secure, utilize the features of device authentication, digest authentication, authorization, transport security, message integrity, and signal/media encryption.

As access devices, IP phones and switches provide security features and interfaces at the user end. With the IP phone, disable unused PC ports, enable Gratuitous ARP, isolate voice VLAN, restrict access to the built-in web server, and integrate authentication/encryption with VoIP servers. With the switch, configure the security features for preventing MAC CAM flooding, illegitimate port access, fraud DHCP server, DHCP DoS attack, and ARP flooding.

End Notes

1 Cisco Unified Communications Solution Reference Network Design (SRND) based on Cisco Unified Communications Manager Release 6.x, http://www.cisco.com/en/US/products/sw/voicesw/ps556/products_implementation_design_guide_book09186a008085eb0d.html.

2 RFC 2663, "NAT Terminology and Considerations," P. Srisuresh, M. Holdrege, August 1999.

3 Cisco Unified Communications Manager Express Security, http://www.cisco.com/en/US/netsol/ns340/ns394/ns165/ns391/networking_solutions_design_guidance09186a00801f8e30.html.

4 Cisco CallManager Security Guide Release 5.0, http://www.conft.com/en/US/docs/voice_ip_comm/cucm/security/5_0_1/sec50.html.

References

RFC 2617, "HTTP Authentication: Basic and Digest Access Authentication," J. Franks, P. Hallam-Baker, J. Hostetler, S. Lawrence, P. Leach, A. Luotonen, L. Stewart, June 1999.

RFC 3261, "SIP (Session Initiation Protocol)," J. Rosenberg, H. Schulzrinne, G. Camarillo, A. Johnston, J. Peterson, R. Sparks, M. Handley, E. Schooler, June 2002.

RFC 3711, "Secure Real-time Transport Protocol (SRTP)," M. Baugher, D. McGrew, M. Naslund, E. Carrara, K. Norrman, March 2004.

RFC 4346, "Transport Layer Security (TLS) Protocol," T. Dierks, E. Rescorla, April 2006.

PART III

Lawful Interception (CALEA)

This chapter covers the fundamentals of Lawful Interception with the following topics:

- Definition and background
- Requirements from law enforcement agents
- Reference model from an architectural perspective
- Functional specifications
- Request and response interfaces
- Operational considerations

CHAPTER 10

Lawful Interception Fundamentals

Many of the previous chapters in this book have presented the general meaning of VoIP security; the main topics are, in short, what threats exist and how to mitigate them. However, this chapter focuses on a different aspect of VoIP security that is defined from the government's perspective, which is known as Lawful Interception (LI). LI is based on a government law requiring service providers to provide interception of user information.

The general consensus is that LI belongs to the category of VoIP security even though some people may not agree with it.

The purpose of this chapter is to provide the following information on LI:

- Definition and background
- Requirements from law enforcement agents
- Reference model from an architectural perspective
- Functional specifications
- Request and response interfaces
- Operational considerations

The details of implementing LI with examples will be discussed in the next chapter.

NOTE   The content in this chapter does not represent any legal requirements or obligations for a certain country, but provides general guidelines based on common specifications so that you may understand the concept and the service architecture at a high level. Readers who are planning or implementing LI in their VoIP service need to look at country-specific requirements and standards. For Europe and America, there is more information on the following section.

TIP   For more information on country-specific requirements and standards, go to your favorite search engine and search for "Lawful Interception," "Communications Assistance for Law Enforcement Act (CALEA)," or "Wiretapping" with the country name.

Definition and Background

LI, also known as *wiretapping*, is the lawfully authorized interception of communications (call content) and call-identifying information (call data) for a particular telecommunication subscriber (target subscriber), requested by a law enforcement agency (LEA).

The call content (CC) is, for example, voice or video. The call data (CD) is a dialed number, call direction, call duration, signaling information, and so on. The target subscriber is identified generally by a phone number.

The LEA could be any agency that is able to request lawful interception; for example, the FBI or local police in the U.S. requests it with a corresponding warrant.

LI in public switched telephone networks (PSTN) has been executed for more than 20 years in most countries. The scope of LI in this context is the VoIP network, managed by telecommunication service providers (TSP) who are being asked to meet legal and regulatory requirements for the interception of voice and data communications in IP networks in a variety of countries worldwide.

Almost every country has its own LI requirements and has adopted global standards (or proposals) fully or partially, developed by standard organizations. There are two groups of leading organizations in Europe and America:

In Europe:

- European Telecommunications Standards Institute (ETSI, 102-xxx series)

In America:

- Alliance for Telecommunications Industry Solutions ([ATIS], T1.xxx series)
- Telecommunications Industry Associations (TIA, J-STD-xxx series)
- PacketCable (PKT-SP-ESP series)
- Cisco (Service Independent Interception [SII])

In Europe, the European Council Resolution of 17 January 1995 on the lawful interception of telecommunications (96/C 329/01) declared electronic surveillance as a mandatory requirement, even though some countries did not fully accept it because of privacy issues.

In America, the U.S. Congress passed the Communications Assistance for Law Enforcement Act (CALEA) in 1994 to make clear a telecommunications carrier's duty to cooperate in the interception of communications.

Although Europe has a single organization, ETSI, as just shown, America has multiple organizations (ATIS, TIA, PacketCable, and Cisco) with different proposals, even though those are fairly similar at a high level; actually, some specifications inherit the other. The standardizing is still in progress.

This chapter focuses on common concepts and methodology based on the proposals in the U.S., referring to the following specifications:

1 **ATIS T1.678**[1]—Defines Lawfully Authorized Electronic Surveillance (LAES) for voice-over-packet technologies in wireline telecommunications networks, written by ATIS.

2 **TIA ANSI/J-STD-025A**[2]—Defines the interfaces between a TSP and an LEA to assist the LEA in conducting lawfully authorized electronic surveillance. ATIS T1.678 inherited this specification.

3 **PacketCable PKT-SP-ESP1.5-I02-070412**[3]—Defines the interface between a TSP that provides telecommunications services to the public for hire using PacketCable capabilities, and an LEA to assist the LEA in conducting LAES.

4 **RFC 3924**[4]—Describes Cisco's architecture for supporting lawful intercept in IP networks, and provides a general solution that has a minimum set of common interfaces.

Now that you are aware of the basic concept, definition, and background of LI, the next section shows what the requirements of LI are, as an initial step.

Requirements from Law Enforcement Agents

LEA requires TSP to provide certain capabilities or information for LI. As a precondition for TSP's assistance, LEA has to serve TSP with the necessary legal authorization identifying the target subscriber (or subject), the communications and information to be accessed, and service areas where the communications and information can be accessed. After this authorization is obtained, the TSP shall perform access and delivery for transmission to the LEA's procured equipment, facilities, or services.

The requirements for TSP vary from country to country, but many requirements remain common. The purpose of the following list of requirements is to provide an understanding of the motivation behind the architecture and some of the requirements imposed on components and interfaces that are described in the later sections of this chapter.

- LI must not be detectable by the target subscriber (or subject)—that is, it must be confidential.

- Mechanisms must be in place to limit unauthorized personnel from performing or knowing about lawfully authorized intercepts.

- There is often a requirement to provide the intercepted call data separately from the actual call content.

- If call data is delivered separately from content, there must be some means to correlate the data and the content with each other.

- If the information being intercepted is encrypted by the TSP and the TSP has access to the keys, the information must be decrypted before delivery to the LEA or the encryption keys should be passed to the LEA to allow them to decrypt the information.

- If the information being intercepted is encrypted by the target subscriber and its remote party and the service provider has access to the keys, the service provider may deliver the keys to the LEA.

- There is often a requirement for TSP to be able to do multiple simultaneous intercepts on a target subscriber. The fact that there are multiple intercepts should be transparent to the LEAs.

- There is often a requirement that the service provider should not deliver any unauthorized information to the LEA.

Now that you are aware of common requirements, the next section takes a look at the basic architecture of LI.

Reference Model from an Architectural Perspective

The functions needed to perform LI are broadly categorized as access, delivery, collection, service provider administration, and law enforcement administration functions. These functions are described herein without regard to their implementation. The relationship between these functional categories is shown in Figure 10-1.

Figure 10-1 *Lawful Interception Reference Model*

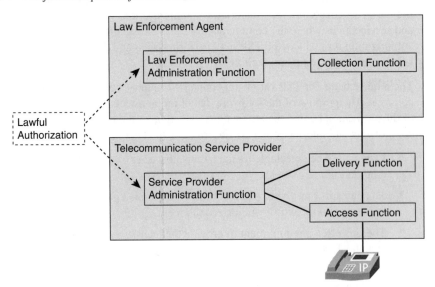

As shown, the access function, delivery function, and service provider administration function are the responsibility of the TSP, and the collection function and law enforcement administration function are the responsibility of the LEA. The use of these functions to perform an interception is initiated by receipt of a specific lawful authorization. The following sections present a brief description of each function.

NOTE   All LI functions use an initial capital letter for each function's name followed by the letter "F," such as "AF" for "Access Function" because these names are defined by LI specifications and not as general terms.

AF (Access Function)

The AF consists of one or more intercept access points (IAPs), accesses and intercepts the target subscriber's call data and content confidentially.

IAP may be an existing device that has intercept capability or it could be a special device that is provided for that purpose; for example, a Session Border Controller (SBC).

The AF typically includes the ability

- To intercept the target subscriber's call data information unobtrusively and make the information available to the DF (Delivery Function).

- To intercept target call content unobtrusively and make the call content available to the DF.

- To protect (for example, prevent unauthorized access, manipulation, and disclosure) intercept controls, intercepted call content, and call data consistent with TSP security policies and practices.

The intercepted information by the AF is delivered to the next function, Delivery Function.

DF (Delivery Function)

The DF delivers intercepted communications to one or more CFs (Collection Functions) in the form of call content and data.

The DF typically includes the ability

- To accept call content for each target subscriber over one or more channels from the AF(s).

- To deliver call content for each target subscriber over one or more call content channels (CCCs; see the following Note) to a CF.

- To accept call data or packet-mode (see the following Note) content information for each target subscriber over one or more channels and deliver that information to the CF over one or more call data channels (CDCs; see the following Note).

- To ensure that the call data and content delivered to a CF is authorized for a particular LEA.

- To duplicate and deliver authorized call data and content for the target subscriber to one or more CFs (up to a total of five).

- To protect (for example, prevent unauthorized access, manipulation, and disclosure) intercept controls, intercepted call content, and data consistent with TSP security policies and practices.

NOTE   Call content channel (CCC) is the logical link between the device performing an electronic surveillance access function and the LEA that primarily carries the call content passed between an intercept subject and one or more associates.

Call data channel (CDC) is the logical link between the device performing an electronic surveillance access function and the LEA that primarily carries call-identifying information.

NOTE   *Packet mode* is a communication in which individual packets or virtual circuits of a communication within a physical circuit are switched or routed by the accessing telecommunication system. Each packet may take a different route through the intervening network(s).

After receiving the intercepted information, the DF sends them the next function, Collection Function.

CF (Collection Function)

The CF is responsible for collecting lawfully authorized intercepted communications (call content) and call data for an LEA. The CF is the responsibility of the LEA.

The CF typically includes the ability

- To receive and process call content information for each target subscriber.

- To receive and process information regarding each target subscriber (for example, call associated or non-call associated).

SPAF (Service Provider Administration Function)

The administrator of TSP receives the information of a target subscriber and call type (call data or/and content) from LEA, and uses this Service Provider Administration Function (SPAF) to control the Access Function and Delivery Function. The SPAF interface is described in the next section.

Unlike other LI functions (AF, DF, and CF), most standard documentations do not define the specification of SPAF and handover to solution providers. Therefore, the implementation of SPAF is various from vender to vendor. The detail of SPAF is beyond the scope of this book.

LEAF (Law Enforcement Administration Function)

LEAF provides the provisioning interface for the interception as a result of a court order or warrant delivered by the LEA. It could involve separate provisioning interfaces for several components, but more typically is a single interface to the service provider administration function, which takes care of provisioning of other components in the service network. Because of the requirement in some laws to limit accessibility to authorized personnel, the provisioning interface has to be strictly controlled. In many cases, the identity of the target subscriber received from the LEA has to be translated into an identity that can be used by the network to enable the interception.

Unlike other LI functions (AF, DF, and CF), most standard documentations do not define the specification of LEAF and hand over to solution providers. Therefore, the implementation of LEAF is various from vender to vendor. The detail of LEAF is beyond the scope of this book.

Now that you are aware of five different functions of LI, the next section takes a look at the interfaces between the functions.

Request and Response Interfaces

Figure 10-1 illustrates the functional reference model of Lawful Interception with the information of who owns which functions. This section looks into the internal and external interfaces among access, service provider, and LEA domain.

Figure 10-2 illustrates the interfaces between the functional modules that are renamed to make the names closer to the actual implementation. The Service Provider Administration Function has an interface (HI-1) with LEA and receives provisioning request. The Mediation Device (MD; see the following Note) has mainly a delivery function interfacing with IAPs to provision interception and receive call data and content.

NOTE   A Mediation Device (MD) is maintained by TSP and is the center of the LI process. It sends configuration commands to the various IAPs to enable intercepts, receives intercept information (call data and content), and delivers this information to the LEA. If more than one LEA is monitoring an intercept target, the mediation device duplicates the intercept information for each LEA. The mediation device is sometimes called the delivery function.

In some cases, the mediation device performs additional filtering of the information. It is also responsible for formatting the information to be compliant with the country or technology-specific requirements for delivery to law enforcement.

Figure 10-2   *Interfaces of Lawful Interception*

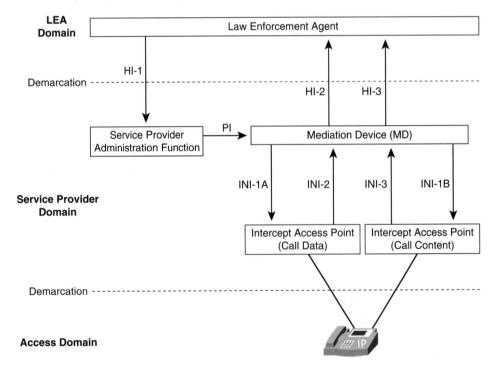

Note that there are demarcation points between LEA, Service Provider, and Access domain in Figure 10-2, assuming that the service provider does not manage the subscriber's access network.

Table 10-1 provides a brief description of the interfaces in Figure 10-2, based on what information is sent to which direction.

Table 10-1 *Description of LI Interfaces*

Interface	Description
HI-1	**Handover Interface 1**—The law enforcement agent provides intercept information to the service provider administration function. The information could be the phone number of the target subscriber, time of interception, message format, encryption key, and so on.
HI-2	**Handover Interface 2**—The interface between the mediation device and law enforcement agent (for example, collection function) for delivering call data, such as call duration, time, call direction, message headers, and so on.
HI-3	**Handover Interface 3**—Interface between the mediation device and law enforcement agent (for example, collection function) for delivering call content, such as voice or video.
PI	**Provisioning Interface**—Provisioning interface from the service provider administration function to a mediation device. The parameters include target identifier, duration of interception, type of interception, and so on.
INI-1A	**Internal Network Interface 1A**—A mediation device provides interception information (for example, target identifier, duration) to the intercept access point for call data.
INI-1B	**Internal Network Interface 1B**—A mediation device provides interception information (for example, target identifier, duration) to the intercept access point for call content.
INI-2	**Internal Network Interface 2**—The internal access point sends call data information to the mediation device through this interface.
INI-3	**Internal Network Interface 3**—The internal access point sends call content to the mediation device.

Additionally, to provide a generic interface for intercepting, replicating, encapsulating, and transporting content packets to the MD, the content intercept interface (INI-3) should specify the following:

- A filter specification for classifying the packets to be intercepted
- The destination address of the MD (where to send the packets)
- Encapsulation and transport parameter
- A timeout value for the interception should be specified, which defines a limited lifetime so that failures will not result in interceptions remaining beyond their authorized lifetime

The flow of interception in general can be exemplified as follows:

Step 1 A warrant from a court.

Step 2 LEA decides corresponding TSP.

Step 3 LEA sends the request through HI-1.

Step 4 TSP receives the request and configures it with SPAF.

Step 5 SPAF provisions the interception through PI.

Step 6 MD receives the provisioning request and decides corresponding IAPs.

Step 7 MD sends the interception information to IAPs through INI-1A and/or INI-1B.

Step 8 IAPs intercept the call data and/or content of target subscriber.

Step 9 IAPs duplicate and send the call data and/or content to MD through INI-2 and/or INI-3.

Step 10 MD forwards the call data and/or content to LEA through HI-2 and/or HI-3.

Now that you are aware of LI interfaces—that is, what information is sent to which direction—the next section shows operational considerations when practicing LI.

Operational Considerations

There could be a variety of operational issues in LI, depending on the requirements and unique circumstances country by country. In particular, security-related issues are outstanding because of the sensitive nature of LI, both from the standpoint of the need to protect sensitive data and to conceal the identities of law enforcement agencies and the intercept targets.

The following section describes typical issues that need to be considered when implementing and operating LI. The content refers to Cisco SII architecture.[5]

Detection by the Target Subscriber

A common requirement is to ensure that the target subscribers are unable to detect that they are being intercepted. It assumes that they have the following capabilities:

- **Able to check IP addresses or routing path**—You can do this by capturing signal or media packets locally and checking the destination of those packets. If the destination is different than usual, you may detect that an interception device is involved and those packets are rerouted.

- **Able to check if any unusual signaling is occurring on their customer premises equipment (CPE)**—You can detect this by capturing signal packets locally and comparing with usual signals.

- **Able to detect degradation or interruptions in service**—You can detect this by comparing the voice quality with usual quality when using the phone. If media is rerouted for interception, the quality of voice could be affected.

Because of these assumptions, the interception mechanism described here does not involve special requests to the CPE, rerouting of packets, or end-to-end changes in IP addresses. Instead, content intercept is done on a device along the normal content path (for example, no rerouting has occurred) that is within the service provider's network. A convenient content IAP is an SBC or router at the edge of the service provider's network to which the target subscriber connects.

NOTE   In a case where there is multihoming (two or more routers connected to provide access for the CPE), intercept taps may have to be installed on more than one access router. If the CPE is multihomed to multiple service providers, the interception will have to be installed on each service provider separately and the LEA will have to correlate the data.

Address Information for Call Content Interception

In some cases where the location and/or addressing information for the interception is not known until the target subscriber registers (or makes a call in the case of voice), the call data may provide needed information in order to do the content tap.

Example 10-1 shows an example with SIP messages (INVITE and OK). It assumes that the target subscriber, UserA (4085556666), makes a call to UserB (4157778888), and the proxy server in the middle is working as a back-to-back user agent (B2BUA) as well as a media gateway. When the IP phone of UserA sends INVITE, the service provider detects that this call request is from a target subscriber by looking at the phone number (4085556666) in the From header, and finds that the IP address of target subscriber is 192.168.100.10 (as shown in the "c=" line) and the media port is 49172 ("m=" line). The service provider enables LI function on the B2BUA and responds OK with the media gateway's IP address (172.23.10.10) and port (3456). All media going through this IP address and port will be duplicated and forwarded to a mediation device.

Example 10-1 *Address for Call Content Interception in SIP*

```
INVITE sip:4157778888@example.com SIP/2.0
   Via: SIP/2.0/UDP userAclient.example.com:5060;branch=z9hG4bK74bf9
   Max-Forwards: 70
   From: UserA <sip:4085556666@example.com>;tag=9fxced76sl
   To: UserB <sip:4157778888@example.com>
   Call-ID: 2xTb9vxSit55XU7p8@example.com
   CSeq: 1 INVITE
   Contact: <sip:4085556666@userAclient.example.com>
   Content-Type: application/sdp
   Content-Length: 151

   v=0
   o=UserA 2890844526 2890844526 IN IP4 userAclient.example.com
   s=-
   c=IN IP4 192.168.100.10
   t=0 0
   m=audio 49172 RTP/AVP 0
   a=rtpmap:0 PCMU/8000


SIP/2.0 200 OK
   Via: SIP/2.0/UDP userAclient.example.com:5060;branch=z9hG4bK74bf9
   From: UserA <sip:4085556666@example.com>;tag=9fxced76sl
   To: UserB <sip:4157778888@example.com>;tag=314159
   Call-ID: 2xTb9vxSit55XU7p8@example.com
   CSeq: 1 INVITE
   Contact: <sip:4157778888@userBclient.example.com>
   Content-Type: application/sdp
   Content-Length: 147

   v=0
   o=UserB 2890844527 2890844527 IN IP4 userBclient.example.com
   s=-
   c=IN IP4 172.23.10.10
   t=0 0
   m=audio 3456 RTP/AVP 0
   a=rtpmap:0 PCMU/8000
```

Content Encryption

If the call content is encrypted and the service provider has access to the encryption keys (for example, receives keys in Session Description Protocol [SDP]), the keys can be sent via the call data. It is, however, possible for end users to exchange keys by some other means without any knowledge of the service provider, in which case the service provider will not be able to provide the keys. This kind of encryption could make decryption at the LEA impossible. This is why the original packets are provided on interface INI-3 rather than attempting to convert them to some other format.

Another consideration in encryption is interfaces between LI functions. All interfaces must be able to provide strong cryptographic authentication to establish the identity of each party, and must correlate the identity with the action they are attempting to perform. That is, it is not sufficient to expect that authentication alone implies any specific authorization. Because LI is an interesting target for attackers, all interfaces must perform some sort of cryptographic message integrity checking such as Hash-based Message Authentication Code (HMAC)-Message Digest 5 (MD5). Message integrity checking must also counter replay attacks. Because of privacy and confidentiality considerations, the architecture should allow for the use of encryption. Although encryption is not necessarily a requirement, it is highly recommended and may be a requirement in some LI deployments.

The next topic, unauthorized creation and detection, is another type of security consideration.

Unauthorized Creation and Detection

Another concern is the prevention of unauthorized creation and detection of intercepts. This is particularly important when a network element such as a router is used as a content IAP. Those routers that have the capability should be carefully controlled with access to intercept capability and information only via authorized personnel. In one approach using the model in Figure 10-2, the mediation device is in a controlled environment and it does the intercept request to the content IAP over an encrypted link. Logging and auditing are used to detect unauthorized attempts to access the intercept capability.

Because legal intercept is expected to run on the wide-open Internet, very few assumptions should be made about how well the networks of the LEAs and the TSPs can be secured. Although this book does not examine the issues of physical security, operating systems, or application hardening within the LI architecture, they are clearly important considerations. In particular, both the MD and LEA servers must be considered prime targets for attacks by hackers. Hardening measures commensurate with other highly vulnerable servers, such as key distribution and authentication, authorization, and accounting (AAA) servers, must be considered in any design.

Call Forwarding or Transfer

The feature of call forwarding or transfer that is often provided as a local service feature makes interception more difficult. If call forwarding is invoked, a call that was intended to terminate on the target subscriber may be forwarded anywhere in the network resulting in the media stream bypassing the original content IAP. Also, because call forwarding can often be set up on a call-by-call basis, the location of the content IAP will often not be known until the call is set up.

Capacity

Support for lawful intercept on a network element supporting customers consumes resources on that equipment. Therefore, support for lawful intercept requires capacity planning and engineering to ensure that revenue-producing services are not adversely affected.

The CPUs of the following devices will be impacted by LI:

- **Edge router**—Must be able to intercept and replicate all intercepted IP communication on its section of the network.

- **Trunking gateway**—Must be able to intercept and replicate all intercepted calls that are forwarded off-net.

- **Mediation device**—Must be able to support the required maximum number of simultaneous intercepts.

The following interfaces must be engineered with sufficient bandwidth to support LI traffic:

- IAP (for call data) <-> mediation device

- IAP (for call content) <-> mediation device

- Mediation device <-> collection functions

You should also understand that three-way calls require twice the bandwidth of regular calls because they require two pairs of transmit and receive channels.

You may also need to provision a network management system for LI, such as domain name server (DNS), DHCP server, simple network management protocol (SNMP), network time protocol (NTP) server, and so on.

The various devices involved in LI have minimum software and memory requirements that must be met. Because of the number of possible devices, these requirements are subject to change.

The several issues in this section should be considered before implementing and operating LI service.

Summary

LI is the lawfully authorized interception of communications (call content) and call-identifying information (call data) for a particular telecommunication subscriber (target subscriber), requested by LEA.

The call content is voice or video. The call data is a dialed number, call direction, call duration or signaling information, and so on. The target subscriber is identified generally by a phone number.

Almost every country has its own LI requirements and has adopted global standards (or proposals) fully or partially, developed by standard organizations. There are two groups of leading organizations: ATIS, TIA, PacketCable and Cisco in the U.S., and ETSI in the EU.

In America, the U.S. Congress passed CALEA in 1994 to make clear a telecommunications carrier's duty to cooperate in the interception of communications. Although Europe has a single organization, America has multiple organizations with different proposals, even though those are fairly similar at a high level.

As a precondition for TSP's assistance, LEA should serve TSP with the necessary legal authorization identifying the target subscriber, the communications and information to be accessed, and service areas where the communications and information can be accessed. After this authorization is obtained, the TSP shall perform access and delivery for transmission to the LEA's procured equipment, facilities, or services.

The requirements for TSP vary from country to country, but many requirements remain common at a high level, such as: the LI must not be detectable by the target subscriber, must have a capability of encryption, must provide a separate interface for call data/content, and must be able to do multiple simultaneous intercepts on a target subscriber, and so on.

The functions needed to perform LI are broadly categorized as AF, DF, CF, SPAF, and LEAF. The AF, DF, and SPAF are the responsibility of TSP, and the CF and LEAF are the responsibility of LEA.

Interface INI-1 is used for MD to request IAP interception of call data and content. Interface INI-2 is used for IAP to send call data to MD. Interface INI-3 is used for IAP to send call content to MD. Interface HI-1, HI-2, and HI-3 are used between LEA and MD to send the request and receive the response of interception.

There could be a variety of operational issues on LI, depending on the requirements and unique circumstances country by country. The typical issues are detection by the target subscriber, identifying location/address information for call content interception, content encryption, unauthorized creation/detection, special call type (call forward/transfer), and capacity.

End Notes

1   ATIS T1.678, "Lawfully Authorized Electronic Surveillance (LAES) for Voice over Packet Technologies in Wireline Telecommunications Networks," Alliance for Telecommunications Industry Solutions, http://www.atis.org.

2   TIA ANSI/J-STD-025A, "Lawfully Authorized Electronic Surveillance, Telecommunications Industry Associations," http://www.tiaonline.org/.

3   PacketCable PKT-SP-ESP1.5-I02-070412, "Electronic Surveillance," PacketCable, http://www.packetcable.com.

4   RFC 3924, "Cisco Architecture for Lawful Intercept in IP Networks," F. Baker, B. Foster, C. Sharp, October 2004.

5   Cisco Service Independent Intercept Architecture, Cisco Systems, http://www.cisco.com/en/US/technologies/tk583/tk799/technologies_design_guide09186a0080826773.pdf.

This chapter covers the methodology of deploying Lawful Interception in the following interfaces:

- Intercept Request Interface
- Call Data Connection Interface
- Call Content Connection Interface

CHAPTER 11

Lawful Interception Implementation

Chapter 10 covered the fundamentals of Lawful Interception, such as definition, requirements, basic architecture, and so on. This chapter covers the next step, how to implement each of the fundamentals in the VoIP service environment.

Even if the requirement from Law Enforcement Agent (LEA) is fixed, the implementation varies depending on a Telecommunications Service Provider (TSP). The primary reason for this variance is that there is no single standard that rules the method of implementation for whole LI architecture. In fact, most standard specifications provide partial implementation for the interface between functional modules.

To show you how to implement these fundamentals, this chapter focuses on the following interfaces with corresponding specifications in the United States, in order to give you guidelines:

- Intercept Request Interface (INI-1)
    - SIP P-DCS
    - Cisco SII (Service Independent Intercept)
- Call Data Connection Interface (INI-2, HI-2)
    - PacketCable Electronic Surveillance Specification
- Call Content Connection Interface (INI-3, HI-3)
    - PacketCable Electronic Surveillance Specification

NOTE The content in this chapter does not represent any legal requirements or obligations for a certain country, but provides general guidelines based on common specifications. Readers who are planning or implementing LI in their VoIP service network should look at country-specific requirements and standards.

Intercept Request Interface

This section focuses on the interface between a mediation device (MD) and an intercept access point (IAP) for intercepting call data and content. Figure 11-1 illustrates a simplified view of the interfaces between functional modules; MD and IAP could be multiple devices.

Figure 11-1 *Interface Between MD and IAP*

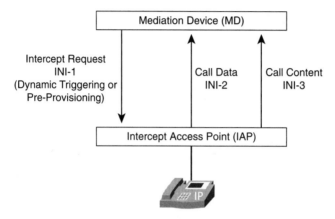

There are two methods of requesting interception: dynamic triggering and pre-provisioning.

Dynamic triggering means that the MD has full control of VoIP signals and sends a request message to the IAP when the target subscriber is detected in the signaling path. That is, the MD keeps monitoring all signals between endpoints and detects the target, whereas the IAP has no information about the target beforehand and just responds passively according to the MD's request. Some VoIP protocols provide this kind of interface, such as SIP P-DCS-LAES header (RFC 3603).

Pre-provisioning means that the MD provisions the request to the IAP beforehand so that the IAP may send back intercepted call data or content when the IAP detects the target subscriber. That is, the IAP should know information about the target beforehand and monitor the traffic passing by. This kind of interface is usually proprietary, and Cisco's Service Independent Intercept (SII) is an example.

The following sections cover the details of SIP P-DCS headers and Cisco SII to give you a better understanding of intercepting between the MD and the IAP.

NOTE Both SIP P-DCS headers and Cisco SII define only the requesting interface. The response interface (for example, formatting call data or content) is defined by other organizations like PacketCable, which is described in the section "Call Data and Content Connection Interface" in this chapter.

SIP P-DCS Header

SIP P-DCS-LAES and P-DCS-Redirect extension headers are used for dynamically triggering the intercept request, which is defined in RFC 3603,[1] which this section refers to.

The P-DCS-LAES extension contains the information needed to support Lawfully Authorized Electronic Surveillance (LAES). This header contains the address and port of a mediation device for delivery of a duplicate stream of call data (event messages) related to this call. The header may also contain an additional address and port for delivery of call content.

The P-DCS-Redirect extension contains call data information needed to support the requirements of LAES of redirected calls. This header is only used between proxies and trusted User Agents (for example, TSP's PSTN gateway).

Use of P-DCS-LAES and P-DCS-Redirect is controlled by a combination of legislation, regulation, and court orders, which must be followed.

In certain cases inclusion of these headers will be mandated, and therefore must be present in the requests and responses indicated. In other cases (for example, communication with untrusted user agents), inclusion of these headers will be forbidden, and therefore must not be present in the request and responses indicated.

The P-DCS-LAES and P-DCS-Redirect headers have the following parameters:

- P-DCS-LAES
    - Laes-sig (hostport)
    - Laes-param (Laes-content/Laes-key/generic-param)
    - Laes-content
    - Laes-key
- P-DCS-Redirect
    - Called-ID
    - redir-uri-param
    - Redirector
    - redir-count-param
    - Redir-count

The values of Laes-sig and Laes-content are addresses of the mediation device (or Delivery Function [DF]), and used as the destination address for call data and content, respectively. Laes-key is a string generated by the proxy that is used to securely transfer information.

The P-DCS-Redirect header contains redirection information. The redir-uri-param indicates the original destination requested by the user (for example, dialed number), the Redirector indicates the new destination, and the Redir-count indicates the number of redirections that have occurred.

The intercept process flows with the P-DCS headers are as follows. The first one is for outbound calls.

Intercept Process Flow for Outbound Call

Figure 11-2 illustrates an example of intercept process flow when a target subscriber originates a call, based on a common call scenario.

Figure 11-2 *Intercept Process Flow When Initiating a Call*

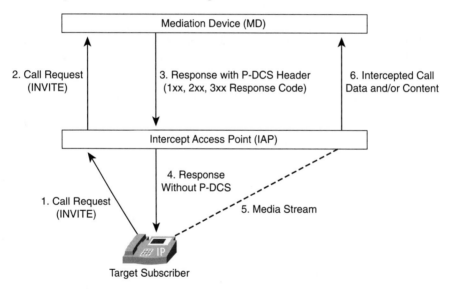

The description of each step in Figure 11-2 is as follows:

Step 1 A target subscriber initiates a call with SIP INVITE.

Step 2 The IAP receives the INVITE and sends it to an MD having proxy function.

Step 3   The MD checks for an outstanding lawfully authorized surveillance order for the originating subscriber, and decides whether it triggers or not. The presence of the P-DCS-LAES header in the first reliable 1xx (except 100), 2xx, or 3xx response, indicates that the IAP should trigger the interception.

If a 3xx-Redirect response is received to the initial INVITE request, and if a P-DCS-LAES header is present in the 3xx response, the IAP should include that header unchanged in the new INVITE for redirecting. In the new INVITE, the IAP should also include a P-DCS-Redirect header containing the original dialed number, the new destination number, and the number of redirections that have occurred.

Step 4   The IAP relays the response without the P-DCS header so that the target subscriber cannot recognize any detection involved.

Step 5   After call setup, media channels are opened and the target subscriber sends and receives media through the IAP that could be different from the IAP handling signals.

Step 6   The IAP sends intercepted (duplicated) call data or/and content to the MD that could be different from the MD handling signals.

An IAP that includes a Refer-to header in a REFER request, when the originating subscriber has an outstanding lawfully authorized surveillance order, should include a P-DCS-LAES header attached to the Refer-to. The P-DCS-LAES header should include the address and port of the delivery function (MD) for a copy of the call data and call content.

The IAP and MD should not send the P-DCS-LAES and P-DCS-Redirect headers to an untrusted entity.

Now that you are aware of the intercept process flow for outbound calls, the next section looks at the flow of inbound calls.

Intercept Process Flow for Inbound Call

Figure 11-3 illustrates an example of intercept process flow when a target subscriber receives a call, based on a common call scenario.

Figure 11-3 *Intercept Process Flow When Terminating a Call*

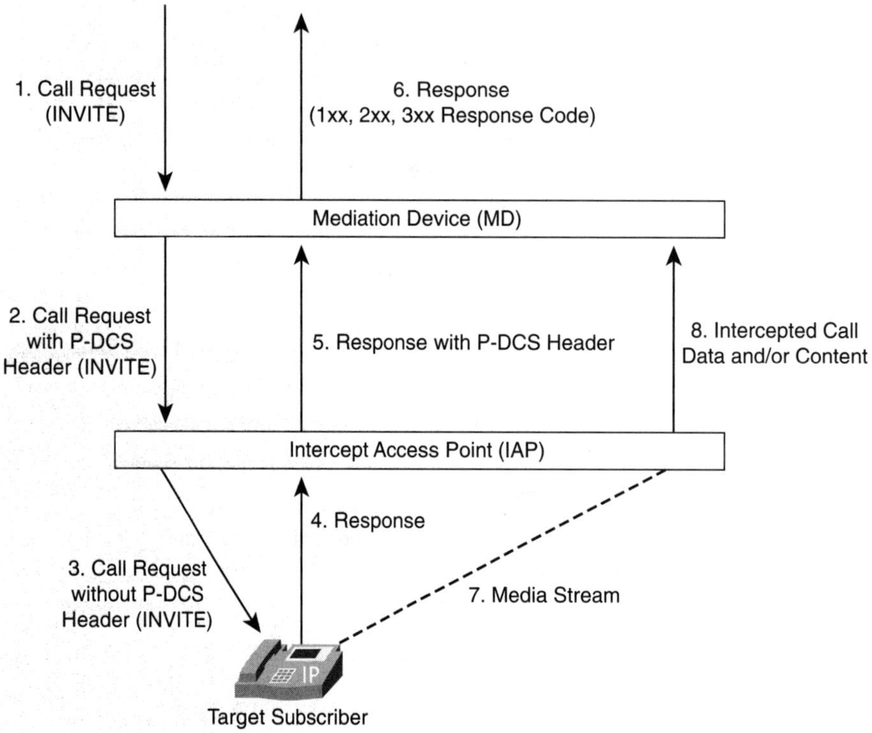

The description of each step in Figure 11-3 is as follows:

Step 1   An MD having proxy function receives a call request (INVITE) from another proxy server. The MD checks for an outstanding lawfully authorized surveillance order for the terminating subscriber, or the presence of the P-DCS-LAES header in the INVITE request. If the terminating subscriber is under surveillance, MD adds a P-DCS-LAES header to the INVITE with IP and port information for the delivery of call data and/or content, as well as security key information if needed.

Step 2   The IAP receives the INVITE with P-DCS-LAES header and triggers the interception for the target subscriber.

Step 3   The IAP sends the INVITE without P-DCS-LAES header to the subscriber. The P-DCS-LAES header is removed so that the target subscriber cannot recognize any detection involved.

Step 4   The endpoint of the target subscriber responds for the call request.

Step 5   The IAP sends the response.

Step 6   The MD sends the response to the originating proxy. If the IAP is unable to perform the required surveillance, the MD should include a P-DCS-LAES header in the first reliable non-100 response requesting the originating proxy to perform the surveillance. The P-DCS-LAES header should include the address and port of the MD for a copy of the call data and/or content.

Step 7   After call setup, media channels are opened and the target subscriber sends and receives media through IAP that could be different from the IAP handling signals.

Step 8   The IAP sends intercepted (duplicated) call data and/or content to MD that could be different from the MD handling signals.

In this section so far, you have learned about the intercept process flows for inbound and outbound calls with SIP P-DCS headers, which is the method of dynamic triggering. The next subsection covers the pre-provisioning method with Cisco SII.

Cisco SII

The SII architecture was developed by Cisco to provide compliance with LI legislation and regulations. It is defined in RFC 3924[2] and the Cisco SII Architecture document,[3] which this content refers to.

It provides a common approach for intercepting IP communications using existing network elements. The architecture addresses the key LI requirements and does so in a cost-effective manner. Key features of the architecture include the following:

- Use of standard access list technology to provide the intercept.

- Encapsulation of the entire intercepted and replicated packet so that the original source and destination addresses are available (important information for intercept purposes).

- Use of a control plane for intercept that is different from call control, which prevents network operations personnel from detecting the presence of active intercepts in the network (see the following Note).

- An integrated approach that limits the intercept activity to the router or gateway that is handling the target's IP traffic and only activates an intercept when the target is accessing the network.

- No LI-related command-line interface (CLI) commands that could allow for the detection of intercept activity on a router or gateway.

- LI-related Management Information Bases (MIBs) and traps sent only to the (third-party) equipment controlling the intercept.

- Support for multiple encapsulation and transport formats (for example, PacketCable Electronic Surveillance Specification, described in the section "Call Data and Content Connection Interfaces").

NOTE   A *control plane* defines the transport used for sending or receiving the messages that initiate the LI. Because it is important that unauthorized network operations personnel not know that intercepts are active on the network, it is important to hide or keep separate the active intercept messages from those messages used for routine call setup. However, many TSPs routinely monitor all messages for diagnostic purposes, so the personnel may be able to learn of the interception.

The next topic is the description of device interfaces in SII.

Device Interfaces

Figure 11-4 illustrates the device interfaces in the context of the specific devices that are used in a Cisco SII network. Note that Call Management Server (CMS), edge router, and trunking gateway have the call data and call content IAP function in this picture. Access server and authentication, authorization, and accounting (AAA) server are used for "data" interception that is beyond the scope of this book.

Figure 11-4   *Cisco SII Device Interfaces*

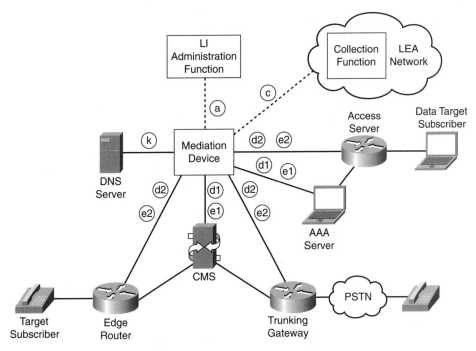

Table 11-1 shows the description of each interface in Figure 11-4.

Table 11-1   *Cisco SII Device Interfaces*

Interface	Description
a	The LI administration function sends intercept provisioning information (target identifier, duration of intercept, and so on) to the mediation device.
c	The mediation device delivers intercept information to the Collection Function (CF). If more than one LEA is intercepting the same target, the mediation device must duplicate the intercept information to send to the CF of each LEA. This interface meets the specifications found in the PacketCable Electronic Surveillance Specification document.[4]

continues

Table 11-1 *Cisco SII Device Interfaces (Continued)*

Interface	Description
d1	This is the delivery interface. The call data IAP uses this interface to deliver call data to the mediation device. For voice, this is according to the PacketCable EventMessages Specification document. For data, this is Remote Authentication Dial-In User Service (RADIUS) accounting messages.
	For voice intercepts, the IAP is the call control entity (call agent, SIP proxy, or H.323 gateway). For data intercepts, the IAP is the AAA server (or a sniffer monitoring RADIUS traffic).
d2	The call content IAP replicates call content and sends it to the mediation device. The call content IAP encapsulates the packets with additional User Datagram Protocol and IP headers and a 32-bit call content connection identifier (CCCID) header, based on the PacketCable Electronic Surveillance Specification document. The CCCID is used to associate the call content with the target.
	The CCCID is included so that the mediation device can map intercepts to the appropriate warrants. Usually, the mediation device will rewrite the CCCID before forwarding intercept information to CFs.
	The call content IAP is an edge router, trunking gateway, or access server.
e1	The mediation device uses Secure Shell (SSH) to provision an intercept on the call data IAP.
e2	The mediation device uses Simple Network Management Protocol version 3 (SNMPv3) to instruct the call content IAP to replicate call content and send it to the mediation device. The call content IAP can be either an edge router or a trunking gateway for voice.
k	The mediation device queries the Domain Name Service (DNS) server to determine the fully qualified domain name (FQDN) of the call content IAP.

Intercept Process Flow for Standard Call

Figure 11-5 illustrates the topology for a standard Cisco SII voice intercept at a trunking gateway or aggregation router. Note that this is a high-level call flow that does not include all details of the protocol messaging involved.

Figure 11-5   *Standard Intercept Process Flow*

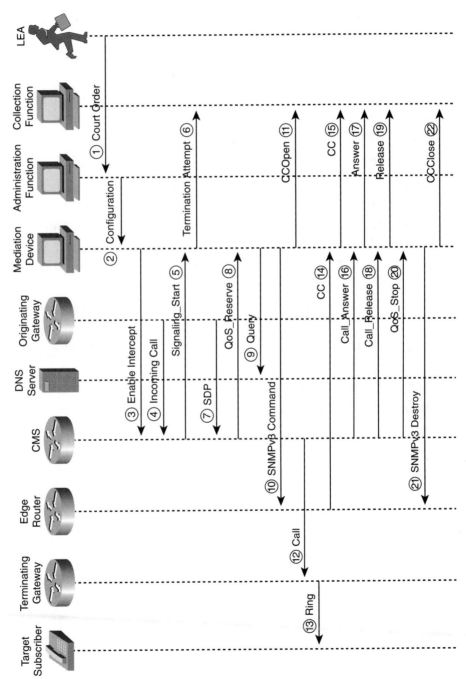

The description of each step in Figure 11-5 is as follows:

Step 1 The LEA physically delivers a court order to the network administrator who operates the LI administration function.

Step 2 The LI administration function sends a configuration command to the mediation device that enters the intercept.

Step 3 The mediation device sends a configuration command to the CMS to enable the intercept.

Step 4 The intercept target receives an incoming call.

Step 5 The CMS sends a Signaling_Start message to the mediation device.

Step 6 The mediation device sends a termination attempt message to the Collection Function (CF).

Step 7 The originating gateway sends Session Definition Protocol (SDP) information to the CMS.

Step 8 The CMS sends the SDP information to the mediation device in a QoS_Reserve message.

Step 9 The mediation device queries the DNS server to determine the IP address of the edge router (based on the IP address of the target gateway).

Step 10 The mediation device sends an SNMPv3 command to the edge router to initiate the intercept.

Step 11 The mediation device sends a CCOpen message with the SDP to the CF.

Step 12 The CMS delivers the call to the terminating gateway.

Step 13 The terminating gateway rings the target phone.

Step 14 The call is connected end-to-end, and the edge router intercepts and replicates all voice packets and sends the packets to the mediation device.

Step 15 The mediation device delivers call content to the CF.

Step 16 The CMS sends a Call_Answer message to the mediation device.

Step 17 The mediation device forwards this message as an Answer message to the CF.

Step 18 When the parties hang up, the CMS sends a Call_Release message to the mediation device.

Step 19 The mediation device forwards this message as a Release message to the CF.

Step 20 The CMS sends a QoS_Stop message to the mediation device.

Step 21 When the mediation device receives the QoS-Stop message, it sends SNMPv3 messages to the edge router instructing it to destroy the call content monitoring sessions and the mediation device MIB. Three destroy messages are sent: one for each of the two call content streams and one for the mediation device MIB.

Step 22 The mediation device sends a CCClose message to the CF.

This is the intercept process flow for a standard call. The next topic is the process flow for a forwarding call.

Intercept Process Flow for Forwarding Call

Figure 11-6 illustrates the topology for a Cisco SII of a voice call that is forwarded to voicemail.

Figure 11-6 *Standard Intercept Process Flow*

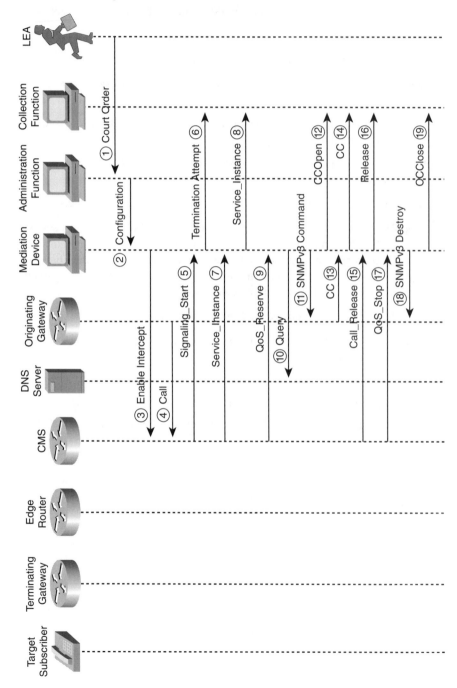

The description of each step in Figure 11-6 is as follows:

Step 1 The LEA physically delivers a court order to the network administrator who operates the LI administration function.

Step 2 The LI administration function sends a configuration command to the mediation device that enters the intercept.

Step 3 The mediation device sends a configuration command to the CMS to enable the intercept.

Step 4 The target receives a call from the public switched telephone network (PSTN) that is not answered, which triggers call forwarding to voicemail.

Step 5 The CMS sends a Signaling_Start message to the mediation device.

Step 6 The mediation device sends a termination attempt message to the CF.

Step 7 The CMS sends a Service_Instance message to the mediation device indicating that the call is being forwarded.

Step 8 The mediation device forwards the Service_Instance message to the CF.

Step 9 The CMS sends a QoS_Reserve message to the mediation device.

Step 10 The mediation device queries the DNS server to determine the IP address the call is being forwarded to. When the mediation device determines the call is being forwarded to the voicemail system, it knows that the call must be intercepted on the originating side.

Step 11 The mediation device sends an SNMPv3 command to the originating gateway to enable an intercept (if call content is to be intercepted).

Step 12 The mediation device sends a CCOpen message to the CF.

Step 13 The originating gateway duplicates all packets and sends them to the mediation device.

Step 14 The mediation device delivers call content to the CF.

Step 15 When the caller hangs up, the CMS sends a Call_Release message to the mediation device.

Step 16 The mediation device forwards this message as a Release message to the CF.

Step 17 The CMS sends a QoS_Stop message to the mediation device.

Step 18 When the mediation device receives the QoS_Stop message, it sends SNMPv3 messages to the terminating gateway instructing it to destroy the call content monitoring sessions and the mediation device MIB. Six destroy messages are sent: three for each part of the three-way call.

Step 19 The mediation device sends a CCClose message to the CF.

This is the intercept process flow for a forwarding call. The next topic is the process flow for a conference call.

Intercept Process Flow for Conference Call

Figure 11-7 illustrates the topology for a Cisco SII of a three-way voice conference call.

Figure 11-7 *Intercept Process Flow for Three-Way Conference Call*

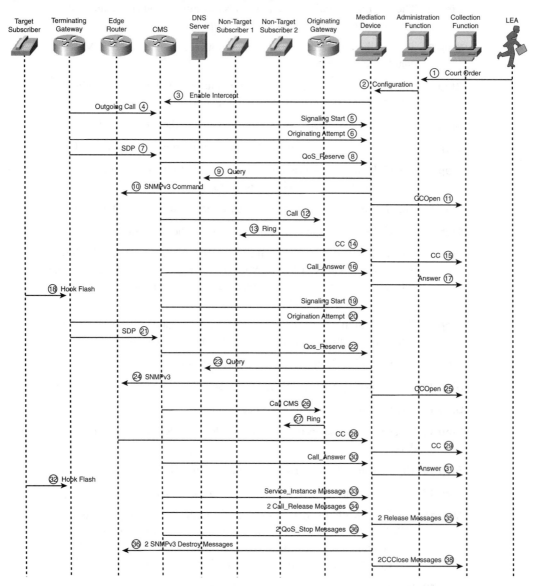

The description of each step in Figure 11-7 is as follows:

Step 1 The LEA physically delivers a court order to the network administrator who operates the LI administration function.

Step 2 The LI administration function sends a configuration command to the mediation device that enters the intercept.

Step 3 The mediation device sends a configuration command to the CMS to enable the intercept.

Step 4 In this scenario, the intercept target initiates an outgoing call.

Step 5 The CMS sends a Signalling_Start message to the mediation device.

Step 6 The terminating gateway sends an originating attempt message to the mediation device.

Step 7 The terminating gateway sends SDP information to the CMS.

Step 8 The CMS sends the SDP information to the mediation device in a QoS_Reserve message.

Step 9 The mediation device queries the DNS server to determine the IP address of the edge router (based on the IP address of the target gateway).

Step 10 The mediation device sends an SNMPv3 command to the edge router to initiate the intercept.

Step 11 The mediation device sends a CCOpen message with the SDP to the CF.

Step 12 The CMS delivers the call to the originating gateway.

Step 13 The originating gateway rings nontarget subscriber 1.

Step 14 The call is connected end-to-end, and the edge router intercepts and replicates all voice packets and sends the packets to the mediation device.

Step 15 The mediation device delivers call content to the CF.

Step 16 The CMS sends a Call_Answer message to the mediation device.

Step 17 The mediation device forwards this message as an Answer message to the CF.

Step 18 The target hook flashes to put the Hook nontarget subscriber 1 on hold and initiate a second call.

Step 19 The CMS sends a Signalling_Start message to the mediation device.

Step 20 The terminating gateway sends an originating attempt message to the mediation device.

Step 21 The terminating gateway sends SDP information to the CMS.

Step 22 The CMS sends the SDP information to the mediation device in a QoS_Reserve message.

Step 23 The mediation device queries the DNS server to determine the IP address of the edge router (based on the IP address of the target gateway).

Step 24 The mediation device sends an SNMPv3 command to the edge router to initiate the intercept.

Step 25 The mediation device sends a CCOpen message with the SDP to the CF.

Step 26 The CMS delivers the call to the originating gateway.

Step 27 The originating gateway rings nontarget subscriber 2.

Step 28 The call is connected end-to-end, and the edge router intercepts and replicates all voice packets and sends the packets to the mediation device.

Step 29 The mediation device delivers call content to the CF.

Step 30 The CMS sends a Call_Answer message to the mediation device.

Step 31 The mediation device forwards this message as an Answer message to the CF.

Step 32 The target hook flashes to create a three-way call.

Step 33 The CMS sends a Service_Instance message indicating Three_Way_Call to the mediation device.

Step 34 When the parties hang up, the CMS sends two Call_Release messages to the mediation device, one for each part of the three-way call.

Step 35 The mediation device forwards these messages as Release messages to the CF.

Step 36 The CMS sends two QoS_Stop messages to the mediation device.

Step 37 When the mediation device receives the QoS_Stop message, it sends SNMPv3 messages to the terminating gateway instructing it to destroy the call content monitoring sessions and the mediation device MIB. Six destroy messages are sent: three for each part of the three-way call.

Step 38 The mediation device sends two CCClose messages to the CF.

This is the intercept process flow for a conference call. The next section covers what you need to consider before implementing LI in your network.

Predesign Considerations

Before configuring your network for LI, you should establish or verify reliable end-to-end IP connectivity on your existing network. The main concern when designing an LI network is ensuring that the network has sufficient bandwidth and CPU capacity to handle the anticipated load of intercepts. This section focuses on the following considerations as an initial stage of designing an LI network:

- Bandwidth and processing power
- IP address provisioning

The CPUs of the following devices will be impacted by LI:

- Edge router

  It should be able to intercept and replicate all intercepted IP communication on its section of the network.

- Trunking gateway

  It should be able to intercept and replicate all intercepted calls that are forwarded off-net.

- Mediation device

  It should be able to support the required maximum number of simultaneous intercepts.

The following interfaces should be engineered with sufficient bandwidth to support LI traffic:

- Between call data IAP and mediation device
- Between call content IAP and mediation device
- Between mediation device and CFs

You should also take into consideration that three-way calls require twice the bandwidth of regular calls because they require two pairs of transmit and receive channels.

You should also provision a network management system to perform DNS and DHCP, such as Cisco Network Registrar.

The use of SNMPv3 in SII requires that Network Time Protocol (NTP) is enabled and that all network elements involved in LI are synchronized to a stable time source.

The various devices involved in LI have minimum software and memory requirements that must be met.

In general, Cisco recommends that service providers do not use static IP addresses, particularly for Customer Premises Equipment (CPE). Static provisioning of IP addresses is time-consuming, expensive, and error-prone. On the IAPs, it can be helpful to use loopback interfaces for the interface with the mediation device because the loopback interface remains constant if physical interfaces go out of service or if the routing path changes.

Security Considerations

Given the sensitive nature of lawful intercept—both from the standpoint of the need to protect sensitive data, and to conceal the identities of law enforcement agencies and the intercept targets—the LI architecture must contain stringent security measures to combat the following types of threats:

- Impersonation of LEAs and mediation devices
- Privacy and confidentiality breaches
- Message forgery
- Replay attacks

Because LI is expected to run on the wide-open Internet, very few assumptions should be made about how well the networks of the LEAs and TSPs can be secured. Although this section does not examine the issues of physical security, operating system, or application hardening within the principles of the LI architecture, they are clearly important considerations. In particular, both the MD and LEA servers must be considered prime targets for attacks by hackers. Hardening measures commensurate with other highly vulnerable servers, such as key distribution and AAA servers, must be considered in any design.

All interfaces must be able to provide strong cryptographic authentication to establish the identity of the principles, and must correlate the identity of the principle with the action they are attempting to perform. That is, it is not sufficient to expect that authentication alone implies any specific authorization.

Providing the ability to use strong crypto is not identical to requiring its use. Because many Cisco devices do not have crypto accelerators, actual use of crypto accelerators is the choice of the TSP, and is dependent on how the device is deployed and its relative exposure. For devices placed in open, hostile environments (such as access routers), TSPs must consider customer requirements for LI when making decisions about crypto acceleration hardware.

Because LI is an interesting target for attackers, all interfaces must perform some sort of cryptographic message integrity checking (such as Hash-based Message Authentication Code—Message Digest 5 [MD5]). Message integrity checking must also counter replay attacks. Because of privacy and confidentiality considerations, the architecture should allow for the use of encryption. Although encryption is not necessarily a requirement, it is highly recommended and may be a requirement in some LI deployments.

- **Interface between MD and call data IAP: Control**—SSH is used for the control interface between the MD and the call data IAP.

- **Interface between MD and call content IAP: SNMPv3 Control**—SNMPv3 View-based Access Control Model (VACM) and User-Based Security Model (USM) are used for the control interface between the MD and the call content IAP. The native SNMPv3 security module mechanism must be used, and the minimum requirement is that preshared keys must be supported. The additional requirement is that the IAP must support the ability to protect the LI MIBs from disclosure or control by unauthorized

USM users. In general VACM should provide the necessary tools to limit the views to particular USM users, but there are also special considerations given that USM and VACM provide the ability to create arbitrary view/user mappings to authorized entities.

The security requirements of the Cisco Lawful Intercept Control MIB (CISCO-TAP-MIB) with respect to SNMP require the following actions: The MIB must be accessed (or accessible) only via SNMPv3. By default, no access must be granted to the MIB. Access to the MIB must be granted only by an administrative authority with the highest privileges: the CISCO-TAP-MIB can be added to a view only at privilege level 15 (the highest level), and including CISCO-TAP-MIB into a view on a router via the SNMP-VACM-MIB will be disallowed.

SNMPv3 must be configured correctly to maintain security. The MD acts as a network manager and the call content IAP acts as an agent.

- **Interface Between MD and call data IAP**: **Data**—The call data is delivered from the call data IAP to the MD. This information is delivered in RADIUS format. Currently, this information is not encrypted.

- **Interface Between MD and call content IAP**: **Content**—The call content information is delivered from the call content IAP to the MD. IP security (IPSec via standard router cryptographic features) is used for this interface.

These are security considerations when designing SII architecture. The next section shows configuration examples with a few Cisco devices.

Configuration Example

Because it would be impossible to show all configuration examples of devices according to each service scenario, the purpose of this section is to give a glimpse of configuration with a few Cisco devices: aggregation router, Cisco BTS 10200, and Cisco PGW 2200. Note that the example of a mediation device is not shown here. You may need to contact MD vendors, such as SS8 or Acme Packet, for configuration examples with Cisco devices.

Aggregation Router

The following aggregation router platforms support version 1.0 of Cisco LI MIB:

- Cisco 7200 series routers
- Cisco 7301 router
- Cisco 7500 series routers
- Cisco 10000 Edge Services Router (ESR)
- Cisco 12000 Gigabit Switch Router (GSR)
- Cisco Universal Broadband Router (uBR) 7246
- Cisco uBR 10000

The following configuration enables Cisco SII on an aggregation router using version 1.0 of the Cisco LI MIB:

```
7200-egw(config)# snmp-server view tapView CTapMIB included
7200-egw(config)# snmp-server group tapGroup v3 auth read tapView write tapView
  notify tapView
7200-egw(config)# snmp-server user mduserid tapGroup v3 auth md5 mdpasswd
```

The following configuration synchronizes the router's clock with the mediation device and enables SNMP traps to be sent to the mediation device:

```
7200-egw(config)# snmp-server enable traps snmp authentication linkdown linkup
  coldstart warmstart
7200-egw(config)# snmp-server host 10.15.113.9 version 3 auth mduserid
7200-egw(config)# ntp server 10.15.113.9
```

The "mduserid" username and "mdpasswd" password must match the username and password that are provisioned on the mediation device for this particular router. In this case, the router's clock is synchronized to the mediation device's clock. A better option is to synchronize all devices in the network to an NTP time server.

Cisco BTS 10200

The following call agent profile must be provisioned on the Cisco Broadband Telephony Softswitch (BTS) 10200 softswitch call agent:

```
ADD CALL-AGENT-PROFILE
ID=CA146
CMS_SUPP=N
MGC_SUPP=N
DQOS_SUPP=N
CDB_BILLING_SUPP=N
EM_BILLING_SUPP=N
GTD_SUPP=N
ES_INTERCEPT_TYPE=SERVICE_INDEPENDENT_INTERCEPT
CMS_ID=12345
MGC_ID=56789
FEID=54321
```

Because the BTS 10200 call agent has no information about network topology and is not aware of aggregation routers, no configuration is necessary for aggregation routers.

On the call agent's profile for trunking gateways, local hairpinning (that is, sending a call back in the direction that it came from) must be disabled. The following line in the trunking gateway profile disables local hairpinning:

```
MGCP_HAIRPIN_SUPP=N
```

Cisco PGW 2200

The Cisco PSTN Gateway 2200 (PGW 2200) softswitch call agent only operates in SII mode using PacketCable Event Messages Specification version I03. Provisioning on the Cisco PGW 2200 requires enabling the LI feature and identifying the mediation devices.

Before adding an MD to the Cisco PGW 2200, you should verify that LI is enabled by verifying that the "SysConnectDataAccess=true" and "LISupport=enable" parameters are set as shown in the /opt/CiscoMGC/etc/XECfgParm.dat file.

Following is an example of provisioning a mediation device using default RADIUS timeouts and retries. The recommended RADIUS key of 16 zeros is automatically provisioned.

```
mml> prov-add:extnode:name="mdname",type="LIMD",desc="Mediation_Device"
mml> prov-add:lipath:name="md-path",desc'"MD_Path",extnode="aqsacom"
mml> prov-add:iplnk:name="md-link",desc="MD_link",svc="md-path", ipaddr="IP_
Addr2",port=14146,peeraddr="192.168.9.2",peerport=1813,pri=1
```

In the preceding example, the "ipaddr" value is selected from the /opt/CiscoMGC/etc/ XECfgParm.dat file and must match the physical interface that has connectivity to the mediation device.

In this subsection, you have learned about Cisco SII interfaces, intercept flows for various calls, predesign, and security considerations. The next section covers call data and content connection

Call Data and Content Connection Interfaces

There are two interfaces for call data and content connection in the LI architecture, as shown in Figure 11-8: between IAP and MD, and between MD and LEA.

Figure 11-8 *Call Data and Content Connection Interfaces*

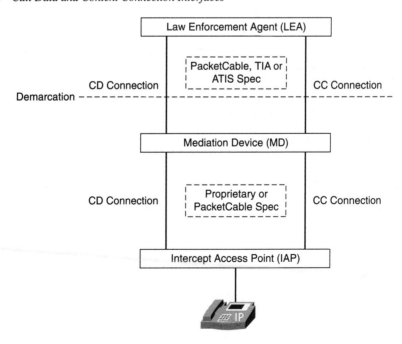

The specification of call data and content interface between IAP and MD is various and mostly proprietary depending on the TSP's preference. They may deliver original call signal and media (RTP packets) without any formatting, or encrypt them with their own method, or apply one of the known specifications like PacketCable Electronic Surveillance.

However, the specification of call data and content interface between MD and LEA is relatively fixed: Europe adapts ETSI (102 series), and America adapts either PacketCable (PKT-SP-ESP), ATIS (T1 series), or TIA (J-STD series), which are very similar at a high level.

This section focuses more on the connection interface between MD and LEA, and refers to the PacketCable PKT-SP-ESP specification.[5] The first topic is the Call Content Connection Interface, as described in the following section.

Call Content Connection Interface

The content in this section describes the mechanism for delivery of call content, via call content connections (CCC) from the TSP's DF to the Law Enforcement's CF.

NOTE   All LI functions use an initial capital letter for each function's name followed by the letter "F," such as "DF" for "Delivery Function," because these names are defined by LI specifications and not as general terms.

The CCC datagram should contain a timestamp that allows Law Enforcement to identify the time at which the corresponding information was detected by the DF. This timestamp should have an accuracy of at least 200 milliseconds. The CCC datagram should be queued at the DF for transmission to the CF within 8 seconds of detection of the corresponding packet by the IAD 95 percent of the time.

The delivery of a particular CCC datagram to the CF depends on many factors not under the control of the TSP, such as the bandwidth between the DF and CF. These factors may affect the ability of the TSP to meet the transmission criterion, and this specification does not require the TSP to take steps to counteract delays caused by such factors.

Call content should be delivered as a stream of User Datagram Protocol (UDP)/IP datagram, sent to the port number at the CF as provided during provisioning of the interception. The UDP/IP payload should adhere to the format shown in Figure 11-9.

Figure 11-9   *Payload of CCC Datagram*

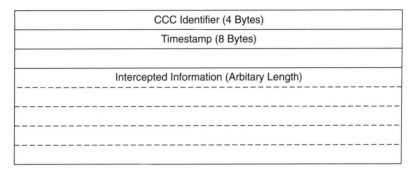

The CCC-Identifier in Figure 11-9 is provided by the DF in the CCOpen message (beginning of call content delivery in PacketCable specification). It is a 32-bit quantity and is used to identify the intercept order to the LEA.

A conversation typically consists of two separate packet streams, each corresponding to a direction of the communication. Both are delivered to the demarcation point with the same CCC-Identifier. The party listening to the communication is identified by the combination of Destination Address (from Original IP Header) and Destination Port (from Original UDP Header). The Destination Address and Destination Port for both parties involved in the communication are provided in the SDP information provided to the LEA as part of the CCOpen message.

The DF should generate a CCC-Identifier that is different from all other CCC-Identifiers in use between that DF and a particular LEA. That is, two streams of content delivered to a single LEA must have different CCC-Identifiers, but a single stream of content delivered to multiple LEAs may use a single CCC-Identifier, so long as no other stream being delivered to one of the LEAs is using the same CCC-Identifier.

The Timestamp in Figure 11-9 should adhere to the NTP time format: a 64-bit unsigned fixed-point number, in seconds relative to 0000 on 1 January 1900. The integer (whole seconds) part is in the first 32 bits and the fractional part (fractional seconds) is in the last 32 bits. The timestamp should be accurate to within 200 milliseconds of the time the DF received the datagram.

Intercepted Real-time Transport Protocol (RTP) information will be of the format shown in Figure 11-10.

Figure 11-10 *Intercepted RTP Information*

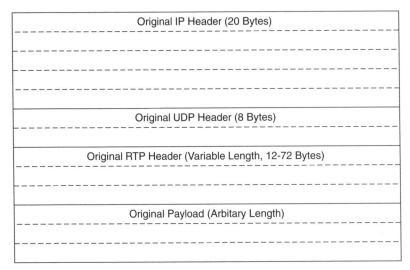

Note that protocols other than RTP may be intercepted, such as for T.38 fax relay.

The brief description of each header in Figure 11-10 is as follows:

- **Original IP header**—The IP header sent by the endpoint. Contained in this IP header are the IP Source Address (SA) and IP Destination Address (DA), which identify the Internet addresses of the source and destination of the packet.

- **Original UDP header**—The UDP header sent by the endpoint. Contained in this UDP header is the Source Port and Destination Port, both of which are 16-bit quantities that identify the connection to the two endpoints.

- **Original RTP header**—The RTP header sent by the endpoint identified in the SA and Source Port. This header contains the packet formation timestamp, packet sequence number, and payload type value, as generated by the source endpoint.

- **Original payload**—The bit sequence as sent by the endpoint identified in the SA and Source Port. The payload typically contains the voice samples, as encoded and encrypted by the sending endpoint. Encryption of the payload is by use of a stream cipher, or other method. Encoding of the voice may be done through use of one of the Internet Engineering Task Force's (IETF's) defined coder-decoder (codec) algorithms (for example, G.711 or G.729) or through a dynamic payload type defined in the SDP (for example, dual-tone multifrequency [DTMF] with RFC 2833). See the following Note for transcoding.

NOTE	*Transcoding* occurs whenever a voice signal encounters an edge device without compatible codec support. The transcoding of communications content between encoding algorithms does not effectively alter the original content if the new encoding algorithm supports at least the same capabilities (that is, encoded frequency range) as the original encoding algorithm. Intercepted content may be transcoded into a different encoding format if the new encoding format provides at least the same level of information as the original encoding format. For example, the G.711 encoding algorithm is acceptable for use in transcoding content originally encoded in the G.728 or G.729E algorithms. If G.711 is used for the intercepted call, the DF may pass the original RTP packets, unaltered and unencrypted. The DF should support the ability to disable transcoding on a per-intercept basis.

Call Data Connection Interface

The content in this section describes the mechanism for delivery of call-identifying information (call data), via Call Data Connections (CDC) from the TSP's DF to the LEA's CF.

Call-identifying information is formatted into discrete messages using a specialized protocol called the Packet Cable Electronic Surveillance Protocol (PCESP). The PCESP messages are transported to LEA over a CDC interface.

The call data connections in the PCESP are implemented as TCP connections, established by the DF, to the CF designated by LEA in the surveillance provisioning. A TCP connection shall be capable of transporting the call-identifying information for multiple surveillance cases to a single LEA.

The PCESP messages must contain a timestamp that identifies the time the corresponding event was detected by the IAP. The requirement of the timestamp is the same as the CCC datagram. The delivery of particular PCESP messages to the CF depends on many factors not under the control of the TSP, as described in the CCC datagram.

PCESP messages contain an Accessing Element ID to identify the IAP. The Accessing Element ID is a statically configured element number uniquely assigned within a PacketCable domain.

The following section shows the CDC messages and their usage examples.

CDC Messages

The CDC messages report call-identifying information accessed by an IAP. These IAPs provide expeditious access to the reasonably available call-identifying information for calls made by a target subscriber. This includes abandoned and incomplete call attempts, if known to an IAP.

The CDC messages in Table 11-2 have been defined to convey information to an LEA for call-identifying events on a call that result from a user action or a signal. Only the events that are available to PacketCable elements providing intercept access functionality will be reported using the messages shown in Table 11-2.

Table 11-2   *CDC Messages of PacketCable*

CDC Message (Call Events)	Description
Answer	A two-way connection has been established for a call under surveillance.
CCChange	A change in the description of call content delivery for a call under interception.
CCClose	End of call content delivery for a call under interception.
CCOpen	Beginning of call content delivery for a call under interception.
ConferencePartyChange	A third party or more additional parties are added to an existing call to form a conference call, or any party in a conference call is placed on hold or retrieved from hold.
DialedDigitExtraction	The target subscriber dialed or signaled digits after a call is connected.
MediaReport	Exchange of SDP information for new or existing calls for which only call-identifying information is being reported.
NetworkSignal	The PC/TSP network requested the application of a signal toward the target subscriber.
Origination	The IAP detects that the target subscriber is attempting to originate a call.
Redirection	A call under surveillance is redirected (for example, via termination special service processing or via a call transfer).
Release	The resources for a call under surveillance have been released.
ServiceInstance	The IAP detects that a defined service event has occurred.
SubjectSignal	The target subscriber sends dialing or signaling information to the PC/TSP network to control a feature or service.
TerminationAttempt	The IAP detects a call attempt to a target subscriber.

CDC Message Example for Basic Call

This section describes the events that trigger the generation of CDC messages to be delivered to LEA for multiple types of calls. More specifically, it identifies when CDC messages are generated for the call and identifies the information each CDC message contains.

The examples for a basic call are divided into two: originating from and terminating to a target subscriber.

For completed calls originating from a target subscriber under a communication intercept order, nine call-identifying messages are generated for delivery to the LEA: Origination, CCOpen (downstream), CCOpen (upstream), Answer, CCChange (downstream), CCChange (upstream), CCClose (downstream), CCClose (upstream), and Release.

For completed calls terminating to a target subscriber under a communication interception order, nine call-identifying messages are generated for delivery to the LEA: TerminationAttempt, CCOpen (downstream), CCOpen (upstream), Answer, CCChange (downstream), CCChange (upstream), CCClose (downstream), CCClose (upstream), and Release.

In addition to the CDC messages described here, other CDC messages might be generated depending on the events that occur during a basic call. As examples, the NetworkSignal message might be generated for events such as the application of dial tone (originating call) and ringing (terminating call) toward the target subscriber, and the SubjectSignal message might be generated for an event such as fax tone detection.

CDC Message Example for Call Redirection

Call redirection is invoked when a call attempts to terminate to a target subscriber, and the CMS determines that the target has subscribed to special call-handling services, and the conditions for feature invocation are met. When the call redirection is done immediately upon the termination attempt, the following sequence of messages is an example of what will be sent to the LEA, as determined by events detected at the IAP(s):

1 TerminationAttempt (for the original terminating call to the target subscriber)

2 NetworkSignal (for ringsplash)

3 Redirection (to identify the redirection event and the redirected-to party)

4 CCOpen (downstream, if communication interception order)

5 CCOpen (upstream, if communication interception order)

6 Answer (if redirected call is answered by redirected-to party)

7 CCChange (downstream, if communication interception order)

8 CCChange (upstream, if communication interception order)

9 CCClose (downstream, if communication interception order)

10 CCClose (upstream, if communication interception order)

11 Release (when a completed redirected call ends)

If the redirection is done after the termination attempt, but before the call is answered, the following sequence of messages is an example of what will be sent to the LEA.

1 TerminationAttempt (for the original terminating call to the target subscriber)

2 CCOpen (downstream, for the original call, if communication interception order)

3 CCOpen (upstream, for the original call, if communication interception order)

4 NetworkSignal (for ringing [if not busy])

5 CCClose (downstream, for the original call, if communication interception order)

6 CCClose (upstream, for the original call, if communication interception order)

7 Redirection (to identify the redirection event and the redirected-to party)

8 CCOpen (downstream, if communication interception order)

9 CCOpen (upstream, if communication interception order)

10 Answer (if redirected call is answered by redirected-to party)

11 CCChange (downstream, if communication interception order)

12 CCChange (upstream, if communication interception order)

13 CCClose (downstream, if communication interception order)

14 CCClose (upstream, if communication interception order)

15 Release (when redirected call ends, if answered by redirected-to party)

If a call redirected by the target subscriber's service is subsequently redirected again by the redirected-to party's service, an additional Redirection message may be generated for the second redirection.

If a call originated by a target subscriber is redirected by the associate's service, a Redirection message may be generated.

CDC Message Example for Call Transfer

Two different services may be offered to subscribers for call transfer. The first, called *blind transfer*, allows a party of an active call to redirect that end of the call to another party and immediately drop out, whether the redirected call completes or not. This is typically done by switchboard operators, and is also performed internally within a network in implementing other services.

The second type of call transfer, called *consultative transfer*, is a variant of three-way-calling, where the three-way call is first established, and then the initiator drops out and the remaining parties are directly connected.

A blind transfer occurs only on an active call; that is, one that has already generated a Origination or TerminationAttempt, Answer, and (if a communication interception order) CCOpen (downstream), CCOpen (upstream), CCChange (downstream), and CCChange (upstream) messages to LEA. When performed by a target subscriber on an active call, the blind transfer may result in the following call-identifying messages:

1 Redirection (to identify the redirection event and the redirected-to party)

2 CCClose (downstream, of the old connection, if communication interception order)

3 CCClose (upstream, of the old connection, if communication interception order)

4 Release (of the old connection)

5 TerminationAttempt (of the new connection at the redirected-to party)

6 CCOpen (downstream, of the new connection, if communication interception order)

7 CCOpen (upstream, of the new connection, if communication interception order)

8 Answer (if redirected call is answered by redirected-to party)

9 CCChange (downstream, of the new connection, if communication interception order)

10 CCChange (upstream, of the new connection, if communication interception order)

When a blind transfer of a call under surveillance is performed by a subscriber not under surveillance, the following sequence of call-identifying messages is an example of what may be sent to the LEA:

1 CCClose (downstream, of the old connection, if communication interception order)

2 CCClose (upstream, of the old connection, if communication interception order)

3 Release (of the old connection)

4 CCOpen (downstream, of the new connection, if communication interception order)

5 CCOpen (upstream, of the new connection, if communication interception order)

6 Answer (if redirected call is answered by redirected-to party)

7 CCChange (downstream, of the new connection, if communication interception order)

8 CCChange (upstream, of the new connection, if communication interception order)

A consultative transfer results in the same sequence of call-identifying messages as three-way calling up to the point where the initiator disconnects.

For example, consider party A being a target subscriber, and establishing the three-way call with parties B and C.

When the multimedia terminal adapter (MTA) performs the bridging function, and the initiator disconnects, the following sequence of call-identifying messages is an example of what may be sent to the LEA:

1 CCClose (downstream, of the call between A and B, if communication interception order)

2 CCClose (upstream, of the call between A and B, if communication interception order)

3 Release (of the call between A and B)

4 Redirection (of the call between A and C, redirected-from A, redirected-to B)

5 CCClose (downstream, of the call between A and C, if communication interception order)

6 CCClose (upstream, of the call between A and C, if communication interception order)

7 Release (of the call between A and C)

8 TerminationAttempt (at C, of the new call between B and C)

9 CCOpen (downstream, of the new call between B and C, if communication interception order)

10 CCOpen (upstream, of the new call between B and C, if communication interception order)

11 Answer (of the new call between B and C)

12 CCChange (downstream, of the new call between B and C, if communication interception order)

13 CCChange (upstream, of the new call between B and C, if communication interception order)

When a bridge service is used, the initiator disconnects, and the bridge is removed from the connection, the following sequence of call-identifying messages is an example of what may be sent to the LEA:

1 CCClose (downstream, of the call between A and bridge, if communication interception order)

2 CCClose (upstream, of the call between A and bridge, if communication interception order)

3 Release (of the call between A and bridge)

4 CCClose (downstream, of the call between B and bridge, if communication interception order)

5 CCClose (upstream, of the call between B and bridge, if communication interception order)

6 Release (of the call between B and bridge)

7 Redirection (of the call between C and bridge, redirected-from bridge, redirected-to B)

8 CCClose (downstream, of the call between C and bridge, if communication interception order)

9 CCClose (upstream, of the call between C and bridge, if communication interception order)

10 Release (of the call between C and bridge)

11 TerminationAttempt (at B, of the new connection between C and B)

12 CCOpen (downstream, of the new call between B and C, if communication interception order)

13 CCOpen (upstream, of the new call between B and C, if communication interception order)

14 Answer (of the new call between B and C)

15 CCChange (downstream, of the new call between B and C, if communication interception order)

16 CCChange (upstream, of the new call between B and C, if communication interception order)

In this section, you have learned about call content and the Data Connection Interface with message examples. The next section covers general interface requirements between MD and LEA.

Interface Between MD and LEA

The interface between the Mediation Device (DF) and LEA (CF) is defined as the *demarcation point*. The details of call data and content information between them are described in the section "Call Data and Content Connection Interface" of this chapter. This section covers the general interface requirements between them, based on the PacketCable PKT-SP-ESP specification.[5]

The CDC and CCC information will not necessarily be synchronized when received by an LEA. The call content and call-identifying information are delivered to an LEA using the independent services of the CCCs and CDCs respectively, and these services can be provided on independent networks or independent facilities.

Procurement, engineering, and sizing of the physical facilities connecting the DF to the CF is the responsibility of the LEA. Engineering and sizing of the CF is also the responsibility of the LEA.

When the resources necessary for transmission of call content or call-identifying information, as provided by an LEA, are insufficient, the information is not required to be queued by the DF. In other words, intercepted information may be delayed or discarded by the DF if insufficient transmission capacity is provided by the LEA to the LEA's CF.

It is the responsibility of the TSP to deliver CCC and CDC information to a demarcation point. The demarcation point shall consist of a physical interconnect adjacent to the DF. The LEA is responsible for providing the equipment, facilities, and maintenance needed to deliver this information from the demarcation point to the CF.

The TSP should ensure that only those packets that have been authorized to be examined by the LEA are delivered to the LEA at the demarcation point. For example, if there is more than one LEA doing surveillance on the TSP's network at a given point in time, each LEA should see only the data that it is authorized to receive.

The requirements in each network layer can be summarized as follows:

- **Network layer interface**—The network layer protocol for delivery of both CDC and CCC information should be as defined by the IP. The transport protocol for CDC information is as specified in the section "Call Data Connection Interface," whereas transport of CCC information is as specified in the section "Call Content Connection Interface." Both CCC and CDC information may be provided over the same physical interface. Information is available in the CCC and CDC information packets to identify the type of packet (either CDC or CCC) and the particular case. The identification is provided either directly by the packet containing the surveillance case identifier, or indirectly by the packet containing an identifier that can be correlated with the case identifier.

  Contained in the IP header is the source IP address, which is the address of the DF, and the destination IP address, which is the address of the CF provided during interception provisioning. All transfer of packets other than those operationally required to maintain the link should be from the DF to the CF only. At no time may the LEA send unsolicited packets from the CF to the DF.

- **Link-layer interface**—The default link-layer protocol between the DF and CF should be as defined by the Ethernet protocol. However, alternate link-layer protocols may be used at the discretion of the TSP based on negotiated agreements with the LEA.

- **Physical interface**—The default type of physical interconnects provided by the TSP at the demarcation point should be an RJ45 10/100BaseT connection. However, alternate physical interconnects may be provided at the discretion of the TSP.

Encryption need not be supplied by the TSP on the connections between the DF and the demarcation point. However, the LEA may choose to provide encryption from the demarcation point to the CF by supplying the necessary equipment and facilities.

Summary

This chapter demonstrates the methods of implementing Lawful Interception based on standard specifications in United States, focusing on three interfaces: Intercept Request Interface (INI-1), Call Data Connection Interface (INI-2, HI-2), and Call Content Connection Interface (INI-3, HI-3).

Intercept Request Interface has two methods of requesting interception: dynamic triggering and pre-provisioning.

Dynamic triggering means that the MD has full control of VoIP signals and sends a request message to the IAP when the target subscriber is detected in the signaling path. That is, the MD keeps monitoring all signals between endpoints and detects the target, whereas the IAP has no information about the target beforehand and just responds passively according to the MD's request. Some VoIP protocols provide this kind of interface; for example, SIP P-DCS-LAES header.

Pre-provisioning means that the MD provisions the request to the IAP beforehand so that the IAP may send back intercepted call data or content when the IAP detects the target subscriber. That is, the IAP should know the information about the target beforehand and monitor the traffic passing by. This kind of interface is usually proprietary, and Cisco's SII is an example.

There are two interfaces for call data and content connection in the LI architecture: between the IAP and the MD, and between the MD and LEA. The specification of call data and content interface between the IAP and the MD is various and mostly proprietary depending on the TSP's preference, whereas the interface between the MD and LEA is relatively fixed: Europe adapts ETSI (102 series), and America adapts either PacketCable (PKT-SP-ESP), ATIS (T1 series), or TIA (J-STD series), which are similar at a high level.

The call content connection is established by DF as a UDP connection, and the content is sent to the IP/port number at the CF as provided during provisioning of the interception. The packet of call content includes an identifier used to identify the intercept order, timestamp, and intercept information.

The CDC is established by DF as TCP connection, and the data is delivered to the CF designated by LEA in the surveillance provisioning. The TCP connection shall be capable of transporting the call-identifying information for multiple surveillance cases to a single LEA. The call data messages have been defined to convey information to a LEA for call-identifying events on a call that result from a user action or a signal.

It is the responsibility of the TSP to deliver call data and content information to a demarcation point. The demarcation point shall consist of a physical interconnect adjacent to the DF. The LEA is responsible for providing the equipment, facilities, and maintenance needed to deliver this information from the demarcation point to the CF.

The TSP should ensure that only those packets that have been authorized to be examined by the LEA are delivered to the LEA at the demarcation point. If there is more than one LEA doing surveillance on the TSP's network at a given point in time, each LEA should only see the data that it is authorized to receive.

End Notes

1 RFC 3603, "Private Session Initiation Protocol (SIP) Proxy-to-Proxy Extensions for Supporting the PacketCable Distributed Call Signaling Architecture," W. Marshall, F. Andreasen, October 2003.

2 RFC 3924, "Cisco Architecture for Lawful Intercept in IP Networks," F. Baker, B. Foster, C. Sharp, October 2004.

3 Cisco Service Independent Intercept Architecture, http://www.cisco.com/en/US/products/ps6566/products_feature_guide09186a008060dece.html.

4 PacketCable Electronic Surveillance Specifications, PacketCable, http://www.packetcable.com/specifications.

5 PacketCable PKT-SP-ESP1.5-I02-070412, Electronic Surveillance, PacketCable, http://www.packetcable.com.

References

RFC 2833, "RTP Payload for DTMF Digits, Telephony Tones and Telephony Signals," H. Schulzrinne, S. Petrack, May 2000.

INDEX

Numerics

3DES (Triple Data Encryption Standard), 87

A

access
    control, Unified CME, 259–261
    devices, 13, 277
        deployment, 284–286
        IP phones, 278
        Switch, 278–282
        VLAN ACLs, 282–284
    policies, 213
    ports, preventing, 279
    SBCs, 208
Access Control Engines. *See* ACEs
Access Control Lists. *See* ACLs
Access Function (AF), 116, 295
access gateways, 74
ACEs (Access Control Engines), 216
ACF (admission confirm), 50
ACLs (Access Control Lists), 108, 215
    DoS protection, 216
    VLANs, 282–284
Active-Active mode, 231
Active-Standby mode, 230–231, 250
Address Resolution Protocol. *See* ARP
addresses
    alias address modification, 50
    call content interception, 301–302
    limited-use, 171
    NAT, 21, 109–113
    obfuscation, 170
    translation, 49
    traversal, 222–224
address-of-record (AoR), 69
AddRoundKey() function, 92
admission confirm (ACF), 50
admissions, control, 49
AES (Advanced DES), 89–92
AF (Access Function), 116, 295
aggregation routers, 327–328
ALG (Application Layer Gateway), 253

algorithms
    DES, 87. *See also* DES
    DSA, 95–96
    hashing, 96
        MAC, 99–100
        MD5, 97–98
        SHS, 98–99
    RSA, 95
    SHA, 84
alias address modification, 50
Alliance for Telecommunications Industry
  Solutions (ATIS), 292
alteration
    media, 37–38
    messages, 35–37
amplification, DoS and, 197
Analog Telephone Adapter (ATA), 117
analysis, 160
    flooding attacks, 135–137
    malformed messages, 150–153
    service policies, 234–237
    sniffing/eavesdropping, 158–161
    spoofing, 164–165
    unintentional flooding, 139
anchoring media, 240
ANMPv3 (Simple Network Management
  Protocol version 3), 316
Annex D (H.235) baseline security, 54
Annex E (H.235) signature security, 55–56
Annex F (H.235) hybrid security, 56–57
Answer messages, 334
AoR (address-of-record), 69
Application Layer Gateway (ALG), 253
applications
    pkcs7-mime types, 183
    VoIP, 12
architecture
    Cisco SII architecture, 313, 329
    connectivity, 232–234
    hardware, DoS protection, 215–216
    LI, 294–297
    networks, 8
    SBC locations, 224

F

fake (spoofed) messages, 24–30
features, rich, 8
file authentication, 270
filtering
    content, 168
    SIP messages, 158
Find-Me-Follow-Me (FMFM), 8
firewalls, 249–251
    ASA and PIX, 251–256
    deployment, 250
    FWSM, 256–258
    limitations, 258–259
    SBCs, 207
    VoIP-aware, 108–109
First Available, 221
flooding
    calls, 20–22
        control, 129
        request, 129
    DoS attacks, 114, 128
        intentional, 129–138
        unintentional, 138–143
    MAC CAM, mitigating, 278–279
    messages, 132, 137
    ping, 129
    registration, 129
    SBCs, 206, 213–216
    traffic, 132
flow
    calls
        digest authentication, 176
        through SBCs, 210
        SIP, 60–61
    process. *See* process flow
    traffic, 239–244. *See also* traffic
FMFM (Find-Me-Follow-Me), 8
formatting S/MIME bodies, 186–188
forwarding calls, 303
FQDN (fully qualified domain name), 316
fraud
    COR, 264–266
    DHCP servers, preventing, 280
    toll, 26

full cone NAT, 109
fully qualified domain name (FQDN), 316
functionality, SBCs, 208, 226–228
    DoS protection, 213–216
    LI, 224–225
    NAT traversal, 222–224
    network topology hiding, 208–212
    overload protection, 216–222
functions. *See also* commands
    AddRoundKey(), 92
    hash, 97–98
    MixColumns(), 91
    ShiftRows(), 90
    SubBytes(), 89
fuzzing, protocol, 22–24
FWSM firewalls, 256–258

G

gatekeepers, 50
gateways, 50
    ALG, 253
    EIGRP, 252
    media, 119
    MGCP, 74–77
    trunking, 328
    Unified CM, 267
        authentication, 269–273
        configuration, 275–277
        encryption, 273–275
        integrity, 269–273
        security, 267–269
    Unified CME, 259
        access control, 259–261
        after-hours call blocking, 266–267
        COR, 264–266
        phone registration control, 261–262
        secure GUI management, 263–264
geographical limitations, 7
Gigabit Switch Router (GSR), 327
global power outages, 139
government law, LI. *See* LI
gray traffic, 214
GSR (Gigabit Switch Router), 327

H

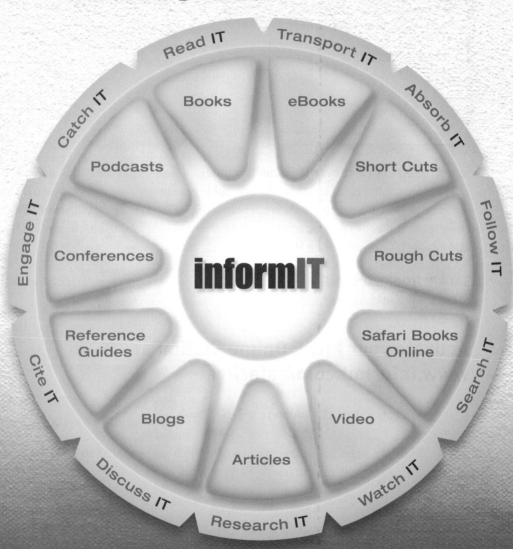

FREE Online Edition

Your purchase of **Voice over IP Security** includes access to a free online edition for 120 days through the Safari Books Online subscription service. Nearly every Cisco Press book is available online through Safari Books Online, along with over 5,000 other technical books and videos from publishers such as Addison-Wesley Professional, IBM Press, O'Reilly, Prentice Hall, Que, and Sams.

SAFARI BOOKS ONLINE allows you to search for a specific answer, cut and paste code, download chapters, and stay current with emerging technologies.

Activate your FREE Online Edition at www.informit.com/safarifree

> **STEP 1:** Enter the coupon code: NKMKSAA.

> **STEP 2:** New Safari users, complete the brief registration form.
> Safari subscribers, just login.

If you have difficulty registering on Safari or accessing the online edition, please e-mail customer-service@safaribooksonline.com